ADVANC[...]

Published by
LID Publishing Ltd.
Unit 204, The Record Hall,
16-16A Baldwins Gardens,
London, EC1N 7RJ

31 West 34th Street, 8th Floor,
Suite 8004, New York,
NY 10001, US

info@lidpublishing.com
www.lidpublishing.com

A member of:

BPR
Business Publishers Roundtable

www.businesspublishersroundtable.com

Printed in Great Britain by TJ International
ISBN: 978-1-910649-32-9

Cover and page design: Caroline Li

China photos by Ji Dong

JONATHAN GELDART

INSIDE THE MIDDLE KINGDOM

INSIGHTS INTO MODERN CHINA
– A COLLECTION OF 50 PERSONAL STORIES

LONDON   MONTERREY
MADRID   SHANGHAI
MEXICO CITY   BOGOTA
NEW YORK   BUENOS AIRES
BARCELONA   SAN FRANCISCO

CONTENTS

Foreward		7
Frontispiece		8
Introduction		20
Chapter 1	The wisdom of tea	28
Chapter 2	A woman of substance	38
Chapter 3	Rebel with a cause	46
	There is no chapter four	56
Chapter 5	Being gay in Beijing	60
Chapter 6	Pollution and window cleaners	68
Chapter 7	Lilly	72
Chapter 8	The man who met the Queen	80
Chapter 9	The driver	90
Chapter 10	The regional manager	96
Chapter 11	Fit for China	106
Chapter 12	The journalist	112
Chapter 13	Hungry for brands	120
Chapter 14	A hard act to follow	124
Chapter 15	The professor	130
Chapter 16	A Russian love affair	140
Chapter 17	The Welsh/Chinese oil man	146
Chapter 18	Facing West	152
Chapter 19	The Chinese-American	164
Chapter 20	The travel blogger	174
Chapter 21	Breaking with tradition	180
Chapter 22	The Classical impresario	184

Chapter 23   Creative Friends   192

Chapter 24   The fruit man   198

Chapter 25   The online entrepreneur   206

Chapter 26   The diplomat and two baskets
                 of pineapples   212

Chapter 27   The WeChat millionaire   224

Chapter 28   Reading between the lines   234

Chapter 29   Youth culture   240

Chapter 30   Books in the rafters   248

Chapter 31   The dentist and the dog   258

Chapter 32   The children who never cry   266

Chapter 33   The dream-chaser   276

Chapter 34   A perspective on Chinese film   284

Chapter 35   Of heroes and legends   294

Chapter 36   Marriage and women's empowerment   304

Chapter 37   Of names and animal rights   312

Chapter 38   The lawyer   322

Chapter 39   The Chef   328

Chapter 40   Wang the wise   336

Chapter 41   Dong the destroyer   346

Chapter 42   Porridge and marriage   356

Chapter 43   A proud member of the Party   366

Chapter 44   Tea and history   374

Chapter 45   The power of believing   384

Chapter 46   The Daoist Abbot   394

Chapter 47   The government travel agent   404

Chapter 48   Against all odds   412

Chapter 49   The Canadian   424

Chapter 50   Made in modern China   432

Postscript: A letter to the reader   442

Acknowledgements   444

An introduction to Jonathan Geldart   446

To Clare.
Without whose support none of this
would have ever been written

FOREWARD

I met Jonathan through a mutual business associate who felt our shared fascination with China could lead to an interesting discussion over lunch. In fact, it led to a book, The Thoughts of Chairmen Now, a unique look at business which we co-authored and first published in 2013 and reprinted in 2015.

Jonathan and I share a passion for China, its fast-growing and vibrant economy has created some of the greatest and most valuable brands on the planet and its long history and fascinating culture has absorbed and captivated us both. However, it is the daily interaction with ordinary and extraordinary people that is the most compelling aspect of living and working there. *Inside the Middle Kingdom* tells the stories of some of these people. You will find a full range of experiences and emotions, lessons and insights enshrined not only in the words of the people but also in the personal notes and commentary from Jonathan.

I have been particularly impressed at how Jonathan has obtained access to these people and how they have opened up to him. The Chinese are often thought to be 'closed' and difficult to read. These personal stories are anything but.

Through a series of, sometimes impromptu, interviews Jonathan has let the voice of Chinese people be heard. I recognise many of the stories as I too have heard them told across China during my many years in the country but I never recorded them. I am so glad that Jonathan has. They deserve to be told and the extraordinary insights they uncover to be explored.

David Roth
CEO, The Store Worldwide WPP Group

FRONTISPIECE

Having spent more than seven years in Beijing, at first as a 'fly in' and 'fly out' visitor, and recently feeling much more like a resident, I have developed a survival strategy as a *laowai* (老外), *waiguo ren* (外国人) or foreigner in this fast-moving, heavily-polluted capital:

Coffee and curiosity

With coffee, I started with Starbucks and moved through McDonalds (once was enough) to Costa and even Subway (once). Now I have made it my business to seek out what I, at least, regard as the better locations to indulge my beverage vice.

I was never really a big coffee drinker and, of course, tea is the thing in China, but I just can't help myself. It seems fitting for a number of reasons that I seem to conduct almost all of my meetings, interviews and discussions with 'a large coffee with hot milk' within easy reach. The better ones have air con (essential in a Beijing summer) and heating (just as essential in the bitter Beijing winter). One benefit is they all pretty much have access to the internet. Most are reasonably priced and nearly all of the ones I've been to, with a few notable exceptions, have coffee which is drinkable. They are, by and large, also places where my interviewees, well almost all of them, have felt comfortable to sit and chat.

Curiosity is the other thing I have in almost limitless naivety. I was taught to be curious about the world by my mother and father, particularly my father. As a scientist of long training, he was always encouraging my brother and me to ask questions and seek out truth. It was good training and I think also made me inclined to listen as well as talk. It remains a total mystery to me why these people agreed to tell me their stories, and even more so that they were happy for me to write them down. No one asked to remain anonymous and most were happy to be quoted in full.

These are not the deranged ramblings of a disordered mind, though some of the stories are quite amazing. They are all true and real. The people are real, the stories are real and the places are real. The result is a perspective on China that I believe is a little different. The chapters here are a compilation of a series of my personal insights into Chinese life, traditions, places and culture through the eyes and mouths of the Chinese people who live and work there. It is also their perspective on the Western world. There is nothing particularly new in the stories of these people, but it is the first time their stories have been told. The comments and reflections which accompany their words are my own, drawn from a good deal of additional listening and personal experiences in China and, more specifically, Beijing. I have listened hard and reflected at length both on what was said to me, and the window into ordinary Chinese life that the words opened. If I have misinterpreted any comments or missed important things, then I apologize unreservedly.

As a result, this book is not only a reflection on the words of those whom I spoke to, but also my personal commentary on modern China as it appears to me every day that I am here.

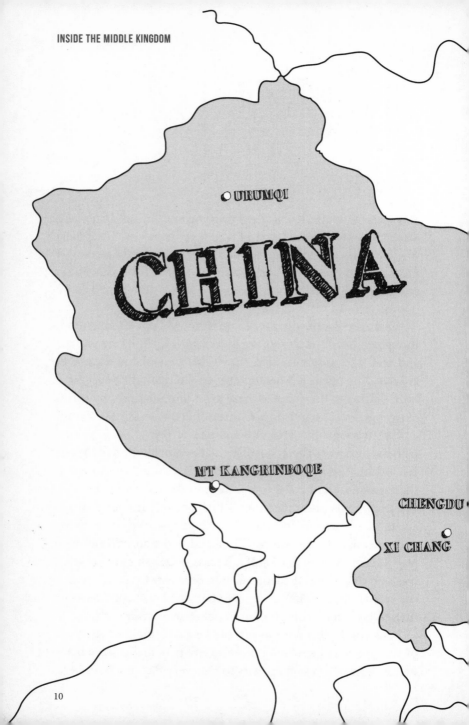

HARBIN

TONGLIAO   SHENYANG

HOHHOT   BEIJING   DANDONG

BAOTOU   TANGSHAN

TIANJIN

TAIYUAN   DALIAN

YINCHUAN

JINAN
SHOUGUANG

XI'AN   SHAOLIN TEMPLE   QINGDAO

ANKANG   NANJING

CHUZHOU
YIXING   SHANGHAI

WUHAN   HANGZHOU
SHAOXING

CHONGQING

CHANGSHA   XIAMEN
ZHANGZHOU

SHENZHEN
GUANGDONG

HONG KONG

Beijing Confucius Temple

The Bell Tower

Xicaoshi Street

13

The Donglishiying Hutong

The Luogu Alley

Imperial College coffee shop

The Forbidden City

Yandaixia Street

Xicaoshi Street

Shanjiankou Street

INTRODUCTION

I have found that, despite all the reading and pre-preparation that many people do before arriving in China, be it for a holiday or for business, nothing really prepares them for the layers of subtlety and complexity that is everyday life there. I have learned more by living, working, eating, drinking, oh and singing, with Chinese colleagues and friends, than any book or tourist trail guide could ever have taught me. The more I listen, the more I learn and the more I learn, the more I appreciate that I know so little about this sometimes strange and contradictory country.

This book is an effort to allow what I believe to be the real China, behind the rhetoric of the media and the stereotypes of prejudice, to emerge through the words of ordinary citizens. True, they are almost all living and working in Beijing, but they are predominantly not 'Beijingers', 'Beijing ren' or 'Beijing people' in Chinese. Beijing is the political heart of China. It is also a magnet for everyone across the country who see its streets as the place to make money and seek their fortune. While Shanghai is often seen as the international centre, and there are many cities and places across China which are very different, the capital has a quality all its own. It is a melting pot of Chinese from all provinces and ethnicities. It is Chinese. Foreigners are very much in the smallest of minorities and, as such, unlike so many of the capitals of the world, Beijing is a more accurate cultural barometer of the country than you may find in the likes of Washington DC, London, Paris or Moscow.

There are insights here on all aspects of Chinese life should you choose to pause and reflect on them. There are stories of marriage, of gender inequality, of religion, of tea, of animal rights, traditional culture and gay life. It is a deliberate mixture of every aspect of China.

The reader should also be aware of a few other aspects of Beijing life, which may help in their understanding and appreciation of some of these stories. These are my personal observations and will probably not be found in any guidebook; throughout this book there are repeated references to a number of key aspects of Chinese and Beijing life. To help the reader understand these better I have provided some additional explanations here:

The *hukou* (户口) is referred to often. This is the certificate of residence that every Chinese person possesses. It divides those from the cities from those in the rural areas. It denotes where individuals live; their 'home town'. The *hukou* is probably the single most important document possessed by any Chinese person. It used to be that if you didn't have a *hukou*, you didn't receive any food coupons; in the Cultural Revolution, this meant you starved. Today those with a rural *hukou* are treated differently from those with one from a city, specifically the larger ones such as Beijing or Shanghai, who are afforded additional privileges in terms of job opportunities, pensions, medical support and education. After the Cultural Revolution, the information stored on your identity card was based on your *hukou*.

WINTER IN BEIJING

The wind is cutting through the brightly coloured long coats, parkas and quilted jackets that bespeckle the streets of Beijing. The temperature has dropped 10 degrees in the past two days and winter is here. The trees are being stripped of their leaves, which swirl everywhere into coats and crannies, and trail into public buildings, offices and homes alike. Ice flecks the pavements, some of it from the rather disgusting personal habit of loudly clearing the throat followed by random spitting, that even known government displeasure seems to have failed to stamp out. You also have to watch out for restaurant spillages as you navigate the huddled pavements. But one blessing comes with the biting cold. It blows away the heavy layer of soot and carbon-filled haze that otherwise smothers the city like an unwelcome duvet on a hot summer night.

People complain about the pollution in Beijing. It is not good in many cities but Beijing is the capital and bears the brunt of the criticism and noise. I can attest that it is terrible and everyone complains about it. Most days, it exceeds all World Health Organization guidelines for air worth breathing. About 95% of the population don't bother to wear protective face masks and those that are for sale seem to be more decorative than effective. The masks that are recommended to keep out the worst of the airborne micro-soot which can clog your lungs are expensive and usually out of stock (if they ever were in stock in the first place). Everyone complains, but we all just suffer and those who can afford to do so buy air filters for their houses. Those who can't just accept it. You can tell the good days when you can see the mountains that ring Beijing to the west and north. You can tell the bad days when you can't see the buildings over the road!

The subway is amazing: fast, efficient, on time and air-conditioned, but the crush of humanity is overwhelming during rush hours, which last from around 07.30 to 09.00 and 18.00 to 19.30. The rest of the time it is just bad, then it shuts. At the end of 2016, there were almost 345 stations and more are scheduled. The authorities are building more and more lines – at the moment there are 18. More than 10 million people use the subway each day, and it feels like it. It is incredibly cheap with a base cost of ¥3 (£0.33) and only ¥10 (£1.10) for the longest of journeys. Once you learn to navigate the labyrinth of intersecting lines and connecting access tunnels it gets you to most places, most of the time. Link that to the buses, which are even cheaper and go to more inaccessible locations, and you are transported around the city with a surprising degree of ease. The longer distance buses will take you out to the suburbs an hour away for ¥20 (£2.20) and even further if you can bear the commute. Many do.

Taxis are the other heavily subsidized transportation in Beijing. For less than ¥30 (£3.40) you can cross the city and for ¥100 (£11) make it out to the airport from the centre, including the road toll of ¥10 (£1.10). They are everywhere but have no obligation to stop and pick you up if they don't want to. Foreigners are studiously avoided by many – no driver I have been picked up by has ever spoken English and they just don't want the hassle. You soon learn to stand waving a piece of paper in your hand as they assume it is an address. Drivers are usually visibly relieved and thankful if you get in speaking even basic Chinese.

Traffic in Beijing is a nightmare. The main routes are clogged and fume-ridden from early morning to late at night. Of course, many cities around the globe are the same. But you would have thought that with arterial expressways, of which there are many, having three lanes each way and a bus lane as well, this would be enough to whisk you around the city with consummate ease. You'd be wrong. The traffic crawls and snarls its way through the wide streets and narrow ones at the same frustrating snail's pace. Three lanes often are made into four by impatient drivers. Indicators are seemingly decorative and driving quality appalling, which makes the whole experience more an application of sixth sense and blind faith over rules and standards. Accidents are rare, but insurance rarer still. If there is an accident, everything stops where it is, in the fast lane sometimes, while it is all sorted out, with or without police involvement.

SPRING

It just cannot be spring. But all the shops and public buildings have removed the tell-tale heavy cloth and felt flaps which normally shut out the biting cold from across the few doors that are not locked and barred against it. The apartments are freezing too and the people inside can be seen in their coats as the heating has been switched off and the sun has still to show its reluctant face through the pollution. There are some signs of life around though. The trees and hedges of the parks and public space have been unwrapped from their winter coats of green fabric, secured with wooden batons and weighted ropes. In early December it is always rather endearing to see the workers carefully wrapping up the city in its green coat of protective wrapping. It is a very practical, if enormously expensive, exercise to wrap every public hedge and many

23

For businesses, most people will only schedule two meetings a day in Beijing, one in the morning and one in the late afternoon. The traffic is the main reason for the scheduling. Arriving on time is difficult and lateness often accepted, if accompanied with a rolling of the eyes and a "the traffic was terrible" comment. If a meeting is scheduled for 11.00 or later, you will probably go to lunch together; if later in the afternoon, then dinner is quite likely. If dinner is for business purposes, then drink yoghurt! It lines the stomach and offers some small protection against the *Baijiu* (白酒) or strongly distilled spirit you will almost certainly be served.

Lunch in China is at noon and the entire country stops to eat. Watching millions of people being served at the same time is a sight worth seeing. There are food stalls and restaurants of every size, type and taste everywhere. Be aware that eating food is about relationship building, not usually discussing business. In the evening, dinner will start at 18.00 or perhaps 19.00 and you'll be done by 21.30. If red wine and Baijiu-toasting has been involved, then you really will be 'done' by 21.30. There can often be an invitation to karaoke after food and you should be prepared to be singing *Hey Jude* at the top of your voice with a bunch of spirited, often spirit-fuelled, colleagues until the early hours. I find I have learned to develop recurring heartburn and to retire early.

Relationships or *guanxi* (关系) are critical in China. They drive every aspect of business and social interaction. They are built over considerable time and with effort. Don't expect to do anything, particularly business, if you have not expended time on building the personal relationships first. It may seem like you are wasting time – you are not. Long-lasting relationships will open doors you never knew existed. Most business deals I have seen fail have done so on the back of Westerners trying to short-cut the relationship building. Also, relationships are passed from one person to another. So, if you are introduced by one person to another, they are showing you a lot of 'face' (see below) and, as such, you should treat the new 'friend' with the same respect as your mutual contact. Relationships build up a web of connections which will serve you well in getting on in China, from helping you find a good place to eat, to doing a deal. Do not underestimate their power or importance.

The notion of 'face' or *mianzi* (面子) in China is often referred to and a reference here is important. The idea of 'face' is disarmingly simple. It is about showing the right level of respect to others. No one likes to be embarrassed, especially in front of friends or colleagues and this is no less the case in China than anywhere else in the world. However, it is a bit easier to make a mistake in China due to the complexity of the culture and layers of meaning attached to so many things. In addition, people can take offence at things that Westerners shrug off as either unimportant or irrelevant. It is possible to step on a cultural or social 'landmine' without even knowing it has gone off, until you are refused another meeting or find people politely but permanently 'unavailable'. The simple rule is to be polite to everyone. It costs nothing and pays dividends.

It is also important to pay as much attention to what is not said as to what is. Reading between the lines is an art form in China and it is easy to make mistakes here too, on both sides. Be as precise and explicit about what you mean as possible, to avoid ambiguity. There is

of the bushes, shrubs and low trees across Beijing individually. I wonder if the greenery appreciates this touching care as it absorbs all that carbon belched out by the factories and transport system that otherwise choked Beijing for much of the year in a cough-inducing fug.

SUMMER

I feel the heat at the best of times, but Beijing in 'flaming June' is a hell-hole of the first order; 40 degrees is just unpleasant by any standard. This city of changes is beset by pollution of apocalyptic proportions for much of the year and the summer is no exception. Face masks are almost useless against the smallest carbon particles abound. The hospitals and pharmacies see a surge of complaints and clotted lungs. The smog is just plain gritty and you can taste it. This place needs a good spring clean! So do my lungs. I am escaping back an assumption by most Chinese people, who might not have experienced a Western culture before, that you will be meaning something additional to your words when you speak. If you feel there may be something being left unsaid, there probably is. Asking outright for clarification will be taken as a loss of face so be sure to have someone around to 'interpret' for you as well as 'translate'.

The Chinese can be incredibly direct, which can be seen as rude in the eyes of many Westerners. I have often had someone look me in the eye and, without a shred of irony, ask why my hair is grey and why I don't dye it black, like every other senior leader in China. I just smile and apologize for being English! People will comment on your hair, clothes, taste in food, use of cosmetics or accent, without a blink of the eye. Sometimes it is to tell you that you look good, but not always. My advice here is to roll with the punches. It is not meant badly and to respond negatively will be to tread on the broken glass of face.

Finally, from a business – and indeed a social – perspective, gifts are important in China. At the root of this is the notion of face and respect but it is also simply that we all appreciate people being thoughtful. Gifting has had a bad name in China in recent years as extravagant gifts were connected to the corruption and 'graft' the current leadership is fighting to destroy. However, the giving and receiving of small, inexpensive, but thoughtful, gifts is really appreciated and reciprocated. Not to do so could well be taken badly, unless you know each other well and agree that gifts are unnecessary for each visit. But don't forget gifts at the major festivals or it will go down very poorly! My habit now is to take sweets from my home town in the north of England. Most Chinese people have a very sweet tooth and the personal connection is understood and always elicits smiles. You may well end up with a lot of tea in return, but it makes great 'regifting' presents for those at home and everyone understands that there is only so much tea you can drink.

The Chinese have been trying for more than 2,000 years, since the Qin dynasty, to organize their enormous country into some form of hierarchy. The government today divides the People's Republic of China into five administrative divisions, roughly based on geography and population: province, prefecture, county, township and village. Separately, and with some overlap, an unofficial system organizes cities into tiers. In part, this is based on size, but mostly on economic development. Despite its shortcomings, the tier system is a useful classification device. The municipalities of Beijing, Shanghai, Guangzhou and Shenzhen are widely referenced as being 'tier 1' cities. There are 32 'tier 2' cities at provincial capitals (roughly), 238 prefecture cities at 'tier 3' and 383 county cities at 'tier 4'. A remaining group of around 1,643 towns are said to be 'tier 5'. I am indebted to Millward Brown, a WPP research company, for this definition.

Of course, I could go on and on. But suffice to say that you can browse many books and the internet to learn more about Chinese history and culture. I advise that you do. Even a broad understanding of the long and complex history of China will be very much appreciated. At the end of the day, however, no one expects you to be Chinese.

to the UK! Pity the poor souls that have to suffer here 100% of the time and of whom it is said have a reduced life expectancy of at least five years as a result. The untold long-term effects and damage to the young, as well as the old, seems a heavy price to pay for progress.

AUTUMN

It's hot in the coffee shops and shopping malls now. Being someone who never likes operating at anything over 0 degrees since my time in the Arctic, it is snug beyond reason. The date is 16 November and the heating in Beijing was turned on, by local government decree, yesterday. I forgot the date and expected to need the woollen black polo neck that I thought looked rather cool, but is decidedly not. Back to layers tomorrow. I make a mental note. I guess I'll complain in March next year when it goes off again – always too early!

THE
WISDOM
OF TEA

Behind the big wooden doors tucked away in the maze of *hutong* streets, Datangchun (大唐春) near Nanluoguxiang (南锣鼓巷), just off East Gulou Street (鼓楼东大街), is a haven of quiet and wooden buildings. Professor Zhao Weimin is the director of Peking University's Culture Research and Development Centre. He is revered amongst the intelligentsia of Beijing, if not China, as a thinker and teacher on traditional Chinese culture and the private courtyard is an invitation-only centre of contemplation and policy debate.

We gather around a long wooden table in a traditional Tang dynasty-style room of books, calligraphy and teapots. At the centre of the table seems to be one of the oldest tea tables I have ever seen. Delicate tea cups neatly arranged beside an old tea mixing utensil and small handmade teapot.

Professor Zhao is dressed in traditional clothing modelled on the end of the Qing dynasty, as far as I can tell, and carves a lump of 100-year-old *pu'er* (普洱) tea from a tea 'cake' to mix with a 20-year-old one. He moves with flowing arcs of hands to cut and mix tea, boil water, warm pots and bowls, at the same time as explaining the art of tea.

"The main function of pu'er tea is to lower the blood fat. But now it has become a cultural phenomenon amongst Chinese scholars. In the process of making and drinking tea comes the essence of Chinese traditional culture. Our ancients always talked a lot about tea and we are now reviving this tradition."

Professor Zhao empties the mixed tea into the delicate earthred, enamelled pot. It is dark, almost black in colour. His actions are slow and methodical, almost reverential. This is a process which is not to be hurried. The very consistency and tight twisted leaves of the tea create an impression of timelessness and dignity.

"There are four levels to drinking tea. Firstly, of course, we drink when we are thirsty, to refresh the palate and the body. Secondly, we taste the tea and determine its quality from its aroma and its effect on the palate, the lingering aftertaste and satisfaction of the senses. Thirdly, is the talking about tea. Tea is a carrier, a vehicle for our thoughts and words and contemplative reflections. This is a focus on the tea itself, its origin, its provenance, its journey and its history to arrive with us as the drinker. Fourthly, people do not just talk about the tea but about life, society and the world. This is the philosophical level. When drinking tea, people must think and share deeply about their own life, society, the Zen and appreciate the doctrine of Daoism and Buddhism to connect themselves to the higher dimensions, the fourth and even the fifth dimension. Generally, the first two levels are about the experience of drinking tea. The second two are about wisdom."

He grunts with satisfaction as he pours the second pot, the first having been used to wash the tea and warm the serving chalice and cups. Then he slowly fills an ancient tea cup before him. It is a simple ceramic wide-topped shallow bowl-like container. The dark liquid first swirls around the sides then fills the cup.

"Watch the surface of the tea."

We all lean forward. It is almost like worshipers at the altar, bowing to the chalice. Then slowly, almost imperceptibly, the tea shimmers and starts to become opaque. Across the surface a delicate white film forms.

"The tea chi is being released," whispers Professor Zhao.

I have never seen this before. But I have never taken tea with a tea master before. The white vapour rolls, almost boils, across the surface of the liquid. It has no texture and almost no form at all, reminding me of stories from my youth of the 'Will-o'-the-wisp', or 'fairy fire' and the moment hoar frost forms on the surface of a high mountain pool in the first light of a sharp frosted winter dawn. We are transfixed, all hold our breath. The room is utterly silent. Then it is gone.

"That, is the chi," Professor Zhao says quietly.

"In the ancient times of the Song dynasty, scholars held competitions as to who could make the best tea. They would put hot water and the tea powder into a bowl and then stir it in their special way. The one who could create the most tea chi foam was the winner."

He studies me intently.

"This shared experience draws us together to form philosophical considerations in the moment of contemplation. The development of human beings in different countries has much in common but nowadays people do not come together to discuss the ultimate goal of human existence. If this is discussed well and accepted by human beings from all countries across the tea table, then there would be no conflicts in this world."

He gazes at me thoughtfully. We are sitting directly opposite each other and our eyes lock. Suddenly there is no one else here. We slowly consider each other. There is no need for an exchange of words. His deep dark eyes are quietly penetrating and inescapable. After what seems like an eternity of scrutiny, he speaks again.

"Now the conflicts are small. Even the wars. They are but family quarrels. If everyone can rise above the detail to the level of principle then they can be solved, just like a quarrel between brothers. This is because almost every human being actually wishes to live in peaceful harmony. It is not known how long human beings will exist in this world. What is important is the meaningful things that people do in the allocated span of their lives. Let me tell you about history."

He pours more tea and we breathe again.

"Every person in every country is making their own contribution to the world, to the development of the human race to be strong and rich. China was strong once because of the inventions it created and nurtured in the times of ancient history. The civilization of the world was pushed forwards through Chinese enlightenment. Then, with the Industrial Revolution, the UK went up and made significant contributions to the world and humanity. Later, in the Electronic Age, the US grew up and its peoples pushed global development and the pace of human progress. Now it changes again. The world will progress in an orderly manner and on the basis of mutual understanding, mutual respect and learning, then hatred will have no space amongst us all."

He locks eyes with me again. I have a feeling of deep mutual respect and our conversation enters a higher level. Perhaps the tea chi is working

"If we consider traditional Chinese culture to be a bird, then Confucianism, Buddhism and Daoism are the bird's body. Traditional Chinese medicine and tea are the two wings and *Guqin* (古琴 (the ancient Chinese musical instrument)), playing chess, calligraphy and painting are the feathers. Tea culture dates back to the Tang dynasty (618–907). It was at its highest point in the Song dynasty (960–1279). Many emperors from the Song dynasty liked tea very much and so did the scholars. Tea culture went to Japan from the Tang and Song Dynasties."

He reverentially prepares another pot of tea and I am aware that time has passed. In that small panelled room with its wooden floor, history seems very close. As I handle the ancient cups and sit at the ancient table I feel transported to a different era. It is exactly as Professor Zhao desires.

I am intrigued by the delicate dark-red enamelled pottery teapot he is using.

"I started to design this type of pot about 15 years ago. I believe I have a mission in life to create the perfect pot. Some years ago, when one of your Prime Ministers, Mr Tony Blair MP, came to China I designed, made and gave him one of my teapots. I did so not just because you English have a tradition of tea, but also as a sign of the fraternity between our nations." It dawns on me that I am at an audience with one of the top and most influential people in traditional Chinese cultural studies.

"When I first started to think about the design of this teapot I went to consult with Professor Zhang Shouzhi. Professor Zhang was one of the first ceramic artists after the founding of the People's Republic of China. Now he is over 80 years old. One day Professor Zhang invited me for lunch and he explained that from a design perspective, the form of the dark-red enamelled teapot had reached its peak. This ancient design had never been improved upon and had reached a bottle neck. He felt the design could be improved if it was accompanied in the design phase with a deep insight from culture. The old professor hoped that I could study the teapot design and extend the scope of knowledge and design to perfect it further. Then Professor Zhang bought two train tickets for us both. We travelled to Yixing (宜兴) city in Jiangsu (江苏) Province, the centre of dark-red enamelled teapot design in China and the source of Yixing clay used for these special teapots. We visited many teapot masters. As a result of that visit and the faith in me shown by Professor Zhang I resolved to design the perfect teapot."

"Beautiful," I muse.

Professor Zhao recalls his time as a youngster in Fujian Province.

"As a boy I used to like reading. I never thought I'd be a university professor. I just wanted to get a good job that would give me the spare time I wanted so I could read and study. As I grew up I liked to read the Chinese classics. I really liked the quiet to contemplate what I had read. My father was a government officer in Zhangzhou (漳州) city, near to Xiamen (厦门) on the coast."

It didn't seem right to quiz Professor Zhao on his past but he proffered a little explanation as to how he had come to be one of the foremost Chinese scholars of traditional culture.

"I was a student at PKU at the end of the 1970s. My major was in literature and I studied under some of the most famous professors of the day, such as the curator of the Research Institute of Culture and History. I stayed on after graduating and have been here ever since, now over 40 years. I am the Director of PKUs Cultural Research and Development Centre, as well as the Director of the PKU School of Journalism and Communication. I believe it is essential that the contribution of PKU to society is through education and thought, not business and the creation of Chinese millionaires. I wrote a paper to PKU leadership on this matter and they agreed with me. As a result, we set up this centre of contemplation and study."

"You have had many students in all your years as a professor. Do you believe they have listened to your thoughts and adopted any of your teachings of traditional Chinese culture?" I asked.

"My students have all been intelligent people. PKU is the foremost university in China. My students have gone on to become government officers, the highest of government policy makers, university professors and school headmasters, as well as leaders at the top of state media operations. I am privileged that many return to seek my guidance and opinion. Every evening people gather in this courtyard, equal before each other, regardless of external rank, to debate and discuss the important matters affecting society in China today. A good student can make a contribution to society if they hold in equal measure the three values of truth, beauty and virtue."

Among the gatherings of the great and the good in this courtyard are the main people driving socio-political change in China today. The reason the courtyard has become a crucible of contemporary Chinese thinking is down to five cultural features, which Professor Zhao explains.

"First is respect. Anyone who enters this courtyard is already special. We require all who enter here to recognize that they cannot operate in isolation of their fellows. So, people cannot be selfish. We should show respect to the heaven, the earth, our parents, our elders, our friends and all who enter the courtyard. All are equal in personality.

"Second, tranquillity. The courtyard is located in the centre of Beijing. Nanluoguxiang is a very busy area but the courtyard is very quiet. Not only is the environment quiet but we have reconstructed the courtyard in the old way so that it inspires tranquillity and quietness of spirit in the hearts of those who enter here. When people are not blundering around being utilitarian then they can judge the world objectively, impartially, with tranquillity. Tranquillity is important to people's growth. One should give one's self the time to think about life. The courtyard is an enabler for that. People can give themselves over to one route in their lives without consideration. They can spend their whole lives doing the wrong thing and then find out, too late. That is a shame. People all over the world are pursuing unlimited material things in a life which has finite limits. Is it good or bad to pursue unlimited materiality? For what end? For what good? Balance and moderation are good.

"Third, purity. I want this courtyard to be pure of spirit. This is designed to be the spiritual home of society. It is the gathering ground of the culturally rich and famous. When people come here they do not talk of love or business. They talk of culture, literature, history, life and soul.

"Fourth, ideology. People should develop an ideological level of existence while they live in this world. The ideological level of human existence relates directly and proportionally to social development. The richer the society, the higher the ideological level it needs to attain. If it fails to develop a high ideological level, then society cannot attain a level of tastefulness and refinement that is required to move it to the next level. We espouse and encourage the development of refined ideological thinking here.

"Fifth, mirror. To be able to look into or consider the future one has to understand the mirror of the past. Everyone who comes to the courtyard must look at themselves and at society honestly and purely. They must become each other's mirror. Success and failure are all reference points for human beings. This is the real meaning of friendship around the courtyard; honest reflection of each other and to each other will allow the creation of enlightenment here."

We sit in reflective silence for a moment until interrupted by a small bell. Professor Zhao crosses the room to a discrete but high-tech entry phone system. A few words are exchanged. A student will join us shortly.

We wait.

The student turns out to be a high-ranking government official from a southern Chinese province. We exchange bows and business cards.

"I will continue."

All sit before the teacher. Regardless of external rank, the rules of the courtyard are to be respected. Our discussion turns to the development of classical Chinese writing and the need to create the new classics of the future, including the highest level of thought in Chinese arts and academic circles. Poetry.

"Poetry is an important part of an experts' life. In ancient times people could not go to school or be government officials unless they could write poetry. Poetry is an essential skill of the past and of the present. If people can express themselves through poetry and through the use of the right words, then the true essence of Chinese character can be espoused."

Professor Zhao is completing a book of poetry to be published this year. This is no mean feat, requiring as it does the highest level of ideological thinking to be accepted by his peers and so be worthy of dissemination.

We have almost overstayed our welcome but Professor Zhao has a few more thoughts for us before we leave.

"The open-door policy of China comes after many years of economic development. Now China is going out into the world consciously with a better and wider understanding. There are four sayings of a very eminent PKU professor, Professor Fei Xiaotong. First, different people's cultures and civilizations all have their good points. Second, we should respect other peoples' culture and their good points. Third, different cultures may blend and exist at the same time. Fourth, then there will be one peaceful world."

Professor Zhao continues, "Chinese people can now accept different cultures and will no longer reject Western cultures as in the past. We must not criticize the West all the time. We should remember the old Chinese saying: 'If you want to correct others, first correct yourself.' The Chinese culture is conservative and self-disciplined, so we Chinese will never do anything wrong. Some peoples' culture is to fight but ours is harmony. This is at our core. To judge a country, one should learn its history and development to have an objective judgment. We are agriculturalists and have developed, after thousands of years, a culture enshrined in an agrarian experience. We have an altruistic and collectivist mentality in our DNA. In Europe, you had a mainly marine civilization; you are better traders and paid deep attention to rules, regulations, contracts and laws to protect yourselves. Which is the better civilization? It's hard to say. Balance is good, moderation is good. China cannot bring everything from the West and the West cannot absorb every aspect from China. Only with mutual respect and understanding will the world be a better place."

Eventually we leave with photographs and handshakes. Outside, in the cold courtyard, the peace and tranquillity of the tea room pales a little, but not much. Every aspect of the courtyard has been considered in detail, from the offset entrance complete with water trough to mirror the sky and prevent the entering of bad luck. The inspiring calligraphic carvings over the solid doors support contemplation and the ancient trees at each corner show this is not a new build. It has been sympathetically and empathetically restored, a powerful metaphor for China, steeped in history yet newly reconstructed on the solid foundations of its cultural past.

I pause at the entrance as the wooden doors close solidly behind me. I have emerged again into modern China but I have been changed. The tea chi foams in my mind and I feel I've caught a bit of that Will-o'-the-wisp.

A WOMAN OF SUBSTANCE

Yuan Rui Ming is an elegant and poised woman. Born in 1952, she wears her years gracefully, but you can see the pain in her eyes as she talks of the history which makes her the woman she is today. Mother of Oliver Zhang (interviewed in Chapter 38), she speaks no English, so her son acts as a patient and respectful translator.

"My grandfather was from Jiashan (嘉善县), a small town in Zhejiang (浙江省)," she begins. "He was an accountant. My grandmother was from another small town, Shaoxing, not far away, a housewife. She brought up my father and ..." She pauses. "Is this what you want to hear?"

"Of course," I reply. Her eyes search mine for clues. She doesn't want to bore me or say too much perhaps?

"Where did you grow up?" I ask.

"Hangzhou (杭州). In those days, it was a small historical city, quiet, not like today. Now it is an international tourist city. The railway station at that time was shabby. We lived close to the railway tracks then. Now, Hangzhou East Railway Station is the biggest railway station in Asia. The house we lived in was demolished to make way for the West Lake Avenue. There has been such significant change. I never dreamed about that level of change. It has been so fast."

Like many of her generation, Rui Ming has experienced more and seen more change in China than any generation from before. Her story is that of the rise of China's economic supremacy.

"You have to be proud of China, to make these changes in just 30 years. It never happened in the West." But there is no pride in her quiet voice, only facts.

Rui Ming was at school in Hangzhou; she tells me that the elementary school is still there. She graduated from elementary school after six years and entered high school. Just six months later, the Cultural Revolution started.

"It was 1966. School stopped. I was only 14 years old. I was supposed to graduate in 1968 but I couldn't. We were forced to stop. We all had to go to the rural areas to help the peasants to do farming. It was called *chadvi*. We had to go."

The words are flat and precise, clear and unemotional. She was sent to a small countryside village called Jianshan (嘉善县). She remembers it very clearly.

"Only a few neighbours of a similar age went to the same area with me, but not to the same village. I was on my own. After schooling stopped, all the students were brought together at a local resident committee. We were registered and the committee sent us, allocated us, to different places. It was quite fast. I can remember thinking, 'Wow! What just happened here?' I felt it was a total waste of four years. I cried a lot. I lost my golden years as a girl."

Her eyes never leave mine as she speaks. As I make my notes she pauses and picks up the story with my eyes. Her gaze is kind and thoughtful. She wants to tell her story. Although one of millions who went through this time, for her it was once. It was her life. She wants me to hear it, understand it from her, first hand. Despite the clear pain of the memories of the time, Rui Ming is purposeful and dignified in the recounting of her story.

"Even the peasants questioned why we were there, why the government had done this. I dressed like a peasant, I ate, I slept, I worked like a peasant. I became a peasant. When the holiday came, the national holiday of Chinese New Year, I remember I was sent to cut down trees in the mountains. I was in tears. On this special day, this important day for family, I was on some unknown mountain hundreds of kilometres from the people I loved. I was very homesick."

She smiles at me. The warmth is palpable. There is no anger or resentment in her voice or her words. Just acceptance of a time now long past, but with strong memories.

"There were no phones then. We could only write letters. In the beginning, I would be able to write about every 20 days. Later, I got used to it and would write about one letter a month. After four years, there was a change in government policy. If you only had one child, then that child was allowed to return to work in a factory in Hangzhou, so they could take care of their parents. So I was allowed to go back.

"There were some changes in Hangzhou but not many in the four years I had been away. I was sent to make clothes in a local garment factory. It was only a 25 minute walk from our house. Although I had to work eight hours a day, compared to the countryside it was paradise. Also, I learned the skill of making clothes."

She is talking more brightly now, her features becoming more animated as she remembers this time, clearly significantly better than before. It was at the factory that she met her husband.

"I was 24 years old. He was the brother of my grandfather's neighbour. He was one of ten children. He was number seven I remember. There were 12 children but two died in infancy. It was unusual to only have one child in those days. I was one of five children but two died in the womb and my two brothers died very early, after only 30 and 40 days. I was the only one left."

The facts fall like rain. It is difficult to take it in at the speed of delivery. The reality of the situation is starkly and simply told. This is a story recounted across millions of Chinese from this generation. It is possible to read of all this in the detached pages of history and to see the pictures in the museums or watch the faded propaganda films of the time. But here it was in front of me, inescapable, personal, poignant and true.

"Are you ok?" she asks. "Should I carry on?"

I am suddenly aware that I have stopped listening. My own mind is full of images conjured up from her descriptions. I apologize and explain that her story is really making me think. She smiles again and seems pleased.

"I spent 15 years in the factory in different departments," she continues. "First, I was on the production line and then in the accounting department. I became an accountant. I moved from peasant, to worker, to management. I got to use my brain. I liked the work and the pressure."

That smile again.

"We were married in 1978 and our only son was born later that same year. My husband was a driver. It was a good job in those days. Good jobs were doctors, soldiers, drivers. He was from Shaoxing. He worked for the Electricity Bureau, which later became State Grid after 2001."

I am curious. These were times of significant change in China, was she aware of the changes going on?

"Oh yes, very aware. Everyone around me watched the news on the TV. We were aware that there was enormous change going on. In general, we felt it was positive. Specifically, salaries were going up so we felt the benefits directly. We had to use ration coupons in the early days to get most things such as food and basics. After the revolution, the coupons disappeared so it was clear change, positive change, was happening."

In meeting people around China and talking about the days of the 1980s, the same story emerges from everyone I speak to, and Rui Ming is no different. There had been immense suffering and displacement of people, true. State enterprise factories required long hours and hard work, true. There were many changes, many difficulties and many problems, true. But for the workers in the factories and for those such as Rui Ming, with her new husband and newborn son, things were improving dramatically in their everyday lives. Listening to those such as Rui Ming provides a different view as to what it was like at the grass roots in society.

"For young people, society became far more open," explains Rui Ming. "The earlier government restrictions were lifted. Department stores had had very limited choice, but slowly we noticed more and more products appearing on the shelves. There was more choice available too of different variants of products for customers. I personally noticed changes in the book stores. First, all the books and pamphlets were on political subjects only, but then I started to see more and more books on culture, history and novels."

In the following ten years, Rui Ming and her husband continued to work in the same businesses, and by the early 1990s, things had taken a further 'leap forward'.

"Compared with the previous ten years there were even more material changes and you could actually feel the economy growing really fast. Importantly, attitudes were changing fast too. We became more and more aware of globalization and that China was part of a much wider world. We were looking for communications from, and with, the rest of the world. There was a real hunger for it. People were willing to exchange views and opinions. Before then, people were very closed. In the early 1990s, everything changed and people were really far more open minded."

There is genuine animation and excitement in Rui Ming's voice as she recounts these years. Married, and her son growing up, life was better for her, her family and her peers than it had ever been before. The days of being a peasant were almost a forgotten memory.

"With our son growing up, my husband and I felt the pressure to earn more money to raise him. We also realized the importance of education. An education we had both lost to history. We studied hard in our spare time. Partly, it was so we could keep pace with our son's education, but also so we could improve ourselves and our own jobs. I learned to become an accountant and my husband studied economics and management."

The energy of her descriptions and words affect me powerfully. It is clear that this young married couple, a product of the revolution, were grasping every shred of opportunity which came their way, and creating more almost out of thin air, through sheer hard work and application.

"The driver jobs were disappearing, but because my husband was a good driver he was promoted to the Head of the Drivers Department at the company. It was his responsibility to arrange all the drivers' schedules and arrangements. Then he was promoted again to the Public Safety Department, in charge of safety in the whole business. He became a superintendent. A very good job. A good job meant that he had to study hard to do it well."

Now she is beaming with pride at me. Undoubtedly, they had now moved from very difficult times to a much better situation. Her husband was clearly a success and through hard work and application, money was more plentiful.

"At that time, we were three generations living together in one house. But with my husband's promotion, we were able to move to a bigger house, though still in Hangzhou."

The pride is palpable. But this story is not boastful, just the truth, proudly told, of achievement, almost against the odds, from an inauspicious start. The next 20 years from the 1990s to today also told a story of change. Both she and her husband retired in 2002 and 2003, respectively. Their son married and had two girls. Now Rui Ming is a grandmother, still living in Hangzhou but visiting her son in Beijing. His wife and daughters are still in Taiwan and she is here to spend precious time with him whilst she can before he returns or moves south to Shanghai.

"Now I have no real worry about the rest of my life," she says. "I am retired, I am a grandmother and my son is a successful lawyer. I am so very proud of my son and his achievements. I have seen him grow through difficult times to be a student and now a father. I hope he will have a prosperous future and achieve much better things than we did."

"And what of China now?" I ask.

"I am very optimistic for China. Particularly after President Xi has taken power there has been, and I am sure there will be, another series of changes in China. As it becomes more prosperous, then the people can enjoy that prosperity."

These are not the words from a recent propaganda pamphlet or the TV news. This articulate, self-schooled and self-improved woman has experienced the recent and most turbulent history of China, from the Cultural Revolution, through the Great Leap Forward to the emergence as a world superpower and influencer of the global economy. She has recounted how it has felt on the ground. Her words are her own, a personal and unabridged perspective, over a cup of coffee in the heart of Beijing. No one is around to listen, other than her son, beaming with pride for his mother.

So what hopes for her grandchildren?

"I hope that my granddaughters will have the opportunity to see the world and travel, to become aware of the world and to increase their understanding of it. There is still not enough interaction between the ordinary people of China and the rest of the world. The more there is in the next generations, then the better it will be for China and for all of us.

"I am so optimistic for the future of China and the next generation. The main reason for this is that people of my age really had to struggle to manage and survive. It is very different now with a much more stable life. This is a better place to start.

"We are lucky. Money is not as important to me as before. My health, and the health of my family, is the most important thing now."

Rui Ming's final comment is a reminder of the reality of the current China. Economic prosperity has brought improvements to all in the country. However, there is a cost.

REBEL WITH A CAUSE

An hour on the Beijing transit system is not unusual for some commuters and we first travel south on Line 5 but then on the Yizhuang (亦庄线) Line to Rongjingdongjia East (荣京东街). New towns and business centres are growing up out of the main city, housing not only the people but the enterprises which are supporting the surging growth of the new China. From electronics and media, to high end design and high tech, the office blocks house corporations from all over the world, as well as the emerging new 'innovation plus' enterprises home grown in China.

Xu Zhidong is a product of the new China.

"I was born in Dangdong (丹东) city in Liaoning (辽宁) Province in 1981 and was the only child, in accordance with the one-child policy. My parents still live there. My mother was a worker and my father was first a government officer before he started his own business. They are both retired now."

We are sitting upstairs at the back of an open plan and well-appointed coffee shop in a smart shopping complex, a short taxi ride from the subway station. Xu Zhidong has driven here from his home 20 minutes away. The whole new town area requires a car. Unlike the centre of Beijing, where taxis and public transport are almost enough to survive, out here it is much more like the suburbs of Los Angeles or Philadelphia, with wide open roads and spaces. A car is almost essential and there are none of the quaint, even redeveloped, *hutongs* or old style residential blocks to be found in the middle of Beijing.

"When I was young I always wanted to be a teacher and, as I grew up through primary, middle and high school in Liaoning, that was my dream. It was a dream I had from when I, myself, was in school and felt that school lessons were boring and I could do much better! I applied to Liaoning Normal University and majored in maths, just as my mother had told me to do. I was a good Chinese son and followed the instructions of my parents, especially my mother. But behind all this was my desire to help kids to find lessons fun and interesting, particularly maths lessons."

Zhidong is a determined man. He clearly takes care of himself and exudes a healthy and fit glow. He has sharp-faced boyish good looks and an energy and enthusiasm which is infectious.

"I suppose I was not a great student, but I could do the work. I just didn't like the way it was all taught! I enjoyed playing football and didn't really bother about the lessons. I even fell asleep in some of them as they were so boring. Just six months into the first year at university I quit. I really didn't like it at all. It was the first time I had ever defied my parents. I did this on my own and without their knowledge. I told them I had quit after I did it, as I knew they would try to stop me if I told them what I was going to do. They were very angry with me and couldn't understand why I'd given up. I said I really wanted to make the decision myself and I would accept the consequences. I just wanted to take my own path in the world and not one organized for me by my parents."

After dropping out of Liaoning Normal University, Zhidong spent the following year studying again. He then sat and passed the Chinese college entrance examinations again. To sit and pass once is a major achievement for Chinese students and is a source of annual stress and strife in the education system, given that passing it is of such importance to parents and grandparents alike. To put himself through it all twice would seem like madness to many ordinary young Chinese. But Xu Zhidong is no ordinary man.

"Kids of my era really were a product of their parents and grandparents. The 1980s generation had little real freedom to choose their own path. They were so protected by their parents, who in turn had experienced the deprivations of the Cultural Revolution and wanted their offspring never to suffer what they had suffered. Those born after 1990 make decisions for themselves. They do what they like and want to do. They are so much more independent than we were. When I started work, after I eventually graduated, I was used to listening to and doing exactly what the team leader in the workplace said I should do. There was little encouragement to think for myself at all or to offer my own opinions. Now I make sure that I ask the 1990s generation workers what they think, how we can do it better, and what we should change to improve things."

Zhidong chose to take his major in journalism for his second time at university.

"After my dream to be a teacher, my other one was to be a news reporter. When I saw reporters on television I sort of saw a halo around them, a kind of aura. I wanted to be like that, to have the freedom to report. My second university course was at the Communication University of China in Beijing. I really enjoyed it. After I graduated I managed to get a job at a provincial TV station. I got it through my uncle who was involved in the media business. Until then my only real sense of achievement was scoring a goal in a football match. I hadn't stretched myself totally until then."

We discussed why he hadn't really bothered at school. I suggested that he seemed to find the work easy but had been a bit of a rebel? He grinned at me.

"I guess you are right. I was never really stretched so just got bored and created a bit of disruption, but I wanted to do something interesting with my life."

The TV station job was interesting enough for him to stay for three years but he found the need to report what was required tiresome and uninspiring.

"The role was to report political and Party news more often than not. It became repetitive with the same stuff time after time. There was nothing really interesting, nothing different. It was not what I had imagined it was going to be like so eventually I quit and decided to come to Beijing. People said I was crazy."

Zhidong has a huge grin on his face again. The rebel in him was out and taking exercise.

"My parents were cross with me. Again. They couldn't understand why I was taking another big risk with my life by leaving a stable job to come to the capital. It was another milestone in my life. I really have to thank my grandmother, my mother's mother, and especially my grandfather, my father's father. My grandmother said I should go to Beijing as it was a good place and my grandfather said that a good man can realize his ambition anywhere in the country. In addition, my grandfather gave me some good advice. He said I should practise Chinese calligraphy whenever I had time, I should learn English well, get computer skills, learn to drive a car and, above all, control my temper!"

"So how did you survive coming to Beijing with no job to come to?" I ask him.

"It was a big time of change for me. When I arrived, I was just like everyone else. I didn't stand out as being different and I had to get in the queues again; being a journalist had always given me a pass to the front of the queue, but not in Beijing. My biggest fear when I got here was that if I failed, then I would have to go back to my home town as a failure and that wasn't an option for me!"

"So you managed to get a job?"

"Thankfully my uncle, the one who was in the media world, told me about a job going at a national TV station. I managed to get a position as a programme editor on an interview programme as a contract worker. It was 2007. I worked there for a year but then left when the contract ended. Then I managed to work for a communications company involved in producing and providing programming to a national TV station. That lasted a year and then, again, the contract expired. It was a great help to me though as it allowed me to become reasonably well known in the Beijing media scene. The new job helped me understand how to commercialize the work I did. It woke me up to the fact that a programme is not just a programme. It is a product!"

So, he was out of a job again at the end of 2008. Though the programme had been a big success, there was a backlash from the general public, criticizing aspects of it and the TV company decided not to keep it going. It is unclear what the circumstances were and Zhidong does not elaborate.

"It was my uncle who spurred me to the next role. He told me to write 50 resumés and send them to the top 50 companies in the TV industry in China. He said, just take anything you can and go there to learn about the industry fully. Just going to all the interviews meant that I got to see the industry from a different perspective. It was good advice but I had no stable income. I was doing a contract here and another there. It was only a year but it was tough. I lived in the arts district out past the fifth ring road. I learned a lot but I still had much to learn. Then some friends told me that a TV station wanted to make an internet programme for their website. I registered a company with a friend and we put in a proposal and managed to get the contract. We did everything from planning to filming and editing; everything. They gave me a chance and I wanted to do a great job. I had to negotiate with investors too, which was a challenge on top of doing the work."

Zhidong and his friend worked hard and the result was programming which was not only successful in its own right, but also led to other projects. Throughout 2009 he created programme after programme for the TV company's web channel. Then, abruptly, there were big internal changes at the client and, despite the success of the past, the collaboration ceased. It was another break point in his life.

"I decided to go back to teaching again and applied to a lot of organizations until I got a part-time job teaching media and film. I got great feedback from the students, as I was able to mix theory with real life experiences and stories which they could relate to and which were practical. It was my happiest time with little or no pressure on me at all, but I had such a low income! It was a year of bliss but then I had to leave."

I ask him, "Why?"

"The school had a strict rule. Their teachers can't be lovers."

"Ah."

"We put all our money into the company and finally we literally only had ¥1.00 (10p) left. We ended up sleeping on the floor of the studio and had to wear all our clothes in winter as we could not afford any heating. We lived on credit but I managed to get a small contract, then another and another. It was a hand-to-mouth existence but slowly things got better into 2012. And I also managed to get a new part-time teaching job and that helped a lot."

The hand-to-mouth existence continued to 2013 when he got a lucky break. A large communications company wanted a video produced about the business for promotional purposes. He proceeded to learn all he could about the business so any video would be a true reflection of it. After all his investigations, Zhidong went home for two weeks and thought about the business in detail. Then he wrote the proposal and sent it to the president.

"He called me up and met me. He was very surprised when he met me as he thought the proposal had been written by someone much older than me as it was so detailed and thoughtful. He and I worked on the proposal for over a year together, improving it and refining it. Then he asked me to join the company as a Project Department Director."

Zhidong accepted the job and has been there ever since.

"It really fulfilled so many of my dreams as a job. I enjoyed it so much. I was very proud in 2013 when I made the proposal to the president of the company as he told me that not long after he read my proposal, which included a recommendation that the company start to take an international perspective, then President Xi Jinping spoke of the need for the Chinese culture to go out into the world. The company president felt I had seen what President Xi had seen before he spoke of it and that was providential. We shared a great vision – to take the company global – and there is so much opportunity to develop the business to the next level."

"So what next?"

Zhidong looks at me with sadness in his eyes.

"I don't really know. I quit the job two weeks ago," he replies.

"Why? I thought it was your dream job?" I ask.

"It was. It is. I left on a matter of principle. There was a disagreement. A misunderstanding. I felt I had no choice but to resign."

It turns out, after a little probing that I felt somewhat guilty for doing, that Zhidong left in a fit of anger, having felt he had been wrongly and unjustly accused of something. He felt he was the scapegoat for another colleague's misdemeanours. The resulting feeling of injustice had left him somewhat bitter and resentful. Now he feels he has been a bit hasty and driven by his emotions too much. Maybe he should have remembered his grandfather's advice to control his temper?

"You are right. I should go back. I have learned that the guy who spread the rumour has now been fired and the truth of the matter has been made clear to the big boss. I just got a message from his sister, who is also on the board of the company. She sent me a reference to the 1951 book by J.D. Salinger called *The Catcher in the Rye*. It was a sign for me to think again and go back."

I am impressed on a number of counts. Not only has Zhidong read the book, but so has the boss's sister, and knows a reference to it will be enough for him to read between the lines of the message she wants to send. He feels that she is telling him to reconsider his decision. The Chinese are always good at reading between the lines and interpreting the said from the unsaid, but this takes it to a whole new level I think. We debate the matter. Zhidong wants to go back to finish off what he has started and accepts he was a bit hasty, but still feels a principle is worth making a stand on. So, what will he do?

"I'll probably go back after Chinese New Year. My grandfather was right. I've talked a lot with the vice president and they want me back. I just need a little more time to elapse so my point is made. People think I am a dynamic and driven businessman, but I am quite different at home. I am a reflective person really. I dress differently for different occasions; for work I wear a suit, for media visits I wear fashionable stuff and when I am relaxed, then just jeans and a shirt, like today."

We continue to chat about Zhidong and his personal life. He spends a good deal of time reflecting on life and sharing tea with friends or at home alone. It's unclear if the girlfriend is still around and I don't pry.

"I would like to write a book about my life. Maybe even a film. It has been a roller coaster ride and so varied. There have been times when I've had nothing and times when I've had so much. But I've tried to always be myself, to be reflective, to be true to me, to be a good man. Perhaps a bit of a rebel too."

A rebel with a cause I wonder? Sounds like a good title for the film.

THERE IS NO CHAPTER FOUR

My colleague screws up her nose.

"I really wouldn't do that."

"Do what?" I stop in mid-flow of my explanation to the bank clerk that I want to transfer £250 from my international account to my local Chinese one.

"Don't transfer £250."

I wasn't aware she had been listening to my discussion about a personal transaction but I let that pass in my curiosity.

"Why not?"

"It's a bad number."

Some swift-but-delicate quizzing (with an eye to the grumpiness of the next customer in line) was worthwhile.

The Chinese are superstitious when it comes to numbers. Indeed, they are superstitious about many things. Portents, omens and auspicious happenings have been part of Chinese history and culture for thousands of years. There are books written on the subject. It should be taken very seriously indeed by anyone wishing to understand the Chinese and their culture better.

Numbers are important to the Chinese and readers interested in this subject should do their research carefully. Having an important meeting or event on the 'wrong' date can result in no one showing up. I have now gotten used to asking, "What date would be best for you?" or "Is there a better date for this meeting, event or activity?" It is always appreciated, and the choice of a good date, driven by the lunar calendar and not the Western one, will result in smiles and satisfaction. Deals can be won and lost on the signing date being a 'good' or a 'bad' one. In addition, arranging meetings or visits around the major holidays is a disaster. Avoid the times immediately before and after Chinese New Year, Lantern Festival, Mid-Autumn Festival and Labour Day, at the very least. All of these, except Labour Day, which is always on 1 May, are governed by the lunar calendar, so the Western date changes every year.

The lunar calendar governs much of the Chinese annual cycle, and indeed the cycle of life in China. Watch out for birthdays. Since the Chinese use the lunar calendar, don't assume that your friends' or colleagues' birthdays will be on the same Western date each year. They won't be. Most Chinese people working with foreigners opt for a standard birthday date for ease, but they will still celebrate the right birthday date, according to the lunar calendar, with friends and family.

Equally important are phrases and gifts. Weddings, in particular, and certain other events where money is often the main gift, are fraught with numerical complications. The number eight is a good number and 888 is a great one. Apartments in high rise developments on floors eight or 18 or 28 will be much more expensive.

Back in the bank, my colleague explains that when 250 is said in the Chinese language, it sounds very similar to the characters for 'imbecile'. The counter staff are now giggling almost uncontrollably. Rather sheepishly, I amend my transfer to a less 'stupid' number and everyone dissolves into smiles of cross-cultural understanding.

So, I have found to my cost that numbers are important. So important, indeed, that since the sound of the character for the number four is very similar to the sound of the character for death, you will not find a fourth floor button in lifts, there will be no block four in housing estates, no row four or seat four in cinemas and no fourth chapter in this book.

BEING GAY IN BEIJING

Harry (Zhu Wan Yu) is waiting for me outside the coffee shop. It is not even open yet. We are early but I am expecting her. Short cut hair, casual androgynous clothing and boyish features speak of individualism and a strong sense of self.

Born in 1988, Harry is one of the growing number of Chinese who have come out and openly acknowledged that they are gay.

"I left home after middle school and went to Canada at the age of 16. I was 24 when I came back. I was at high school in Vancouver, then attended York University in Toronto and studied economics. Eight years is a long time in China, so when I came back, there were really no friends here who could help me build my career so I have had to build it up from scratch."

Harry is open, engaging and direct. She makes no effort to hide who she is or how she feels. This is in stark contrast to the otherwise broadly closed community of gay people in China. Though they are increasingly more vocal in both Shanghai and Beijing, there is little to tell of their community outside these two more international and cosmopolitan of cities.

"My father always pushed me to do something but never told me exactly to 'do this' or 'do that'. He just asked me to think of what I wanted for myself. I really appreciate that from him. He is still in Tianjin, where he is a self-made man, an entrepreneur. He has a business making sensors for the electronics industry. He worked at a German electronics company for ten years and then set up on his own and has been very successful. I came to Beijing from Tianjin in 2012 as it was too difficult for me there. It was too small and too slow a pace for me."

I think that maybe by staying in her home town, Harry felt she would be recognized as different and it would have been continually difficult for her parents to have her there as an unmarried and so visibly independent and different woman. My feeling is that the loss of face in the local community for her parents may well have contributed to the feeling of claustrophobia and 'cabin fever' which pushed the move to Beijing.

Her look is piercing at times. She has a quiet confidence and self-assurance born of knowing who she is, what she believes in and what she wants from life. She sips coffee between pouring out her words. But there is a pace and clarity to her delivery which draws you into her story and touches you to the core. She is quiet and shy in many ways, but determined to speak out about who she is and what she stands for.

"I went to an international school in Dalian until Grade 10 and they had a strong Canadian connection with the Sentinel School in Western Vancouver. So, I managed to go there for two years, staying with a Taiwanese family who had a house there. It is supposed to be the nicest community in Canada and I really enjoyed it. I came back home for two months in the summer each year but chose to stay over and attend summer school for two months each year too.

"I lived on my own for four years when I did a Masters at York University in Toronto. I rented an apartment not far from the campus. My father helped me. I was not very outgoing and a little shy, so most of the time I kept myself to myself and stayed in more often than I went out. I learned karate in my spare time and didn't have many friends. Actually, I was quite fat in Canada! Too much good food. When I came back home and my mother came to collect me from the airport she didn't recognize me as I looked so different! I was fat and had yellow hair too. The second time she didn't recognize me either as I had lost the weight and changed my hair again."

Her individuality was clear, both to her and to her family, from her teenage years at middle school. Her father supported her from the very start, though her mother has taken a while to accept her difference; maybe, I feel, she still hasn't.

"I came back to China for my family. They never thought about emigration and I was very lonely in Canada so I came home. I didn't feel that economics as a degree would help me develop a career as I really didn't see myself in a bank – I knew I wouldn't fit in. I really wanted and want to be different."

"How?" I ask.

"Everything really – I look different with my very short hair and I never wear a skirt. I have my own ideas and I don't do what people tell me I should do. I don't agree with the pressure from society here, to conform to the expected norm. Most women of my age are supposed to be married. I don't accept it."

She speaks calmly, but there is strength and more than a hint of defiance in the words and tone. Here is a young woman who is a strong individual and has the underlying strength of character to carry it through in the most difficult of circumstances and against the strongest of societal norms.

"My parents accept that I am different. My father just wants me to be happy every day. Most Chinese parents say they want their children to be happy, but in reality, they can't do it as 'being happy' means to conform to social norms. The pressure is really high but I would say that while Chinese society cares that I am gay and sees it as outside normality, 80% of people you meet don't really care. They are just getting on with their own lives. I'd say 90% of Chinese parents care deeply about the sexuality of their children. However, when I told my father, he was not surprised and he encouraged me to be happy. He said it is not important. I am not hurting anyone and no one is affected other than me. I realized I was gay when I was a teenager. It was just clear to me and I accepted it."

"So now, in Beijing, you are working?"

"Yes, I am in the film industry. It is quite a new business, owned by a friend of my father. I worked in the Beijing Bookworm Bookstore (a famous location in Beijing as a library, bookstore, coffee shop and bar) for the first three months I was here. One day, I got a phone call from my father and he asked, "Do you want to go into the film business?" I said, "Yes," and met the guy my father knew. He had expected me to be a big fan of movies, but I wasn't! He was a bit surprised but he wanted to give me a chance, so he sent me to work for a media company he knew in Beijing. They were creating a database of films and I helped to set it up. I was there for a year."

Here lies the story of many people of Harry's generation. Jobs come from connections and, more often than not, connections come from deep-rooted friendships of family. Helping the daughter or son of a friend cements the bond of a relationship, which is so important in China. *Guanxi* are what China has run on for thousands of years and it isn't changing any time soon. It's as much about who you know, or who your family know, as it is about qualifications, intelligence and application. Harry's story is a common one, as the next generation of China's educated middle classes expands and develops. It is repeated across China's society, but among the emerging and burgeoning middle classes, it is particularly strong as a boost to start people off on their careers.

"I stopped that job after a year as I wanted to study again. However, my father's friend said he didn't want me to go back to school but to get more experience. I agreed to work for him and study in my own time. Self study is hard, I have to learn on my own and I do find this really tough. I read a lot of books so I can learn about the film industry and film-making. I have also been reading and learning a lot about Chinese history. I lost all that learning about the history of my own country by going to Canada. I never thought about it as a teenager. However, now I think it is really important. If you can understand your own country's history, then you can understand your culture better. I have read a lot about the culture of my country. History is made up of people, and people make history. This is really important to me now."

To lose a grip on history in China is almost to lose your identity. People tell me that you are not truly Chinese unless you understand the subtleties of the culture, and the culture is driven not just by the language, complex as that is, but by the detailed and ingrained history taught through all schools and across all ages. There is just so much to absorb that coming to it late in life, and on your own, is almost too much. Harry seems to be struggling with this element of her own identity, without which she will always be even more of the outsider she has already chosen to be. I know this from a personal perspective, that despite my lack of language skills, just understanding some of China's deep and complex history has already unlocked an understanding which I would never have achieved if I had just tried to absorb it by working and living here. Even as I barely scratch the surface, I learn more and more and expand my understanding. But I am not Chinese. The power of the draw and the hunger to understand is almost irresistible if you are.

"The film industry in China is very different to that in the rest of the world," continues Harry. "In Chinese films, there is almost no planning. If you are the director, you also have to do everything else, script, lighting, everything. It is a hard job to master everything. The normal rules in the West for films are not applied in China. We have learned much from Hollywood and from the West but the industry here wants to make films that are run to our own, Chinese, rules. Also, the government has a perspective on all films and there are really strong guidelines. We can't tell ghost stories, the bad guy cannot prevail and you can't talk about gay people. We are constrained a good deal, but we have to accept it and things continue to change."

This perspective on film and the industry is also commented on elsewhere (Chapter 34) by Professor Huang, Dean of the Beijing Film Academy. Harry is candid about the influence of censorship on film and its production. Widely known and understood, the Chinese censorship department for the film industry has the right to demand changes to scripts and style right up to the last minute of release. In the words of a friend, "It is what it is," and people just have to accept it as part of the growing pains of this fast-growing economy. Indeed, there are recent examples of films being released and then cut or amended post release. There are strict rules on what you can show, including how much bare flesh in a shot. Low-cut dresses which reveal too much are not deemed appropriate and much debate prevails on the internet of post-production amendments to some quite high-profile films which first passed the reviews only to be subsequently amended three or four days after general release. The industry rolls with these punches and remains highly competitive and is growing at breakneck speed.

I ask Harry what the future holds for her.

"I enjoy doing interesting things. I am really interested in what I am doing and every day at work is different. It suits me and who I am."

And what will she be doing in five years' time?

"I hope my name will be in the credits of a movie. Maybe I will have written a script, which has become a film. I want to make a story about real life, gay life, but I don't know even if in five years' time it will be allowed to be published or released. I want to make a movie about our generation. Many people of my age don't really think about things deeply. They just adhere to the norm, the expectations that society seems to have of them, that parents have of them, that friends and neighbours have of them."

Harry is a very determined and resolute character. Her words are deliberate, thoughtful and heartfelt. She is reticent at times, but there is no lack of self-assurance or confidence in her ideas and views. She wears her sexuality easily and as a matter of fact. There is none of the ambiguity of position so often found in other gay Chinese people who seem to feel the need to conform, even to marry, for the sake of family 'face'. There is not even the slightest hint of that in Harry.

"I want to tell the story of modern Chinese women – the ones who have the inner strength to be different. This will be a new language for the people of China and for my generation. When you learn a language, it is not just the words and the grammar you need to know, but the history and the culture as well, to really understand. I believe that my story and the story of people like me also needs to be told in China. We are part of the new culture of the country and, as such, need to speak out and be heard as equals, contributing equally to making our country successful, as distinctly and proudly Chinese."

I rather think the story will be told more and more, and strongly sense that Harry will be one of the proud participants and active narrators.

POLLUTION AND WINDOW CLEANERS

CHAPTER 6: POLLUTION AND WINDOW CLEANERS

It catches the back of your throat. You wake up with a dry mouth and the feeling that someone has smeared your lips with coal. Welcome to Beijing in smog time. The rasping cough sounded like he'd been on 60 cigarettes a day all his life, but Mr Liang was contorted with the effort of clearing his throat, not due to the cheap cigarettes that stub out any vaguely healthy aspect of restaurants in China, but from living in Beijing.

Mr Liang runs a successful fruit shop just around the corner from where I live in the Chaoyang District of Beijing.

"Sounds like you have had a bad day Mr Liang?" I smile across the room. He shuffles over to my table and collapses in a disorderly heap into the chair opposite me.

"So you are not working today?" he counters, in a gruff and growling manner that belies the smile on his face. He doesn't drink coffee but knows I'll pay, so will have one of his endless teas.

"I'm a foreigner. We get days off!"

"You should have my job; never a day off."

"Bad cough Mr Liang."

I hit a nerve and he is off on his tirade, carefully focused on the failure of the local, rather than national, government to solve the crushingly atrocious smog and pollution in this enormous city. Received wisdom is that the pollution knocks up to ten years off your life here and even small children are in hospital with respiratory problems.

A friend of mine told me at dinner last night that his wife had held their youngest back from kindergarten since the classroom air filter wasn't working. Some schools actually close when the official air quality index rises above 300. World Health Organization figures suggest that anything over 50 is hazardous. It's the noxious cocktail of carbon monoxide, sulphur dioxide and the particulates smaller than 2.5 microns that settle in your lungs and can't be eradicated. It's the grit in the air that you can actually taste when you land at the airport, as the outside air is pumped in to greet you rather than scooped out of the atmosphere up at 10,000 metres.

You can tell when it is really bad because even the locals wear face masks. I must say, I was a little bemused once to see a local with a face mask on and a cigarette in his hand. "How does that work?" I remember thinking. "Which is the lesser of the two evils?"

"Cigarettes," my colleague cynically remarked, "take the taste of the air away!"

Mr Liang directs his well-rehearsed and articulate attack at the singular failure, he opines, of the local authorities to stamp on, in no particular order: factory emissions from poorly run industry to the west and north west of the city, poor-quality diesel used in the increased number of buses, too many cars on the streets, dust from construction of too many office blocks and shopping malls and badly managed licence plate issuing, which allows the rich to have two plates for the same car, to avoid the oft announced 'odd and even' number plate days.

This peculiar, but oft enacted, bylaw of Beijing means that if you have a car licence plate ending in an odd number, you could be banned from driving into the city on alternate days of the week to those with an even number, if that makes sense! Bizarre as it seems, and broadly unenforceable in practice, this is supported by the local population who, by and large, abide by it. Not so the wealthy few, who simply do not bother with the nicety of a plate at all and, if stopped, haggle on the 'fee' payable to the policeman, or buy two plates, through whatever means they have available, and then use one or the other as appropriate.

Mr Liang is still going strong and we seem to have been joined by both the coffee shop owner and the man who I could have sworn was washing the windows a few minutes ago. We all conclude that "something should be done" by "the authorities" and "the powers that be" need to "stop it right now". I could be back in my local pub in Yorkshire talking about traffic-calming measures on the main road through our village. It is the faceless bureaucrats of anywhere in the world at which the general public's venom is directed and, here in Beijing and many of the other severely polluted cities of modern China, it is no different.

The violent agreement subsides and my bill comes. I seem to have been charged for all of our drinks. Some things don't change wherever you are in the world!

LILLY

The Xiehe (北京协和医院) hospital is one of the best in Beijing and so, by definition, in China. I have only visited it once before, in the small hours of an unforgettable day when I needed urgent medical attention and had to subsequently fly back to the UK to get it. There is a public wing, a private one and a specialist international department where the staff all speak English (except those on duty at 02.30!) and the doctors and nursing staff are some of the best in China. However, the international ward and private wings are not the norm in your average Chinese hospital.

I am accompanied by a translator, not least because I thought navigating the hospital protocols to get to my interviewee would be labyrinthine. Lilly (not her real name) is in for treatment. Cocooned in a private ward on the fifth floor of the private wing, she is only prepared to see me on the understanding that the interview is to be anonymous.

We are early. Rather surprisingly, we sail through the hospital without being stopped or challenged. The staff are friendly and accommodating, anxious to help us find where we need to be and, with smiles and nods of acknowledgement, we navigate the lifts and corridors with ease. We have to wait a little to enter the fifth floor private ward via a friendly security guard who unlocks and opens the door for everyone with permission to enter, but other than that it's just like visiting anyone in any Western hospital.

Lilly comes out personally to the reception area to greet us in hospital pyjamas, dressing gown and slippers. She ushers us into a spartan but warm general waiting area where, other than another visitor sitting quietly, we are alone.

"I'm sorry we had to meet here," Lilly explains, "I'm in for some treatment. Do you want to see my room?"

"Sure."

We walk a short distance down a corridor that could have been in any hospital anywhere in the world. It has the same antiseptic smell and same white lights and scrubbed floors, the same slightly blue/white painted walls and the same notices and hand cleaning points. Her room is unremarkable and well appointed, with a TV, small table and cupboard, curtained bed and discrete drip and medical trolley unit. An older woman is sitting on the bed. She gets up suddenly when we enter but is waved back down by Lilly.

"This is my *ayi* (阿姨 – Chinese name for 'home help'), she's taking a rest while we talk."

The woman smiles and bows slightly. It seems Lilly has brought her home help with her to hospital to look after her. Unusual I think.

"Do you like my room?" she asks.

"Sure."

"You should see the public wards. They are terrible, beds everywhere. Even in the corridors. I'm lucky as I can afford to be private. It's not good over there."

I had been 'over there' before. In addition to my previous early morning foray into the international department of this hospital, I have been to others in Beijing with friends who were open to being accompanied. They are overloaded and stretched to breaking point. There are stories of bribes and corruption to jump queues, see the best doctors, or just any doctor. The whole issue of counterfeit and substandard drugs has been in the news in China for several years and counterfeits have been found to be in widespread use. People died, the government stepped in, but there remains huge suspicion and mistrust of the public system. There is a general belief that if you pay and pay enough then you will get the best care and, hopefully, the real drugs and care you need.

"I'm quite ill." Lilly is remarkably candid though even my interpreter and I initially struggle with exactly what is wrong with her. "I've been here a while and have to stay a bit longer. They told me I just have to stop everything and rest. Otherwise I could die."

Lilly is an interesting character. A child of the 1970s, she spent her early years in China then went to the US. She sits curled up in one of the big hospital chairs which are lined up along two walls of the room. I sit next to her, twisting round to face her alongside me. Wrapped tightly in a light dressing gown, she has somewhat dishevelled short black hair and almost androgynous features. She spends the whole time staring at me intently through her large round, black-rimmed glasses. It is a little disconcerting at times.

"I am from Beijing but I went to the US and lived in Los Angeles and California for 15 years," Lilly speaks, with fluent English.

My interpreter relaxes, perfect English needs no translation, or so we think.

"I did a management degree at the University of Southern California and then worked for a professor for three years as a technical assistant. Then in 2012 I watched an interview with Jack Ma, the founder of Alibaba. He was talking about Big Data. He was amazing. I had never used Taobao but he was inspirational. His vision of the future is compelling. He explained then about the platform as one for everyone, he explained how Alipay would work, how big data would be used, how it would change everything. I decided I wanted to work for Alibaba."

It is a stream of consciousness and it starts to explain why Lilly is in hospital.

"I have always been fascinated by data and what it can tell you. My professor told me that 'the best data wins'. I believe that. Data tells you lots of things. People think that we (Alibaba) keep data on everyone. That just isn't the case. It's the big trends that we look at, not the detail. In 2012 there was almost no data but in 2014 the job I got was actually in data! I went to work in Hangzhou for Ali (Alibaba). I stayed for a little over a year. I only survived a little over a year. Ali is going global and it's like a super tanker, it is just shipping so much data. They needed and need people who understand the East and the West so they can exploit the world and achieve their ambitions."

"How did you end up working for Alibaba?"

"My cousin went to the US in 1986, when I was very little. I wanted to go too. My parents were middle class. My father was an accountant and my mother was a lab technician. My mother told me that the only person you should ever compete with is yourself, to be better today than you were yesterday. I managed to get a scholarship to the US later but that was only going to pay for my tuition and basic food. I needed more money so I borrowed money from lots of people, mainly family, so I could go and live and study in the US. I remember one time I only had $2,000 for a whole semester. It was so hard just to survive!"

Lily jumps from subject to subject then back again.

"I've been very affected by the book *Mindset*. (*Mindset: the new psychology of success* by Stanford University professor, Dr Carol Dweck, 2006), which is a seminal book espousing the notion that what you believe affects what you achieve. It has totally changed my understanding of myself. I feel I have a growth mindset."

Dweck's book and research suggests that having a 'growth mindset', rather than a 'fixed mindset', can lead to enhancement of capability and ability, even the strengthening of intelligence itself.

"I believe that becoming is better than being. For 20 years I didn't really know about myself."

She tails off into silence.

So, what about Alibaba?

"I worked there from the end of 2014 to early 2016. I quit because of my health. But Alibaba was not a good fit for me. I couldn't continue. I'm quite hyper and this caused problems that I didn't realize. To me things were obvious, I have very high standards. Even my bottom line was at a much higher level than people around me. There was a huge gap between my bottom line and my teams' top level of performance. I just didn't know how to lower my level of standard to get things done ..." she tails off again.

So?

"The second problem was rules. I have lots of rules and I like rules. It seemed like ..."

Like what?

"Like ... They just have no rules at Alibaba."

She sinks into the chair shaking her head. Her eyes are still fixed on mine, almost imploring an understanding at this impossible situation.

"I need a work life balance and my family. They see Alibaba as your family and your life. I remember seeing Jack Ma speak about Alibaba and his vision. I remember him spending eight minutes on the story and then three minutes for the AliPay demo. I remember him saying something like 'Apple is not tomorrow, Apple is only giving the direction to tomorrow'. I cried when I heard what he said. I was inspired but I just couldn't do anything to help him."

"I made lots of friends ... But ... Life is ... it was a turning point for me. I will not go back and for family reasons I want to stay here in Beijing."

A deep breath and another stream of thinking is unleashed.

"Opportunities are broadening in China for the use of data. It's China's time for big data. This thing about China and big data, why are people (Westerners) worried about it? I just don't understand. When we use data in business we don't look at it on an individual level, we look at characteristics, trends and the macro picture. If companies obey the rules, then there is no reason to worry about data. I really don't understand the problem. Maybe all those things we dread and worry about, maybe they will come true. But why dread these things? Why not see them as opportunities? If you watch the animated kids film *Big Hero 6* (Walt Disney 2014), it's all about big data, it's a sci-fi movie but it's quite interesting how the things we see in movies now, well they are becoming possible and may happen. I truly believe that we are only constrained by our imagination. I agree with Zuckerberg and his wife. It's possible to eradicate illness in the world. We just need to use data to do it. I have fallen in love with medicine. Doctors are such skilled individuals. We can use big data to help them. This time in hospital has given me the space to think."

A long pause hangs in the air. I leave it there.

Then another deep breath.

"Jack (Ma) once said: 'Today is cruel. Tomorrow is crueller. And the day after tomorrow is beautiful'. This is about the dream. People are fighting for resources. There are plenty of resources in the world; it is the distribution system that is the problem. A lot of things I think are wrong in the West. My imagination has no boundaries, that's the problem. My brain can't handle too much. I was nearly dying. I could see what Alibaba could and needed to do and the possibilities we could open with the data."

Lilly teeters on the edge of another deep breath.

So, what next?

"Oh. I'd like to get out of here then to work for my mentor. He is an innovator in big data. I can learn a lot from him. The competitive advantage in big data is around generating knowledge, insights and good processes. He is doing the right things around big data. When I was younger I was a product manager and I created products using data analysis. I liked to define things very specifically using data. I have always been able to understand the very detailed as well as the overview. I can see the map of things, projects, programmes, problems and their solutions from the top level. I'm not sure why but I can see everything that can and needs to be done all at the same time."

We continue to jump backwards and forwards through time, side to side through problems and solutions. It is sometimes difficult to keep up with her ability to stop, turn, jump, explore, return to the place where she left off the previous subject and then back to another one. Each jump is clean and crisp, to exactly the point she had previously left. She holds times, quotes, dates and circumstances cleanly and accurately.

And your dream for the future?

"My dream is to retire to a place I like with all my friends. I don't want much. Just staying healthy would be good. Ask me a year from now."

As we leave, exhausted, after precisely the allocated 60 minutes, my interpreter turns to me.

"I'm afraid I didn't understand a word she was saying. I think she's mad!"

I'm still absorbing the impact of the encounter.

The distance between genius and madness is a very thin line. Lilly walks the line every day.

The security guard locks us out of the ward.

THE MAN
WHO MET
THE QUEEN

Jeffery was born in 1982 in west Beijing. He is a Beijinger. Recently married and living in his own apartment immediately above that of his parents, he is typical of his generation; well-educated, middle-class Chinese. Schooled first in a local kindergarten and junior school, his parents managed to get him into a Canadian school in Beijing. One of the burgeoning international schools in China, the school gave him the international education his parents wanted for their son. Later, he was sent to the UK to complete his A-levels at a Broxtowe College, Nottinghamshire, followed by Keele University, where he studied economics and business administration between 2001 and 2004.

"I sort of see myself as being a little bit British," he says. "I spent so long there, it is almost like a second home to me. I loved it there. I was lucky, because when I finished university, I went to London to train in accounting to get an Association of Chartered Certified Accountants qualification as a part-time student. I was so lucky. I lived in the centre of London in Warren Street for 18 months. My parents served in the military, but a long time ago, and they returned to Beijing in the 1980s. My father was involved in the set-up of the Beijing Stock Exchange. My mother worked at the Beijing Bureau of Finance. They are both retired now."

I ask Jeffery why he decided to return to China.

"I wanted to come back. There is so much opportunity here. I set up a business with a friend in Changsha (长沙). We had a marketing and advertising agency for two years. He had lots of contacts with the local government and we did ok for a while. However, it was hard and we decided to close it after two years and I came back to Beijing. I got a job with an emerging accounting and finance firm here and have been working there ever since. We are now much more international and it's really interesting to see how the business has developed over the years. It's a bit weird sometimes as we are a local company, and very Chinese in management style."

Jeffery sees one overarching difference between the traditional Chinese business and that of the West.

"It is really significant. Traditional Chinese companies are very hierarchical. The boss is really the boss and the workers are the workers and pretty well do as they are told. I work in marketing and it is different as we have a more internationally minded manager. It's a struggle sometimes, though it's much better than it used to be. When we were totally a local business, we were working all hours and weekends, it was so tough and we just had our heads down all the time with a small team. Now, we have a much better way of working with a lot more flexibility. I usually leave at 18.00, so there is time for me to get home and spend time with my wife and to see my parents. Now, I can see my parents every day for at least half an hour a day."

I was fortunate enough to have attended Jeffery's wedding last year, and it seemed appropriate to explore his views on marriage as a newlywed.

"My wife comes from Shenyang (沈阳) in Liaoning (辽宁) Province. A friend of mine introduced us. She works in Beijing. We met in February 2012 and got married in October 2014. We are a good match. I really view marriage very seriously indeed. Not everyone does, you know."

Reflecting on his comments, I am reminded of the many stories from friends and acquaintances of couples marrying for convenience and security, rather than love.

"I think it is a huge responsibility," he says. "You have to be willing to spend the rest of your life with the other person. I must admit that I was a little scared and fearful of getting married. But I overcame my fear since our personalities are so well-matched. We are very balanced together. She is not materialistic either so we have a good shared set of values. I knew she was the one from very early on in our relationship. We hope to have children next year, perhaps. We are a little unusual in China as a young couple since we live separately from both our parents. We have been able to buy our own place in the same block as my parents, so we are close but also separate. It is a perfect way of living."

Our conversation turns to the subject of *sheng nv* (剩女). This is the Chinese name for a group of women in their 30s who are single. Directly translated it means 'the women who are left behind'. In China, it is estimated that by the year 2020 there will be around 30 million more men than women between the ages of 25 and 40, mainly in the rural areas. The reality is that in the cities there are more single women. This goes deep into the Chinese culture. In the rural areas, the pressure to have boys as the single child has led, one way or another, to there being more boys than girls. This pressure historically stemmed from the need for a secure source of labour and income for the future of the family. Stories of infanticide still circulate across China and there is too much 'noise in the system' to ignore it. Unwanted pregnancies in girls under the age of 18 was a factor in the past. The costs and social stigma of fatherless children didn't help either. Certainly, the facts are that women find it easier to live in the cities. More freedom is certainly a factor, and away from the rural pressure to marry and conform, they are either choosing to marry later or simply can't find the right urban partner with the same 'new' attitudes. These girls are in a rush to get married. Their biological clocks are ticking but their attitudes and urbanized freedoms of jobs and money hold them back.

"In the second-tier cities, girls tend to get married before they are 25 years old. In the more rural communities, women will get married in their early 20s. Parents want girls to marry early so they will have grandchildren in time to look after them in their old age. In the big cities, people are more open-minded and see the whole matter of marriage as not just the parents' decision. Also, when these *sheng nv* look for a husband, they will look above to an older man, even a man who might be divorced. The older men look for a younger woman so there is a match but the *sheng nv* don't really have much choice. In big cities like Beijing and Shanghai, the majority of parents expect their daughter to find someone who has a house. They will be much more supportive of their daughter dating a man who owns a house than someone who doesn't."

There is a question I have long been wary of asking people I have met in China, but the conversation seems to allow it here. "Does love matter in marriage?"

Jeffery pauses for a long time.

"Well, even if a couple is in love, they will be under a lot of pressure. Some just don't get married or have to marry someone they don't love because the parents will not agree to them marrying the person they do love. The pressures are very high, from parents, friends, work and even society."

I recently heard of a landlord refusing to take a single girl as a tenant unless they could speak to the girl's parents to establish their support for her as single and of good repute. In another instance, I've heard of women being overlooked for a promotion at work in certain Chinese companies as they were seen as immature, and not ready for responsibility because they were not married and did not have a child.

"In Beijing there is definitely a tradition that the guy provides a house for the marriage. The girl will provide the car. I know it is a bit materialistic, but it is a financial guarantee for a good marriage and a better future. It's very common. In larger cities, there are fewer men who own a house among the ages of 20 and 30, the prime years for marriage. In cities like Beijing and Shanghai, buying a house is a precondition to getting married. Both families will put all they can, all their savings, into a house for the couple. There is a philosophy about houses. It is the most important thing to a Chinese person. Without a house, you don't have a home! No home and you have no family! It means security. It is seen as very bad to live in someone else's house, like a rented place. It isn't good. You need to own your own place. My parents spent their lives saving for me and my wife and I will spend our lives saving for our children. It's the Chinese way."

The Chinese save money. Chinese people will save more than 50% of their salary each year, whereas Westerners will be lucky to save more than 12%.

"Chinese tourists spent ¥6bn in ten days in Japan over this year's Chinese New Year. We have money and we are prepared to spend it. Before the Chinese travelled abroad as we do now, no one knew about this aspect of our culture. Now they do. I hear that 12% of buildings bought in Australia in 2014 were sold to Chinese buyers!"

I know this personally. A friend of mine who lives in Australia is selling his house and advertising it on Chinese websites. He has been advised to search for buyers in China, as Australians are less likely to be able to afford the high price tag on his beautiful and secluded home than wealthy Chinese people with an eye to emigration.

Somehow, our conversation ranges from topic to topic around money until we settle on a personal favourite. Banks. And service. Or the lack of it.

"Banks don't care and they don't put customer service high on their list of priorities," asserts Jeffery. "The big banks are state owned. They are just too big. They are among the biggest banks in the world, let alone in China. ICBC is the biggest in the world, Bank of China is huge too and they get too much money from business to bother about their private customers. Add to that, the restrictions on foreign banks in China, and there is no motivation to improve services at all, there is just no big competition."

The waiting times in China's banks are legendary. The seeming slickness of the electronic ticketing and queuing system belies the true crushing inefficiency. Chronically understaffed branches are the norm, with staff who are generally diffident, disinterested and ponderous. The systems are slow and tedious, with procedures and processes bureaucratic and arcane. Add to this 'random' security scrutiny and senior-level oversight, and you have a recipe for utter customer disservice. Most branches have a 'customer waiting area', usually of some considerable size.

It is not uncommon for people to wait an hour for relatively simple transactions like getting a bank statement printed, which took me 45 minutes last week, in an empty bank branch. Resident Chinese people, on the other hand, can expect to wait two to three hours if they want to do a relatively complex transaction, such as currency exchange between two accounts. This sort of 'specialist' banking usually only has one staff member allocated to it and often, in central Beijing at least, several customers waiting at any one time.

Not surprisingly, there has been a quantum leap in online banking. In digital China, there are more and more mobile banking applications available to do all the things the West is increasingly taking for granted, and several innovations which are yet to hit many 'developed' countries' service providers. You can do pretty much anything you like online if you have money, certainly if it involves depositing it in large quantities. Actually, most ATM machines have a deposit facility and you do see many Chinese people with wads of cash in everything from brown paper bags (yes really) to smart security satchels, feeding the distinctive red ¥100 notes into hungry machines.

The issue is big withdrawals. Even transfers from one account to another in your own name. That is always a trial.

"I am really lucky since I have spare cash, I own my house so have no mortgage," says Jeffery. "My wife and I have more leisure time too, so we spend it with friends, drinking and having food together, we go shopping, to the movies and, of course, time with my parents."

These words are from the heart of the Chinese middle classes. Money to spend and the time to spend it. Priorities of family and the proximity to be able to achieve these priorities.

"I spend time with my parents every day. We will expect our children to look after us when we are old and I am doing that for my parents now. It's the Chinese way. My wife goes back to visit her parents regularly too. She went back for the Chinese New Year to be with her parents. It's so important. They are so important to both of us. Her parents are older now. Her father has a business selling heavy machinery to construction companies. It is getting harder and harder to make a sale as the real estate market has collapsed across China. It is really tough now. I think he will sell the business soon or just stop. It's just getting too hard to make it all work."

How does Jeffery feel about the prospects for China and himself as the country goes through a time of rebalancing and lower, though still reasonable, growth?

"I think I am normal among my peer group. I have no rent so I can spend my money on what I want. Houses are expensive here. An average small house will cost about ¥30,000 (£3,300) per square metre. Mine was about ¥60,000 (£6,600) a square meter, as we are near the second west ring road in central Beijing. Average salaries in Beijing are around ¥6000–¥7000 (£650–£750) a month so it is really hard for those who do not have a house. Most people will have to spend over 50% of their monthly salary on their rent and the rest easily goes on food, so there is nothing left each month to put into saving for a house."

House prices in Beijing and in Shanghai are holding up. Indeed, they have increased, even though elsewhere across China real estate prices and construction have collapsed, leaving great holes in the ground and the economy. I continue to see block after block of built and half-built residential blocks standing empty, but the cement and steel keeps being produced, the marble quarried and the migrant workers employed as the economy strides along, seemingly impervious to the chronic over-supply and consequent potential social and infrastructure problems this is going to create.

Jeffery is contemplating his future and that of his children.

"We hope to have children next year and we are applying for Canadian citizenship for our unborn child."

This is news to me.

"My wife wants to live abroad and it is also for our children, we always wanted them to be able to be born abroad. My parents are ok with it. The pollution is just so bad in Beijing. It is a real issue. There are also the food safety hazards, the contamination of rice and basic foodstuffs is well known. Overseas, where quality is a given in the food chain, there is more reliability. There is also our children's education. It is now a realistic choice for middle-class Chinese parents, to have their children educated abroad."

I ask him how long he would go for and whether he plans to return to China.

"Of course!" he replies. "It would only be for a few years while our children grow up and are schooled. Then, of course, we would come back. We haven't really thought about it at all really. Staying away isn't really an option. My wife wants our baby to be born in Canada. It is one of the easier places for Chinese people to get citizenship. (Canada has just followed the US in agreeing to issue 10-year visas with China.) It is a big burden on my shoulders but we know the Chinese way is to give your best to your children and then they will give their best to you as you grow old. My parents paid for me to go to school – it's a cycle of life so I will do the same for my children and look after my parents. It has been this way generation after generation in China and it will always be the way here. We all believe in the China Dream, that China will rise again, peacefully."

The paranoia of many Westerners regarding China should be assuaged by comments such as these from Jeffery, and so many of his middle-class cohort.

"The Chinese are happy being Chinese. We don't have imperialism or empire-building in our blood, like some other nations maybe (Jeffery winks at me)."

To the Western mind, this may be seen as an odd comment to make. However, Chinese students are taught, from an early age, of the aggression and imperialist intentions of other nations, including Japan, the US and the UK. Western education of Chinese history will skim over much of the history which is taught in China. All the Chinese people I know have a significant grasp of China's history. Readers wanting to understand more of the attitudes of the Chinese to current events should read widely on Chinese history.

I avoid the temptation to repeat the earlier conversation about food and air quality. The irony isn't lost on Jeffery.

"I know it seems inconsistent to the Western mind, but we Chinese can hold conflicting ideas in our heads at the same time and be comfortable with them both. It is a cost of progress that we have to suffer now but it won't last forever. We will manage things over time so the difficulties will be solved."

Jeffery fishes his smartphone from inside his jacket. After a quick search, he shows me a digitized photograph from long ago. A fresh-faced and cherubic young boy in a group of kindergarten children.

"I wanted to show you this, I hope it is interesting," he says.

"It is," I reply.

"I met your queen."

"Really!?"

"Really. She came to Beijing in October 1986 on her first official visit. I was only four years old and don't really remember, but our kindergarten was chosen by the government to be visited, as it was the best in Beijing at that time. Actually, it is still seen as the best. That was the reason I decided to go to study in the UK, to sort of pay the visit back. I love London, it is such a historic city, you can feel the history in every corner of the city. I really regard it as my second home. I have an unusual connection with the UK and I feel it is very special. China has had a long-standing special relationship with the UK."

"But you are still going to try to become a Canadian citizen?"

"Yes. It's practically impossible to be a British citizen if you are middle-class Chinese."

CHAPTER

9

THE DRIVER

My translator and I arrive outside the appointed place at the agreed hour. The row of restaurants on Lucky Street are all shuttered and locked but a young man scampers out of the shadows as we look bemused and my interviewee emerges as if by magic behind us.

"Sorry about this," says the young man, as he unlocks the huge iron gate blocking the entrance, "there are food safety inspections set this week so we stay locked up except for pre bookings until they go away."

Nothing surprises me in China and rather than be immediately worried that standards are not up to scratch, locals and those in the know simply book ahead at their favourite place regardless. The inspectors are prone to requesting 'additional fees' for health and safety advice, which may be required for passing the tests. Hence, the suite of restaurants all 'shut', save one to take the heat in which everyone then shares the collective 'fees' and fines. It's a lot cheaper that way.

We stumble up the unlit stairwell past the big plastic prawn and broken chairs into a spacious, clean and welcoming establishment. A number of other diners are already enjoying their lunch.

Yu Jingsheng describes himself as half artist, half driver. He works for Beiqi (北汽) Taxis, a state-owned enterprise providing qualified drivers to those who need them, from visiting dignitaries to foreigners with the right contacts.

"I was born in Beijing in 1972 and have two brothers and one sister. I'm the youngest and my first brother is a truck driver and the second works in a kindergarten."

I never find out the profession of his sister but surmise she is a housewife.

"I was quite good at drawing when I was a child so when I graduated from school my mother asked me what I wanted to do. I really didn't know but my mother knew that my uncle, her brother, needed staff so I went to work for him. He was a specialist painter."

It soon transpired that this wasn't just any type of painter and decorator as we might find in the West, but one who specialized in the intricate work which is found in many of the old 'flat' houses of Beijing.

"My uncle taught me the trade but his teacher was a man who worked for a company who repaired the older traditional buildings in Beijing. I really liked the painting job, even though as an apprentice working for my uncle I only earned ¥5 (£0.50) in the morning and ¥7 (£0.70) in the afternoon. I was pretty good though and worked really hard so my salary was soon increased to ¥15 (£1.50) a day. It was 1990 and I was only 18 years old."

Mr Yu then moved to work at a specialist printing company doing vacuum aluminium coating work at a small Beijing factory.

"I worked there for 10 months but then my mother died of cancer and I took over my father's job at a state-owned business. I felt I had to do it to honour my father as he got older. I really regretted doing that job as it paid less than the painting job. Only ¥207 (£20.70) a month, but I worked there for 8 years."

It was there that he met his wife, introduced through friends.

"I decided to change my job once I got married to have more flexibility to raise a family. I joined the Beiqi Taxi Company Limited in 1999 and have been there ever since. It is a very good company and a stable job. My wife was and is a marketing information manager, which allows her time to look after the family. My car belongs to the company. There are a lot of different coloured cars and each colour means it does a different job. Mine is a black car, so my role is usually working for higher level clients including government and congress officials, as well as foreign enterprise leaders."

We eat the shrimps in a hot chilli sauce with vegetables. It is a messy affair with plastic gloves provided. We enjoy the food and there is a good deal of joking and laughed exchanges as we plough our way through the boiled mountains of claws, shells and succulent flesh. It is one of the simpler meals I have enjoyed in

Beijing and all the more pleasurable for it. Sitting with an ordinary Beijinger, a worker from the middle professions of China, I am reminded that the role of 'driver' has been regarded as a better job than average in China. You are not in the fields and not a construction labourer or migrant worker away from home for months at a time. Mr Yu is home with his wife and teenage daughter every evening and his is an uncomplicated and simple existence.

"My work is very flexible and I have a good job. Whenever the National People's Congress and the Chinese Political Consultative Conferences are held, I will always be used to drive government leaders or government officers. These are called 'Special Tasks' and only a few of us are able and experienced enough to do this work."

As we talk it seems clearer and clearer to me that Mr Yu would be similar to a Police Class 1 Pursuit, or Special Branch, driver in the British police but he is tight lipped on his true skills.

"I've met a lot of interesting people in the last 15 years of driving. Some passengers just want me to keep the car moving, they don't want to stop in traffic jams. I am instructed to keep moving, no matter which way I need to go to get to the destination. I just mustn't ever stop. I don't ask any questions and if those are the instructions, all they need to do is sign a special section on the driver manifest and take responsibility for the longer, higher, route cost."

We discuss the advent of the likes of Uber and the other taxi apps which have flooded Chinese cities, and the rest of the world, over the past few years. Mr Yu is scathing.

"These are a disaster. These guys are often not real taxi drivers, no insurance, no skills, no local knowledge and rely on satellite navigation more than their brains. I think it's a totally bad thing and I fully expect the whole thing to collapse in a few years. Basically, you can't trust who you are with. It's all about low cost, not safety. Many of the cars are badly maintained, if they are serviced or maintained at all. In contrast, drivers like those working for Beiqi are all insured and have housing funds to support them and their families. We are professionals, not like that bunch of amateurs!"

Mr Yu doesn't hold back on his vitriol and, while he accepts the point on low fares, he counters with a few insider facts.

"The Didi (嘀嘀打车) (another popular taxi hailing app in China) and Uber guys are usually from other provinces. During the holiday periods, such as National Day or Spring Festival, they go home and there are a lot fewer cars available for the app users. The real taxi drivers are local and know Beijing and the way around the traffic jams better than anyone. They do it for a living. Not just when they feel like earning a bit of money. The pros work from morning to night on proper shifts, getting enough rest and take safety seriously. These other guys sleep in the car, work around the clock, so they may even fall asleep at the wheel. I have heard of and seen Didi drivers who violate the laws of the road. They can cause chaos at intersections by their selfish behaviour. I've even heard some take drugs or drive when drunk. They are a downright liability!"

Mr Yu explains that professional taxi drivers have to take a fitness check and health inspection regularly, as well as have a legal licence which ensures they are properly regulated by the government. There is another aspect too.

"We are all required to report in if we are ill. We are checked on and, if our illness is contagious, we have to go to hospital and are not able to work until a doctor certifies we are fit to do so. That's a major safeguard for the public."

Mr Yu tells stories from the inside of the taxi world which leaves us laughing with incredulity and a serious reconsideration of our taxi app usage.

"Beiqi Taxis pay a good deal of tax to the government every year and do a lot of charity work. They pay a pension, medical insurance, unemployment insurance and housing fund to their staff. It's a properly run business, not like these apps which are only good at taking a slice of the business. They provide no benefits at all to anyone. I believe that it's a fashion and it's only the owners who are making the money."

We discuss the Uberization of everything predicted by the management consultants and doom-mongers.

"We have apps for everything, robots are supposed to be taking over the jobs of everyone but what will happen to society? What real value are these things adding to society? It's good to be able to order your food on an app, get your laundry done via an app, do online shopping, pay online, invest online, pay for your electricity, gas and water and do your bank work online, pretty much everything has an app for it. That's all fine, but where is the progress for society in all this? Real progress should be that everyone has a job, everyone is contributing to society and everyone is upholding the rules of law. If apps and robots do all the work, then the people will be unemployed and idle hands are not good in society. I believe that the quality of people needs to be improved and that is about education. The most important type of education is family education. Those are the important values – family values that give us the right moral grounding for life."

We discuss government support for the taxi drivers of Beijing and fair regulations – in 2016, the price is only ¥13.0 (£1.30) to start and then ¥2.3 (£0.23) per kilometre. We discuss the passenger and the care the driver must take, no matter who they are carrying. His simple humility and care is humbling. His views are not always ones I'd subscribe to, but this straight forward, honest and upstanding man is a solid reminder of the vast majority of Beijingers and, indeed, of the Chinese ordinary working man and woman.

"You have to admit, there hasn't been much of an increase in those prices in 15 years, has there? When people want a taxi they don't really care about the price. They just want to get from where they are to where they are going as fast and as safely as possible. Am I right?"

I have to admit it. He is.

CHAPTER 10

THE
REGIONAL
MANAGER

Lv Zhong Shan is early.

"I quit my job so I have a little more time now," he says.

This is not the introduction I had expected. In arranging the interview, never an easy thing with any Chinese person, I had been led to believe that this 31-year-old senior regional manager from BYD, the Chinese vehicle company, was a very busy man. Flexible due to his regional and mobile role, but busy.

"I was, until very recently, but I have quit my job so I can go to the California Lutheran University to do a one-year MBA. I leave Beijing on Thursday."

I am genuinely taken aback. "You are not staying for New Year?" I ask. It is almost unheard of for any Chinese person not to spend Chinese New Year with their family.

"Actually I am going back to my home town to see my mother first before I go to California."

I have to say I am a little relieved to hear this.

"I was working for BYD company and had done so for seven years. BYD is becoming more and more international. Last year I was supposed to be promoted but the human resources department told me that they need people who have overseas degrees and that they were promoting a younger guy instead. He has an overseas degree. I was really upset. I really couldn't stand it so I decided it was time to go and study abroad."

I am always both impressed and not a little surprised at the way the Chinese can deal with bad news. It is a culturally ingrained defence mechanism, I believe, born out of centuries of collective and continual shared hardship, as well as individual suffering. There is an innate and inbuilt stoicism that seems to carry them through even the most stressful and emotionally painful experiences. Zhong Shan could have just complained about his situation and blamed the business, the system, the other guy, the internal politics and myriad other 'not me' scapegoats as a Westerner in the same situation would have done. But he did not. He applied for and got a place at a university on the other side of the world, which he will fund at his own expense, to get a qualification he believes, but is not certain, will give him the stepping stone to move up the career ladder.

"I have always had a dream to study abroad," he says. "Maybe being overlooked for a promotion was the sign I needed. Two things, my dream and my desire to progress, came together at the right time. My manager and the human resources department both told me that if I get the degree, then I will be able to go back to work at BYD. But maybe I will not choose to do that. Maybe I will be able to get another chance to work elsewhere in this growing and developing new energy car sector."

I ask him how he will be able to afford to leave his job for a year and pay for the flights, the accommodation, the fees and the living expenses.

"Well I did work for seven years at BYD and I was a senior regional manager up until recently."

He seems a little surprised at the question. The truth is that this man has been saving. In the West, mortgages and everyday life expenses drain the average household of their income, so they tend to be living on a debt. The Chinese are savers. Recent data shows that, on average, Chinese workers will save in excess of 50% of their monthly income. Often it is more. As a result, they are buffered, though not always immune from, the vagaries of catastrophe. Zhong Shang is no exception. He has managed to build up enough savings to afford this year-long 'sabbatical'. He has also managed to put a down payment on a rather nice apartment in Beijing, but more of that later.

"I was born in Shandong (山东) Province in a small town called Shouguang (寿光) on 10 October 1983. My *hukou* is there. My father had his own business. In China, Shandong is famous for its vegetables and my father was a vegetable distributor, helping local farmers get their produce to markets all over China."

He pauses. I sense the loss.

"I am sorry."

"It's ok. Thanks."

He gathers himself.

"My mother used to work for China Unicom, the big mobile phone and telephone company. She retired early and is now at home helping my married sister with her first baby. I am going home to see them for New Year."

Wrapped up in this one sentence is the whole of Chinese life. The hard-working father, a self-made man, surviving the Cultural Revolution. The working wife, now widow, dedicated first to her family and now to her grandchild. Everyone living together under the same roof. Savings buffer the loss of the father, while marriage secures the future of the daughter. The focus is on the education of, and building the future for, the only son. Festivals and Chinese New Year, the most important, are at the heart of family life and family is at the heart of everything. Chinese families are the security blanket that the Western world no longer seems to have. Without what some Chinese would describe as a 'laziness-inducing' reliance on the Western welfare system, the Chinese are focused on self-created security, no matter how stretched and stressed they may be. As can be read elsewhere in these Notes, the price can be very high, but financial and emotional security is hard won and not given up without the greatest of struggles.

"I am a very traditional Chinese guy. My home town was the birthplace of Confucius. The people in my home town and my province are among the most traditional in China. I want to spend time with my family, I believe strongly in the Confucius teachings and in fate and I always listen to the opinion and advice of my parents.

"At 18 years old, I went to university in Chongqing, then to Shenzhen in Guangdong Province. I studied electronic information engineering so I went to BYD (a large non-state-owned

Chinese car manufacturer) in Shenzhen. I got a job as an engineer for two years before I got the chance to move to a sales role as a manager. I was lucky as, not long after that, I was able to get a transfer and promotion to Beijing as the regional sales manager for Beijing and Hubei Province. There are around 13 dealerships in Beijing and about 30 in Hubei Province. That was in 2009. I was responsible for managing the dealerships across the area. I had to look at and agree to working practices and policies, as well as sales and marketing and advertising."

Zhong Shan is obviously very proud of the business and enthuses about the "best new-energy automotive company in China".

"Tesla has been successful and invested significantly in new technologies and the new energy segment of the industry, but BYD is a leader. It is going to be very successful in the future."

There is no doubting his enthusiasm, or his knowledge of this industry. This is a bright and ambitious man. But why California and why the Lutheran University?

"I did apply to Peking and to Tianjin Universities and, although I got an interview, I could not go. These are the most difficult universities in China to get into and the tuition fees alone are over ¥300,000 (£32,800) a year. I applied to California. It is a good place and my friends said I would be happy there. Also, the weather is very nice. I got the place and also a study visa for a year too, so I am going to go. I have my personal savings and my mother has also helped me as she has savings.

"I first heard about Lutheran University from my friends. I then went online and looked. I needed somewhere I could get a MBA in a year. I can't afford any longer than that, either financially or from a career perspective. It fits all my criteria – a one-year MBA, a good programme and relatively cheap tuition fees."

Wrapped up in these comments are deep insights into 'the Chinese way'. With the world to choose from, where does an aspiring and ambitious young man look to develop himself and expand his chances for advancement? First, his family. Second, his friends. Zhong Shan's personal commitment of time and money, along with the 'loan' from his mother, will provide the financial security to make the trip and fund the year, but his friends have been instrumental in the decision to go to California. He has several people he knows who are Chinese American and American Chinese (both with quite different perspectives on life brought about from their upbringing in very different socio-political and school systems), as well as Chinese friends who are already there. A ready-made social circle will welcome him. This notion of an extended and ready-made 'family' abroad is enough to swing the decision to the broad location. Subsequently, online research and dogged determination in the application process make up the rest of the jigsaw of temporary emigration.

"I started to buy my own apartment in Beijing last year. Since I am 31 years old and not married yet, I decided to put the deposit down on a new-build. It will be finished next year so the timing will work for me. I felt that if I didn't do it now, then I might never do it."

Again, an insight into Chinese life and, specifically, marriage. An unmarried 31-year-old man without a house is not even going to get on the shortlist of most eligible urban, or many rural, girls. The expectation is that the husband will do his duty, or his family will, to buy the couple a house to live in. No mortgage, no debt. Security again plays the most important consideration for marriage, even above love.

However, my own knowledge of buying a house in Beijing cannot stop me from posing a rather unusually direct question.

"How can you buy a house in Beijing when your *hukou* is in Shouguang? You can't buy here unless you have a Beijing *hukou*. How did you get around that problem?"

Zhong Shan smiles. He is happy to share the inside track and educate this foreigner in something he doesn't know.

"Of course, everyone wants to live in the city. But not everyone can do so. It is very difficult to afford the very high prices and, of course, the regulations around people's *hukou* forbid many from doing so. However, there are two types of property in Beijing. The first is called *zhu zhai* (住宅). For this you are right. You must have a Beijing *hukou*, or have lived here for at least five years. The lease is for 70 years as you know.

"The second is newer. Some properties are in mixed use developments, so there may be a shopping mall, business offices and residential homes for sale in the same place. These are available for 50 year leases and are called *Shang Zhu Liang Yong* (商住两用). It is for this type of house I have put the first payment on."

Such types of property have been around for a while in Beijing and ownership was theoretically open to all – under a local rule that meant certain developments can be used as a place to both live and conduct business from. The literal translation is 'apartment that can be used for residence and business'. However, with the various recent changes in property ownership policies, this is now one of the few properties non–Beijingers can own in the city.

We return to the new challenge of the next year.

"I will live on the campus. I know I will be able to look after myself when I am over there. After living in Beijing and away from home for so long I have no problem managing my daily life. Also, I have really tried hard to develop my spoken English. Although my generation did not learn English until the sixth grade at school (it is now taught from much earlier in schools), I lacked the confidence to actually speak it as I really didn't mix with foreigners very much. Recently, I have made the effort to do this more often."

It has paid off. Our conversation is conducted entirely in almost word-perfect English. I am again shamed at the lack of my Chinese.

"So, in a year's time, do you think Beijing will have changed?"

"Probably not too much in the building of new developments. I think that's already been done, but I think the attitude of the people will have moved on again. Attitudes have changed here even in the past few years and I believe that they will continue to do so. People in Beijing are much more connected with the rest of the world. I really hope that more and more people will care more about the world and less about themselves. I hope that people will care less about money and making money."

I ask him if he thinks he will return to China since so many people leave and never return.

"The US is a developed country," he answers. "Although the weather in Beijing is not so good with the pollution, China is a developing country. I have read research stating that opportunities in my industry will be immense in China. The government has made more and more policies supporting the new energy vehicle sector. Certainly, since 2004 there are more positive policies and more are coming which I know will encourage the industry further."

It is an interesting debate. The increased focus on new and alternative energy is a global issue and in a country the size of China, with undoubted pollution issues, it is high on everyone's agenda. From central government moving high polluting industry away from the major cities, to the private individual buying face masks at the local store and monitoring air quality each day to see if their child should attend school, air pollution is a daily and much talked about hazard.

"BYD started in the new energy sector in China about the same time as Tesla (the US dual fuel car brand) did globally. The US policy is more mature than here in China. The Chinese automotive industry, and the new energy sector within it, is a big cake. Many people want to eat a slice of it. BYD is not a state-owned enterprise. It is basically a private one, so it is more difficult to develop the market than if it were government owned. The critical thing is access to charging points for the vehicles. In the US, there are many chargers, but not in China. The infrastructure is young and underdeveloped. There are now more and more charging places in shopping mall car parks and Tesla have made big investments but more are needed. Everyone in the industry needs to invest so that customers can use the new energy vehicles just as they are able to use any other. I believe it will happen. It is one of the big reasons I want to come back. I can see the opportunity here."

We spend some time discussing the issues. At the heart of the development will be investment in infrastructure. It will need deep pockets. Zhong Shan and I agree that the most likely driver will be central government supporting the major state-owned enterprises in the electricity supply companies and major vehicle manufacturers.

The Chinese market in this area is as complicated as in any other, but we agree that the will seems to be there on all sides. Brands that no one outside China will have heard of are growing. The dual fuel 'Qin' (which BYD brought out to compete with Tesla) took part in and won the first Formula Electric Grand Prix staged in Beijing in 2014. Reporters flocked to see it and many bemoaned the lack of atmosphere from the quiet revolution taking place before them as cars swept past at impressive, but soundless, speeds. "The Qin can reach a speed of 100kph in 5.9 seconds, alarmingly quietly," Zhong Shan enthuses.

"The 'Tang' was also a new dual fuel car produced in 2005 and the 'Teng Shi' was successfully launched as a joint venture between Daimler Benz and BYD at the end of 2014 in Beijing."

Zhong Shan has a real grip on the industry and his enthusiasm for it is genuinely infectious. It is no surprise to me that he was a successful regional sales manager. He is a convert and almost apostolic in his pitch patter.

"It is the smart choice you know. Did you know that the Qin sold more than 10,000 units in Shanghai last year?"

"I did not."

"The Qin is unfortunately not on the new energy-approved list in Beijing or I am sure it would be doing well here too."

I was unaware of such a list existing. I am always surprised by the complex web of local government regulations, rules, policies, subsidies and incentives across China.

"There is a central government subsidy available for the purchase of new energy cars," he explains.

"Is there?!"

"Yes. If you buy such a car in Shanghai, then you get a central government subsidy and you will also get a local government subsidy as cars like the Qin are on the local government new energy vehicle approved list. If you buy in Beijing, then you just get the national subsidy."

I don't bother to voice my thoughts about how the approved list might be compiled or agreed, but it is clearly a critical list to be on across China if you are a manufacturer. I may have misheard him, but I thought he told me that the subsidy could be as much as 50%. Now that is an incentive for greening China's congested city centres.

FIT FOR CHINA

We are sitting in one of Beijing's increasing number of Westernized restaurants. Phoenix Wang orders a bowl of pasta with tomatoes, as well as a carrot and orange blend drink. I have something with a lot of kale and a coffee. Phoenix has spent most of the day in the plush high class gym in the same building. She is a full-time gym instructor, personal coach and very fit. Indeed, Phoenix has been something of a pioneer in China in the fitness business and trains many film stars, and even politicians, in the public eye. She exudes energy and power with no signs of a gram of fat anywhere on her. She wears her fitness with justifiable pride and skin-tight trousers.

"I was born in 1973 in Urumqi, the capital city of what is known as the Xinjiang Uyghur Autonomous Region. My parents are from Jiangsu Province in south China and moved to Urumqi before I was born. I spent all my youth in Urumqi and, when I did the university entrance examinations, I was determined to see another part of China, to see the world and live away from my parents. Both my parents were workers in the city but from an early age they could see that I was a fast runner and good at physical exercise. My father found me a Kung Fu teacher and employed him to actually live in our home so I could be taught every day."

The Xinjiang Uyghur Autonomous Region is to the very far west of China. The name Xinjiang means 'New Frontier of the Western Regions' and has been the source of long running differences of opinion within China for many years. Demands for independence for this largest of the Chinese provinces have met with resistance from Beijing. While clearly the merits of the case are a matter for the politicians, the area has a very diverse set of ethnic groups and a long history of boundary disputes with pretty well all the countries it borders, which include Mongolia, Russia, Kazakhstan, Kyrgyzstan, Tajikistan, Afghanistan, Pakistan and India. It is now China's largest natural gas producing area.

"I wanted to have an independent life. I have liked physical activity from when I was very young and have always been good at it. Before university I did a lot of track and field sports, including the high jump and long jump. I also liked eurythmic and aerobic exercises and body awareness, so I decided to study physical education at university. I went to the Xi'an Physical Education University from 1992–1996. Many students from the far north west provinces tended to apply to the universities in Xi'an. I really enjoyed my time there and found I had a real skill and ability in physical education. When I graduated, I was asked by the coach to stay and teach but I decided I needed to go back to Urumqi to look after my parents."

Phoenix spent the next five years working at a local school teaching physical education, as well as at a number of fitness centres as a coach. As a result of her experience coaching, she felt her skills lay in that direction rather than teaching in schools.

"I found the relationship between music and the arts and physical education to be the most inspiring. That's why I really liked eurythmics, which combines music with physical self-awareness. I also liked to compete in contests. I started entering them when I was in Urumqi and won a lot of awards. I also decided that I wanted to come to Beijing as the opportunities here are so much greater, so I came in 2002."

Having started to enter local physical fitness competitions back in Xinjiang, Phoenix graduated to national and eventually to the international level. Specializing in body building, she rose through the ranks of contestants as the first Chinese woman to ever compete at the Ms Fitness International Finals, run under the International Federation of Body Building and Fitness. She continued to compete and in 2007 she breached the Top 10 and two years later became world champion at the finals in Spain. It was the first time a Chinese woman had achieved such a level and, as such, was also a breakthrough in Chinese fitness history. On the back of her success she became one of the most sought after fitness coaches in China. She is also now one of the judges of the World Ms Fitness Tournament and the only Chinese among a group of Europeans and Americans.

"I really love my job. I have been a coach for many years now.

I'm always appearing in magazines and on fitness programmes. I've even been on CCTV 5 (the ubiquitous China wide sports channel). It's made me quite famous. I have written four books on physical fitness, including Kickboxing, HipHop, Latino and Aerobics. In 2009 I also won the Ms Fitness China championship which really helped me to become even better known."

Phoenix has a whirlwind delivery and the facts come in a torrent of fiercely minded individualism.

"I was the first coach to teach Hot Yoga in China. The first coach to introduce Zumba dance aerobics to the country. The first coach to call on women to build muscles and take control of their physical fitness and the first to introduce a new way of training fitness which emphasises weight training combined with yoga and aerobic exercise."

This combination is Phoenix's own development and uses her own set of principles. Her training techniques are pioneering and she has become one of the top coaches for coaches of fitness in China. Her individualism and strength of character is a powerful cocktail of self-belief, raw energy and grit determination.

Stepping gently aside from the invitation to join a class I enquire about her schedule.

"Every day I am usually taking three classes of up to two hours at a time. All the classes are private and I charge a high fee. I'm expensive because I'm good and I get results."

How much is a lesson?

"¥800 (£80) an hour and you sign up for more than one lesson of course! Most of my clients are VIPs, lawyers and successful people."

So, on an average day Phoenix is earning what many of Beijing's general population earn in a month. With the increase of competition from the myriad instructors in everything from yoga, fitness and even personal grooming springing up around the city, Phoenix continues to tower above them all.

"I think the increase of gyms and interest in fitness is an indication of the increased confidence of our nation. However, the industry is much more advanced in the US, the UK and the West generally. In China people used to pay attention to their health but so many young people are working too hard with long hours and getting ill. If the people are always ill, how can a country develop? I believe it is important to be healthy and then you can work hard but not at the expense of your health."

The focus on health does seem to obsess many Chinese. In every park and public space you can see outdoor exercise machines; there are even public table tennis tables and basketball hoops strategically placed in corners of even the smallest of spaces. Although the smog in Beijing and other places does curtail the exercise of many, you will find the noise of dance exercise classes wafting across the parks from early morning until dusk across China. Couple that with a long history of traditional Chinese medicine and you'd be forgiven for feeling you are living in a nation of hypochondriac fitness fanatics.

"I worry about the focus on money. It seems to be taking over at the expense of health and that's not good. The Chinese are getting fatter and unfit. On the other hand, there is also a genuine increase in the interest people have in well-being. More and more investors are seeing good returns from the fitness industry and other support areas such as fresh food, super fruits, health foods and the like, but it's in its infancy right now. So many people in China live away from home and don't prioritize healthy eating and exercise. Too many people have to commute too far to work and then eat snack foods and rubbish."

Phoenix has an online site which encourages good exercise and a good healthy lifestyle with plenty of practical hints and tips for the busy middle-class Chinese executive.

"So many young people around me are getting ill. The increase in cancer is also all about a lack of health too in my mind. These people tell me they don't have time to stay fit, they are too busy earning money. But to what end? These kids are working all day then all night as well – limited sleep, poor diets and no exercise. It's no surprise to me that they get ill! I want to help people change their lives for the better."

Phoenix runs classes with a holistic approach. She sees herself more as a life coach than just a fitness instructor.

"I use my experience and expertise to encourage my students to exercise their mental health, as well as their physical. It's about your whole life and attitude to it, not just muscle building. I personally experienced this a few years ago when I damaged my knee in 2008. It was not good and the doctor I went to said I had to give up fitness training. I didn't agree and felt I could help myself. I went and studied all I could about the human knee joint so I could repair it. I worked hard on specific exercises and it repaired. Only eight months after I was told to stop, I won the Global Ms Fitness Championship in Spain. I decided I was not going to be a victim or a loser and not to get depressed about it. I learned that you should never give up. I believe that everyone has it within them to succeed and overcome the difficulties they have in life. You need to have a fit body but also a fit mind and will."

But isn't it very difficult for people to just change their lifestyle?

"Anyone can change their lifestyle." Phoenix wags a taught finger at me in rebuke. "You just need the will to do so. It's a choice. Change your lifestyle and you won't get fat and you will get fit. So many people advocate stupid ways to lose fat but I tell all my students that it is about having a healthy lifestyle, then you will be healthy and your body will get rid of the fat it doesn't need."

So, will this resurgence of interest in well-being help the country generally?

"Of course I want China to be stronger and stronger in the world. But it's important that people don't give a useless sacrifice to the country. If people are healthy, then they can make a better contribution. The Chinese fitness industry can help China be fit. It's a big plus for us all. If you can conquer your physical self, then you will win mentally and the core to physical power is to exercise your mind power."

Point taken. Note to self. More kale and less coffee from now on.

THE
JOURNALIST

Yang Yang (not his real name) is a journalist for a financial paper in China. A confident 25-year-old, he nevertheless does not want to be quoted officially. He is, however, happy to talk, via the gauze of partial anonymity.

Yang is still studying journalism at one of Beijing's universities. He has just completed his exams and is not confident of having done well.

"I earn my living as a full-time journalist, so I have to do all my study in my spare time," he says. "I am lucky since my job means I have quite a lot of flexibility, so I have been able to work my studies into my schedule, though sometimes it is very difficult."

His round face and complexion single him out to the trained eye as being from one of the many minorities in China. He hails from Xiang Cheng, a town in Hunan Province in northern China, where his parents are farmers.

"They are simple people and have a simple and quite an easy life. My father is a carpenter, so during the famines he can still work and earn enough money to survive."

The famines occur each year between June and September, when the earth is parched by the dry and arid winds from the Northern Steppes and wilder Mongolian plains. His parents have little education but supported him to have one. He managed to pass the exams to get to University in Nanjing in southern China to study international audit, but dropped out after a year.

"I found it was not for me," he explains. "I just left and went back home to my parents and back to high school for another two years so I could retake the entrance exams. I was lucky. I worked hard and got onto this course in Beijing. My parents could not help me. They didn't understand what or why I was doing what I was doing. I just had to struggle on my own. My parents let me decide everything about my life myself. They could see how ambitious I was and just tried hard to support my decisions. I have a good relationship with my parents but I don't have much time to be able to spend with them. I only go home once a year at Spring Festival for a couple of weeks. I really have nothing in common with the people in my home town. My old friends there are married with kids and have simple, easy jobs in the factories or working for the government. They don't understand why I am not married with children. I am ambitious and I want to be able to grab the opportunities of the new China. I have new friends here in Beijing."

The coffee in front of him grows cold. I bought it without thinking. He sips it occasionally. He only drinks tea.

He interviews me too. But not about business. About life, places I have been, people met, stories shared, experiences of China, family, friends and food. It is an easy conversation.

"I can never talk to my parents like this." His dark eyes seem large behind his equally large glasses. "It is so different. Normally, I interview business people but they don't talk about their lives, the struggle they had or anything. It is just the bullshit of success and business. We have to write what is right for them or we get into trouble when they complain to the editor. They never share their real story. It is difficult.

"When I was young, I was ambitious – it was in my heart, it still is but I don't know why. I always wanted to better myself, not to just survive but to be successful. Right now, I just have to survive. I have no choice. But I will be successful."

We discuss what 'success' means. It has a very different shape and tone to the definition found outside China in the West.

"For the Chinese, owning a house means everything. It means stability; it means security. When men from the country go away to the big cities, often they will do low-wage jobs. However, they will still save and save as much as they can. They will eat little and simply, they will sleep in cheap places. Usually their employer provides basic dormitory accommodation and food for the workers, sometimes actually on the construction site. Everything they save will go home to their wife and children to look after them. But more than that, they will be trying to earn enough money to buy a small bit of land and to build a house. To them, that is success, so their children will have a house to live in."

There is a whole subclass of migrant workers who are the hands behind the infrastructure developments driving much of China's economic growth. These workers leave family behind for up to a year at a time, commuting home, often taking days to do so, for the national holiday of Chinese New Year. The way these workers are paid, or not paid, is little appreciated outside China. Most do not receive any money at all until the company they work for receives their payments at the different stages of a development's completion. In some cases, workers are not paid until Chinese New Year each year. Back home, families struggle to survive until the annual wage arrives, often physically with the worker. Newspapers and the internet report stories of workers who have not been paid for more than a year and unscrupulous contractors who fail to pay at all. In a couple of cases, reports emerged recently of children and impoverished wives committing suicide to draw attention to the plight of their migrant fathers and spouses, unpaid for a year and then told to sue for their wages.

I ask Yang for his definition of success.

"Of course, I send money back to my parents but my mother just saves it. She says they have enough with their simple lives and she will save it all to give to me when I get married so I can buy a house. They give up everything for this common dream of Chinese parents for their children. Success, for me, is to be able to work in finance. My main degree is in journalism but my passion is economics and finance. I hope maybe in five years' time I will be a manager in a finance company. My real dream is to have my own business."

As Yang talks, he becomes more animated and his voice trembles a little as he sketches out the dreams of obtaining a Master's degree, travelling and being his own boss.

"I said, a year ago, that perhaps I would go to do a Master's degree in Canada, the US, or the UK, but now I have changed my mind," he says. "Partly because it would cost me so much money but also because China has changed and I can see more opportunities here. My first choice would now be Shanghai, then Singapore and Hong Kong last." We pause for a moment as he reflects on what he has said.

"I don't see Hong Kong as the gateway of finance to China any more. It used to be, but I can see the change happening. Shanghai is important and all the policies (government) are supporting the development of Chinese finance, insurance and capital markets. Working in financial journalism, I see regulations changing almost every year and there are new ones which will also make a big change. It is happening. China is growing and developing fast. China's world position is changing. I can see the effects of this every day in my job. China is expanding everywhere."

Watching the daily news broadcasts, I could be persuaded to believe this too, through the crafted scripts, but Yang is on the inside, and his is another perspective – truer perhaps?

"The reforms and changes may seem slow to the West, but one or two years in China are fast and if you join up all the dots of the past ten years, you can see the direction changing and it is clear."

I am reminded that the Chinese don't plan for the short term (at least, not for tomorrow or next week), but they do plan for the next 50 or even 100 years. In that context, the changes may seem slow to the untutored eye, but to those living in it every day they can feel the tilt of change as the wind shifts east.

"My daily life is not affected by the movement of China in the world, but my future is."

There is a profundity in this simple statement from the 25-year-old man before me.

Doubtless, he is one of the emerging urban middle class of China. "I have just enough money to live my life ok," he says. But he is also one of the many younger educated and ambitious generation that is the backbone of the future success of China in the world. There is a rawness of determination to succeed that is to be found across China but, in Beijing and some of the other bigger tier 1 and tier 2 cities, you can almost feel it around you in the coffee shops and middle-income eateries. Here, earnest conversations can be overheard planning business, doing deals and dreaming of success. Groups bent over tablets and laptops tap out the future. There is business to be done out there and there are risks worth taking to share in the China Dream.

What are Yang's thoughts on Western society?

"People have an easier life in the West. The Western culture is much more mature than in China. Here, people still have to struggle and work hard all the time. I am just one of those people. But things are changing for the better here. We have many problems and challenges, but although life is hard, it is getting better slowly."

I am intrigued by his perspective and, after some encouragement, Yang explains his views in more detail.

"I believe that Western people have an easier life. It is just my feeling. The ratio between house prices and wages in the West is much narrower. Here, it is so big, it is almost impossible to bridge without the help of family. The living expenses in the West are also lower. Here, prices are going up and up and wages are not. China is also a cash society. We don't do debt! If we need cash, we will borrow from family first. In the West, the attitude to security and the attitude to life is very different to here."

Yang sits back, seemingly exhausted by the enormity of it all.

"Western people want an easy life, but in China no one has an easy life. So, we just have to work hard to earn a living and struggle to build our own security."

We share a long silence. There is not much to say. The chasm of culture and dreams is too great. I endeavour to bring the conversation back home.

What of his extended family?

"I have two older brothers – one is in my home town but the other is in Shanghai. We do not connect often – except, of course, at Spring festival." No more is said. Silence descends again between us like a shroud. The family matter is a closed door. It is his past and not his future. Yang has all the enthusiasm of youth but there is no naivety. His life has already been too hard, too difficult, to remain naive.

He has a girlfriend, also 25, who recently graduated with a degree in English. Will he get married and have children?

"Perhaps one day, but not yet. I am ambitious and I want to grab the opportunities that I can see and dream of. She is not ambitious. She wants a simpler life."

Poor girl.

"Maybe in five years' time you and I will meet in London where I will be on business and I can tell you about my success," he concludes.

There is no hint of irony or the rose-tinted passion of a dreamer. It is simply a statement of fact. He will be successful, he will share in the wider prosperity of China in the world and he will make his parents proud of him.

HUNGRY
FOR
BRANDS

I am accosted as I sit down after a long day of meetings and conference calls. I had hoped to retire to my coffee haven to regroup. The three women are in their mid-20s and keen to practise their English. Already married, one with a little girl at home with her own mother, they all work and are all clinging to their designer handbags as if they were babies.

The conversation starts with the usual Chinese quiz. "Who are you?" "What do you do?" "Where is your home town?" "Why are you in China?" "How old are your children?" On both sides, the pleasantries then move from the mundane to a more interesting topic altogether: money.

One of the things that Chinese people have never really had much of is money, at least until very recently. Although the Chinese invented the stuff a couple of thousand years ago, the masses never really experienced what it was like to have enough to do any more than survive. More recently, that has all changed. There are more than 300 million Chinese people said to be 'middle class' and this number is rising as prosperity and, a very Chinese brand of capitalism, takes hold. These girls are examples of this new found 'emerging' middle class. Brand hungry, and with some money, they shop whenever they can, spending thoughtfully and sometimes lavishly.

Li has the classic Prada, Susan the latest Moschino and Lilly a last season Gucci.

"My husband thinks I'm mad," says Susan, when I comment about the bags and how expensive they must have been. Global brands don't drop their price in China, and in many instances, taxes and 'value pricing' ensures that the prices are appreciably higher than elsewhere in the world on these 'must have' items.

"I would never have been able to afford this unless I gave things up," says Li.

"Like what?" I ask.

"Like food!"

The story unfolds as the girls share the deliberate hardships they have chosen to endure in order to buy these statement goods. The notion of face is well known in China, it revolves around showing and receiving respect and acknowledgement for, and from, others. For these girls, living in a society driven by increasing consumerism and material wealth, 'face' can be gained significantly by the ownership of high-quality and expensive goods. Possession shows or, more importantly, implies status, position and wealth. All these attributes are seen as important in raising you to a new level of stature and status among those around you. However, nowhere have I experienced it in such an extraordinary manner as with these girls. I learn that they are by no means alone and that thousands literally go without food to save enough money to buy certain items that give them huge face with their family, friends and peers.

"Having the latest bag or shoes is really important," admits Lilly. "It shows how successful I have been, or how rich my husband is ..." – though he isn't ... and Lilly is a secretary in a typing pool.

"There is another benefit to not eating so much," muses Li, "I can get into some lovely dresses too!"

As a Western man – or maybe just as a man – I struggle with the concept of giving up food for fashion, but cosmetics, accessories and luxury brands – especially foreign designer brands, are 'in' in a big way for the aspirant Chinese middle class.

Lilly admits that since she had her daughter a year ago, she has not been able to afford to buy anything new. But she has a baby, the other 'must have' fashion accessory for a young woman in China. Her mother looks after the child while she is at work, as most grandparents do in China. Lilly lives more than two hours' commute outside Beijing to the east, where house prices are lower. She still allows herself a once-a-month shop with friends, and often they stay over at each other's houses too so they can have a full "proper shopping day" in one or two of the major Beijing malls.

These young women are professional shoppers. Hours on the internet, swapping stories and experiences on Weibo (微博) and WeChat (微信) with friends and other like-minded value-seekers precede the expedition to try on and review those revered goods. Buying white goods such as new refrigerators, air conditioners and the increasingly popular air filter to manage the Beijing pollution, is usually done during the national holidays (Golden Weeks) in October and Chinese New Year. Personal goods are bought as and when the girls have saved up enough, having gone without 'less essential' things. But they're still looking for a bargain – they will always ask for a discount or seek out items that have an additional gift to go with them. Couple this with the benefit of mall discount cards and offers and somehow, through very rose-tinted spectacles from my perspective, it all seems worth the trouble!

Retailing and brand sales in China have to manage a very different psychology to the West. Those businesses that don't understand the psychology can get it very wrong indeed, but judging by the girls' unwavering focus, international fashion is going to run and run in China. Even as the top end is declining with the anti-corruption focus clamping down on high-cost gifts, the emerging middle class in China is still demanding high-class fashion and foreign brands and will go to extraordinary lengths to possess them.

A HARD ACT TO FOLLOW

I first met Amy Li around a year earlier in an almost empty German Beer restaurant which belonged to a friend of a friend in the east of Beijing. We ate German sausage and drank tea. At that time she was extremely busy expanding her business, a comedy club. Her ambition had always been to bring the unique atmosphere of stand-up comedy to Beijing and there had been some success. We had discussed the difficulties of starting and sustaining such an ambitious venture and her reliance at the time on her main day job, the strain on her and her husband and her dreams of having a child of her own. She and her husband had almost given up having a child of their own and were even considering adoption. She had hinted at a rather unusual solution to her family planning dilemma and I was intrigued to find out what had happened.

We met again recently for lunch, almost a year later in a part of Beijing I had not been to before, outside the fifth ring road. It is an area of unusually clean and wide streets with fewer cars. Now popular with Beijing's growing Muslim community, this is a vibrant and developing light industrial zone with cheaper housing.

I wasn't prepared for what I learned.

"Things are good and bad." Amy smiles. "Now I have a new baby boy!"

Fantastic, congratulations!

"And, of course, our daughter."

A daughter too?

"Yes we adopted my brothers' daughter, as you know."

Well I did know but hadn't dared ask if the audacious and less than usual plan had actually gone ahead. Her brother and sister-in-law had always wanted a son but the first child had been a girl, which had been fine of course – but he really wanted a son, so they tried for another child and were successful. Another girl. The story had unfolded as a plan over a year ago she told me. At that time, and after a long debate with her husband, childless and desperate to have a baby of their own they had decided to adopt her brother's and sister-in-law's child. The family came from a much poorer part of China, Guangxi Zhuang Autonomous Region. Since Amy and her husband had good jobs in Beijing, as well as the plans for the comedy club, which would run in the evenings and draw in more cash, the two couples reasoned that the young girl would have better prospects and an all-important Beijing *hukou* to help secure future education and healthcare in the capital. She would also be cared for by a loving couple, who were blood relatives, so everyone could be happy in the greater scheme of things as an extended family. They would be open and transparent as the child grew older and she would benefit from a wider access to the love, care and attention that all children deserve.

"We adopted her and it was all fine. Then I discovered I was pregnant, with a boy!"

Clearly, this was not at all going according to plan. No doubt the brother and sister-in-law were a little put out by the sudden and unexpected news and subsequent arrival. However, having embarked on the road and signed the papers, there was no going back.

"It has been a little more difficult than we thought. My husband and I are both working hard and the comedy club has not had the success I had hoped for. It's been hard to find and book the right talent. My mother-in-law looks after the babies while we work, but she complains that she just doesn't have the energy to look after them properly."

We discuss the trials of bringing up two young children at the same time. Her adopted daughter, Sammy Wang, is now 18 months old and her son, Yi Wei, is just a few months.

"Our son was named by a Tibetan living Buddha. His name means 'piece of leaf.'"

Despite a couple of goes, I never got to ask her why he was named in this way or how they happened to know a Tibetan living Buddha.

"I was 40 years old when I had our son and I was very worried about having the baby in a normal public hospital. They can be a bit unreliable so I went private. The doctors and nurses are much better and the service was so much better too. It was expensive but we have a beautiful healthy boy now."

I agree with her that private care was a very wise choice. Just pricy.

"Also our daughter's *hukou* is still in Guangxi Zhuang and even though we have done all the paperwork, it will still take almost another two years before we can transfer it to Beijing. And my husband is complaining."

For couples to worry, complain and argue over meeting the wants and needs of their children is not unusual, wherever you are in the world. For this family there is the added complexity of the differences between southern China and, specifically, the autonomous region in which Amy's brother and family live. The autonomous regions have a good deal more flexibility in the rules surrounding children and the traditional family values so well defined in the rest of China. Add to this the frictions and natural disagreements between developed Beijing and the less well developed southern regions, and it creates a heady cocktail of mixed cultures and mixed thinking. I'm not surprised her husband is struggling with it all.

"He is worried about money all the time. He is constantly calculating our long-term financial needs. He complains we are spending too much on two children. He loves both our kids but that doesn't stop him from worrying. My mother-in-law is just wonderful, though hard pressed with the efforts, but she is still brilliant and I am so grateful. I just wish the comedy club could be successful."

Amy originally held on to her job as a producer of comedy shows for CCTV, among others, but had had high hopes for the comedy venture which she started from nothing in 2010.

"It's so frustrating. It's really difficult to find the right talent. I'm very disappointed. However, 90% of the pressure I feel is from my husband about the children and money. I could really do without it. I need to get the club working properly. I was lucky as I was trained in the US and went to the University of Southern California Film School from 2006–2010 with a scholarship. It was a really good experience, so when I came back I started the club. I also worked as a comedy TV show producer for a year and then for the BBC as their China-based partner."

Amy pours out her woes on the ingratitude of staff, particularly the younger generation born in the 1990s, who just want to earn cash and don't care about the experience of developing a skill and gaining experience of the industry.

"They just want the money. If they work in TV directly, they can earn around ¥50,000 (£5,000) per episode but I can only afford ¥10,000-20,000 (£1,000-2,000). These guys are so difficult to work with. You have to be very skilful to deal with them. They have absolutely no loyalty and are so fickle. One really talented young girl, with a great future, just suddenly left because her friend did. She decided to go and set something up with her friend that was totally different. Not in comedy or writing at all. What a waste of talent. I feel sorry for her. However, I'm still reasonably optimistic but it is hard to find what it is that is really funny to Chinese people. I've had to do a few other projects to earn money. The next step is to move the club on to work with a really good film production house. Then we can train script writers and hire more talented young people. I have plans and people are interested. I have an investor who is in his 40s too. He is backing me and my ideas."

In her early 40s, now Amy is predominantly working with people a good deal younger than herself, in their 20s and 30s.

"It's like working with different generations. I feel I'm getting old. It's ridiculous!"

Does she regret her choice of profession?

"No. It is hard but it's worth it. Many of my old classmates are in government jobs or working for research agencies and the like.

They have very stable jobs and are happy and comfortable. They don't need to work every day and many are in half retirement and their life, for the women at least, is really about children."

So, what about the children?

"Well, my brother still wants a boy. He doesn't want to give up."

What about his wife?

"He recently asked me if I could adopt their other daughter so they could try for another child in the hope it will be a boy. I told him he should just treat his daughter like a son. It won't do any harm and, in the future, they can get a live-in son-in-law. It would be fine. But he doesn't agree. He feels it's good for her to have two fathers as they live in different cities. We joke together and say she has a northern father and a southern father. He is very traditional. He really wants a boy. Then he will be happy."

I am not sure how to take this. It is all delivered in a matter-of-fact manner. This is a serious proposition. The extended family are genuinely debating the prospects of the female children born into a low-income environment being 'shipped' north to better prospects. Where will it end? Three girls, four, five? The incomes are finite and the prospects shrinking. However, the drive and urge for a male descendant is clearly as strong in some rural communities as it has always been throughout Chinese history.

How can your brother's wife accept her babies being given away?

Amy shrugs.

"It's not like they don't know where they are or that they are not being cared for."

I guess not.

THE PROFESSOR

Paul Gillis PhD is a leading scholar of the accounting profession in China. He's based at the Guanghua School of Management at the famous Peking University in Beijing. Despite many years working internationally, latterly in China, he has neither lost his distinctive American accent, nor his well-developed scepticism of all things smelling of self-promotion or pomposity. After more than four decades, first in – then observing – the accounting industry, he has seen cataclysmic change both globally and, specifically, in China, where the profession itself is really only 15 or so years old. He has an acute sense of humour and the honed cynicism of someone who has heard every excuse in the book, and a few more besides, from students and business people alike.

"I wanted an international career," he says, rocking back in his chair, which he fills with his considerable frame, developed through his American college football days. "My 28 years in a big international accounting firm working in Singapore, the US and China, as well as numerous other countries, certainly gave me that!" Paul is an intensely likeable man. His personality fills the room with benign benevolence and sharp wit.

"I took early retirement from accounting to do my PhD and then stayed on as a professor here at Guanghua to teach." Later I learned that he chose to leave when the politics and in-fighting took up more of his time than his beloved tax work. He is a principled man.

"I've been fortunate to be able to work closely with the global regulators, specifically the American ones, as well as with leaders here in China for many years. That's given me a really interesting perspective which people seem to want to hear about."

He is a regular commentator on the accounting profession and accounting standards, both globally and their application, or likely application, in China. Paul is the author of a seminal book on the, some would say, arcane subject of 'The Big Four and the development of the accounting profession in China'. He also has a well-followed blog and is oft quoted in the Western press on accounting matters in relation to China.

"I'm not always popular with the profession or some of the firms' leadership for what I say, but I believe it needs to be said. There is a need to expose the illogical and ill-conceived responses and approaches that some people seem to think are acceptable in a world where standards and regulations are pushing for more and more transparency and better and better governance."

Does he ever get told off by the business school or, even worse, by government bodies, for his remarks?

"I have a passion for both the accounting profession, which I study and focus on, and business education in China, which I practise and earn my living from. People know I am speaking from the heart and with significant, deep and experienced knowledge of the subject. Yes, I do get complaints, usually from the big accounting firm leadership, but the Dean of the School here is a supporter and encourages me to speak out on the things that matter. In my mind, if I get no complaints, then I am probably not doing my job!"

"So what of the developments in business education in China? Isn't it rather underdeveloped?" I ask.

"Business education in China started 30 years ago. The Guanghua School is 30 years old this year (2015). It has a long and distinguished history. In reality, the school has been at the forefront of Chinese business education. In the early days, the Chinese imported mainly Western PhDs. Many were US, but ethnically Chinese, returners. There was a hunger for, and adoption of, Western MBA-style education techniques. These people had expertise in business, economics and the Western approach, but none of the Chinese relevance or experience in Chinese business or even a Chinese education. So, really, Chinese business education then was not very Chinese.

"Of course, the lessons on GE, Ford, global conglomerates and the successes of Western entrepreneurs were interesting to the Chinese students of the day from an academic perspective, but they couldn't apply the lessons locally. China was changing then, but it was not changed, we needed to be more relevant."

The past ten years, Paul tells me, have been characterized by the faculty generating much more research and knowledge about doing business in China and the 'Chinese Way'.

"We now teach much more about doing business in China from a Chinese perspective," he attests. "There are unique challenges and issues in Chinese business and we focus on these. Everyone wants to know about Jack Ma and the rise of Alibaba, but there are other stories to be told about the way successful Chinese businesses grow and succeed."

I am reminded that all business schools remain under state control, as education is, by and large, the world over. While this doesn't seem to affect the quality or rigour of the research, it brings with it a degree of inflexibility. However, this is changing. Paul agrees that the business schools will have to focus more on getting closer to business.

"In the West, the school leadership are out in the business community raising finance. In China, they are inside the party infrastructure so academia and business is not as fully integrated as they are in the West. But it is changing and will change further. It has to do so as student demand for education more relevant to the real world is increasing."

"So what are the new insights from the success stories of Chinese entrepreneurs and business?" I ask.

"There has not been much developed about the Chinese business approach as yet – many businesses themselves are young and a product of the extraordinary growth of the wider Chinese economy. However, there are trends and specific issues emerging. One area of study is around how Chinese business leaders have learned the ability to manage large-scale operations. Some of the state-owned and a significant number of non-state businesses have multiple millions of employees. The scale is unimaginable in the West. The skill required to keep such enterprises running is significant, all the more so to keep them profitable and growing."

What will happen now that the growth in China is slowing down? Will the skills to manage the upsurge be matched by those needed when growth evaporates? Also, how do businesses of the size and scale of those seen in China manage without diaries? This seeming reluctance of Chinese business and, indeed, the Chinese people to engage in any form of planning has been a source of long-standing curiosity to me personally, and is often at the root of many Western business failures in China. The difference in planning and executing in the West and in China is a seemingly unbridgeable chasm in the eyes of many Western business people I meet.

"For sure it's a difference and there is a genuine reluctance from Chinese leaders to engage in planning," says Paul. "On the positive side, it means there is immense flexibility and agility in business. However, it also means there is a reticence for leaders and corporations to commit to even medium-term objectives, for fear that it might restrict their flexibility to take advantage of new opportunities. Broadly, I think the jury is out on this. It is a very Chinese thing and a reason so many Western business people get so unbelievably frustrated when working here. The Chinese will never commit to a meeting more than a week in advance, in case they have to offend you by saying they have to go somewhere else; basically, that they have someone more important to see than you. In the West, we all understand that meetings change and so do priorities. Also, senior people's diaries are planned up to a year in advance, at least in principle. However, here in China with the concept of face, they just can't bring themselves to succumb to it."

I was reminded that this happens all the time in China and on the grandest of scales. It was only late in the day on 24 December 2014 that the government released the holiday calendar for 2015. This included the fact that 2 January 2015 was going to be a holiday, and that everyone in China would be expected to work on 4 January to 'make up' for the day of holiday.

It is well accepted in China, and by the Chinese population, that holidays are optional. You don't get paid for them and you only get the national holidays and the government decides when they are. Of course, individual business can add holiday terms to their working practices as they see fit. But the only guarantees are the national holidays. In addition, there is a general practice that if you get a day off, then you work a day the next weekend to make up the time. Time off for extra personal holidays can be taken, at the discretion of management, but you don't get paid for it, unless you either work for a foreign-owned company or are very, very lucky to work for one of the new wave of enlightened Chinese entrepreneurs. I heard a story of an interview with a Chinese business leader who, when asked why he expected his staff to work seven days a week, replied, "Well, what would they do with the time off?"

"Board meetings are not planned." Paul is on the topic of governance. "You could argue that they don't have time for preparing the papers for the meetings, as things change so fast here that the agenda is out of date as soon as it is published, perhaps two weeks in advance. Of course, there are exceptions, but they are few and far between."

So does this lack of forward planning in business affect the competitiveness of China? The government issues regular 'directional' five-year plans and has done for years.

"[It's] hard to say, as we haven't really got the long-term horizons of business here to make a real judgment. However, a lack of strategic planning might reduce competitiveness in the short term, but my belief is that the agility and flexibility they gain is highly competitive. Where Western business can be atrophied by the paralysis of analysis and over-planning, Chinese businesses can turn on a dime and move to take advantage of economic or market changes. I guess the ideal is somewhere in-between. However, there is much to learn from Chinese businesses in the way they adapt to new developments and opportunities. Fortunes have been made by the agility of decision making they exhibit."

How does the accounting profession cope in this environment?

"The Chinese accounting profession is changing and our teaching is based on the technical and societal aspects of accounting, just as anywhere else in the world. There is a disconnect between the needs of the profession and the needs of business. Public accounting in China is less high profile than it used to be. It used to be seen as prestigious and, in the 1990s, many international firms got licences. The supply of graduates was way lower than the needs of the profession. The big international firms mainly recruited people who could speak English and then trained them up. Now it has changed and there is a widespread view that the profession is a tough place to work. Even the domestic firms are having problems recruiting bright young graduates to work for them. The state-owned enterprises and government departments are seen as better opportunities, as are the larger privately held, stock-based businesses and investment banks. Consequently, students are drawn there and not to this profession. It is true around the world, not just in China. The professional services career path is seen as a long and difficult one."

Our discussion turns to the students themselves. Getting into university in China is notoriously difficult, even more so the top ones. Both Paul and I agree that this bodes well for the running of businesses in China in the future. Bright, well-educated, internationally minded, and often experienced students, are moving into the corporate, government and professional worlds alike.

"This is good for the future of business in China and for China itself," says Paul. "Although there is a difference between the foreign approach to corporate governance and that of the West. The basic concept of the foreign approach to governance is that separation of roles at the top of an organization enables mitigation against fraud and poor behaviour. Collusion is theoretically easier in China due to the strict 'laws' of hierarchy, relationships (*guanxi*) and face. So, practices that commonly mitigate against fraud in the West cannot be relied upon in China. This is where the anti-graft focus introduced by the Chinese political leadership in the past two years has worked and is working. There seems to be a greater awareness that there are now real consequences to poor behaviour, corruption and profiteering. You have to hope it will continue to shake people into changing behaviours that, if you read Chinese history, have been around for hundreds of years."

Considering the position on anti-graft, Paul's view is that the widespread, and widely publicized, focus on the misdemeanours of a number of high profile foreign-owned multinationals and joint-owned ventures in the past few years was understandable, even desirable.

"Many of the managers of these businesses didn't understand the rules here in China. They unwittingly stepped over the line. Having said that, there were many who did things that they would never have done in their own countries. It is probably easier to focus on foreign-owned businesses than to do so on domestic-owned ones, where political connections add complexity. But the message is clear to everyone. Chinese businesses are next in line for scrutiny and sanction."

Perhaps the Chinese saying, "You have to kill a chicken to scare the monkey," (杀鸡吓猴) applies here.

After so many years in China observing the accounting professionals and being at the heart of the emerging business education sector, what lessons does Paul have for Western businesses?

He pauses for a while as he considers the question. He is an American through and through. However, he has learned to be Chinese too – he has a Chinese wife and a job that is at the heart of Chinese academia.

"First, I have certainly learned that Chinese and Westerners are much more alike than they are different. Chinese business people are just like you and me. All too often, foreigners here see things as dramatically different and they lose their basic ideals and values. The lesson is to be authentic – be yourself. Authenticity is genuine and true. It will get you further and it will get you more respect."

Again, a long pause, long for Paul anyway, he adds:

"Second, I believe that China's best years are ahead of her. I'm bullish for China. As living standards rise to those of the West, the world does not have the natural and other resources to feed and sustain another 1.3 billion 'Americans'. I feel the answer is neither to hold back China or to reduce the US lifestyle. It needs to be looked at in the round."

CHAPTER

16

A RUSSIAN LOVE AFFAIR

We sit outside to start with. It is only a few days before *Da Han* (大寒) or the 'big cold' in China, which is predicted every year according to the lunar calendar and which never fails to disappoint the calculations. However, it is already below freezing on the concrete patio, but the coffee shop is packed. We are forced to huddle on the wooden chairs scattered next to the back door.

Clutching her cup, Yulia L (she prefers a little anonymity) seems immune to the cold, but she is Russian. Born in Volgograd in 1989, this petite, pretty, bright-eyed young woman is in love.

"I was brought up in Volgograd and was a student there too. I wanted to do science but my parents believed I should learn Chinese. We travelled a lot when I was young. My parents took me away on overseas holidays from when I was only 6 years old, but not to China. They didn't want me to study in Moscow as they thought it would be too dangerous for a young woman, so I studied Chinese in Volgograd. The course didn't have any proper Chinese teachers and they were just trying it out but I spent about two years learning Chinese both there and at Tianjin (Foreign Studies) University. In the first year that I was here it was really hard. I didn't know where to go or what to do to meet people. Slowly I managed to find my way through things. Then I applied to do a further one year course (masters in teaching Chinese to foreigners) at Tianjin in Chinese for my Masters, which was moved to Hangzhou at the last minute by the authorities. I went but after six months I gave up. I realized I was not the studying type. Also, I had fallen in love with a guy I had met there in Tianjin so decided to come back to Beijing so I could be with him."

He was an American.

They are not together any more.

"He was still in Tianjin. That's why we chose Beijing, which is between Hangzhou and Tianjin. But I really wanted to be in

Beijing and he wanted to be in Tianjin. It didn't work. I got a job in the 798 Art District in Beijing and spent a year working there but it was really different to what I knew. I even looked for a job in the US without success. I was without a proper job for six months and so I taught English and Salsa dancing to get by. I actually had a ticket back to Russia, because I never thought I would get a proper job in Beijing."

There is no remorse or sadness in her voice. It just didn't work.

"Then, about six months ago, I heard about a job – I applied and got it. I was, and am, so happy. I organize events at an English language bookstore here in Beijing. It has quite a reputation and we get a lot of different authors who come along, as well as musicians. It's my dream job. I am in love with Beijing!"

My hands are now numb with the cold and my notes, never that easy to decipher at the best of times, have deteriorated to a set of loops and hieroglyphics. We move inside to share a table with a long-haired, cool-looking Mongolian 20-something and his earnest girlfriend. As we encroach on their table with cups and papers they good-humouredly ignore us.

"The Chinese really love the Russians and Russia."

I am interested in what it is like to live and work here for this young Russian and we talk about cultural differences.

"They look at the Russians differently. There is such a history between us. There are so many common threads and connections in our respective histories. Of course, there are differences too, but if you talk to the ordinary Chinese, the taxi drivers and the shop owners, they have a great respect for Russia and what it stands for."

Did you make a lot of Russian friends here?

"No. Actually I really wanted to understand the Chinese and the many other nationalities you can find here in Beijing. It is such a vibrant, safe and open city that it allows you to meet so many different people, so I never really tried to be with Russians. I know what it means to be Russian, so I wanted to find out about the Chinese, as well as other cultures."

There is a part of Beijing the locals call 'Little Moscow' or 'Little Russia'. It has Russian restaurants, Russian shops, and Russian-style buildings. There is a well-known Russian Cultural Centre which runs Russian events with Russian music, art and literature festivals. You hear Russian in the streets and the signs are in Russian first and Chinese second. My local park lies just south of the area and I am often just as likely to be rubbing shoulders with Russian joggers and walkers at the weekend, or in the early mornings, as I am with Chinese ones.

"We try to be as diverse and as inclusive of all authors as we can be, including inviting Russian authors to speak or attend our festivals and book fairs. But they don't see the need to do anything in English. All the Cultural Centre activities are only advertised, promoted and run in Russian and Chinese. The Russians in Beijing are really very insular and self-isolating. They just don't seem bothered or interested in having any involvement in international events."

What about your Chinese friends? What do they think of Russia?

"The older Chinese people respect Russia. Russia is seen as something great. They know about and many have read the works of Russian authors such as Tolstoy and Dostoevsky. They also admire the poets such as Ahmatova and Cvetaeva."

And the younger Chinese?

She is a little more evasive and diplomatic.

"Well. They are young, they have their own opinions and they take a much broader international perspective. They see Russia as a good place to travel to as it is cheap and has so much history. My Chinese friends are not strongly for or against Russia. They see it as a world power and a good neighbour and friend to China."

What is the future for this young, energetic and engaging

Russian woman? Will she stay here in Beijing and in China?

"Yes, for the moment. This is really such a fun place to be. Beijing is a very liveable city, except for the pollution of course! If I went back to Volgograd, it would not have changed much and there would certainly not be the speed of change there that there is here. I think that Moscow is changing a lot but I don't feel I want to be there either."

"I now have a lot of friends here. We live in the Sanitun area of Beijing, which is a bit of a bubble I guess, but the people I know are from all over the world, the US, UK and Europe, as well as elsewhere."

Sanitun is predominantly known for the high number of foreigners both living and working there. It is known for its diversity of cuisine from all over the world, as well as being the site of the largest LED screen in the world, which acts as the ceiling of a huge shopping and leisure area known as The Place.

Yulia's Chinese friends all speak English.

"They all regard themselves as internationally minded. Also, they are all very ambitious, more ambitious than I think young people are back in Russia. There is a feeling of possibility here, that you can try and have a chance to succeed. Of course, there are laws that seem frustrating and impenetrable from time to time but people seem to find a way around things and accept setbacks and challenge more than in Russia.

It's exciting to be here at an amazing time for China. In my job, I meet journalists, people starting up businesses, authors, poets, artists and business people. There is a real feeling of energy and opportunity here that I love. I am in a comfortable zone now. This is a 4G, always on, Wi-Fi place with everything at your fingertips. This is an amazing place with amazing people! Also, it's very nice because of my job, which gives me a great social status and I am welcome everywhere!"

As I listen to and feel the energy, enthusiasm and positivity exuding from every pore of Yulia's body, I think her former boyfriend might have had a hard job competing for her love with that she clearly has for the international aspects of this city and this country. He loved Chinese China. She loves the new vibrant, exciting and increasingly global feel of the capital.

"It's just different," she smiles.

Yes. It is.

THE WELSH /CHINESE OIL MAN

Ling Lai is a Hong Kong-born business executive, raised in Wales and, until relatively recently, working for a Chinese-owned, Australian-based, oil company, while living in Beijing. He is a devout and practising Christian.

"I have to say that I struggled with my identity when I first arrived in the country in 1995," he admits. "I felt I had landed on a different planet. It was a real journey of self-discovery. I was working for BP as a project manager in those days, having joined in the UK, I was then sent to China about 1,000 miles up the Yangtze River into Chongqing in Sichuan Province, to build an acid plant. It was one of the first joint ventures in the petroleum industry between China and the West."

Ling spent almost three years commuting each day across a region of precipitous mountain passes with almost impassable and hair-raising roads. His guest house was spartan and uninviting. To make things even more challenging, he had to manage a workforce of almost 10,000 locals.

"It used to take anything up to two hours on a good day and could be an all-night stress run on sheets of ice in the winter. Today, it takes about 30 minutes on the expressway since they sliced through the mountains a few years ago."

Such is the pace of change in China, and the investment in infrastructure, that the old ways have disappeared under the concrete and asphalt of progress.

Ling continues to search for his identity, caught between his Western upbringing and Chinese roots, with a family originally from Guangdong.

"The danger of being in the middle of the road is that you get run over." He smiles gently. "It's taken me 18 years to feel comfortable in my own skin here. I love this country. I am Chinese racially but can never be truly Chinese. People often call me a banana – yellow on the outside, white on the inside."

It's a common reference to the overseas second or third generation returnees to China. They are never quite Chinese by birth and not quite Western by experience.

"I have stopped worrying about it." Ling's soft and some-what disarming smile appears again. "I am who I am. I can't help it, I do have a Western, international perspective. When I arrived, I had a somewhat misguided and romantic view of China based on my Western upbringing and education. I came down to earth with a bump!

"The accounting and finance office was still using the abacus and rice paper vouchers. But two years later, we had an effective, bilingual, fully-integrated ERP system that could be accessed from the head office in London, 24 hours a day. It was so impressive how fast people learned and absorbed things. The Chinese people had, and have, an incredible capacity to absorb, assess, learn and execute new ideas and approaches. They make them their own, they make them Chinese and there is a hunger for self-betterment and to better people's lives which I just never see in the West."

Ling met his wife in Sichuan and they married in 2003. Now living permanently in Beijing, they return to the UK to visit family as often as they can. She is the head of human resources for a large Chinese corporate, headquartered in Beijing.

"It was my wife who introduced me to Christianity," continues Ling. She was already a member of the church and when we moved to Beijing in 2005, she wanted to attend the international church here. Of course, I loved her very much so agreed to tag along. It was strange showing your passport at the door to get into the church, but that's how it is here."

Ling displays his faith easily and gently. "Man plans the steps, but God has the final say," he sums up. "I was lucky to be sent to Harvard Business School by BP in 2005 and that increased my hunger to learn more about both the world and myself. It also further activated my curiosity about the church and Christ. I became a Christian in November 2006 on my return from the US."

Religion has had a long tradition in China, with Buddhism being more than 1,000 years old in the country. Other beliefs, Taoism in particular, are referenced in Chinese classical literature such as *The Romance of the Three Kingdoms* (*San Guo Yan Yi* (三国演义)). It's China's oldest novel, thought to have been compiled by a 14th century poet, Lo Guanzhong. An epic of blood, brotherhood, treachery and loyalty, it's at the heart of classical Chinese culture, as are its central characters, including a revered-monk-turned-political-strategist.

Ling's experience in the oil industry charts the changes in China's energy business.

"In the early days, it was all about using the Chinese labour and supply chain to transfer technology and experience from the West into China. Then, between 2006 and 2010, I noticed a real shift in emphasis. The game got significantly bigger and more commercial. The Chinese energy companies ceased to be shy about where they went in the world to source energy and reserves. Not everyone agreed with their move into Africa and the Middle East, but from 2010, they really started to compete on the global stage much more effectively. They were using their labour, supply chain, political and commercial skills and know-how to leverage their position."

In 2010, Ling found himself sitting in the middle of an Iraqi desert with Chinese riggers and drillers, leading a joint venture project with BP, Sinopec and the Iraqis.

"In 2001, I would never have believed I could ever be part of China's overseas oil exploration. It would have been unimaginable. It shows how far China has come in such a short time, from domestically focused development to taking to the world stage."

The project was one of the early successes of the overseas expansion of China's energy business. It has been followed by many more ventures all over the world, as the country's energy industry goes further and further afield in search of natural resources the super power needs to sustain its econom-ic growth and development.

Until a few months ago he was working for an Australian company owned by a Chinese asset management business, which also owns interests in German and Portuguese enter-prises. Ling was in the middle of the new China ownership and stakeholding model.

"It's a sign of the times and of the emerging powerhouse of China," He says. That smile again. "I was very comfortable with it. It seems a natural move in the greater scheme of things. China has gone global and there is no stopping it. You can feel it and experience it changing around you. It is one of the won-derful things about working here."

I ask Ling if he sees this change in the values of its people. "Are those changing too?"

"No. I think it is still about self-improvement, about face and about family. These are core to Chinese thinking, and while the pace of change picks up, I see these staying the same. With the focus on family, and pleasing mum and dad by being successful, there are emerging tensions and stresses. Some of these exist between the young, who want to embrace new opportunities, and the older generation, who venerate the past, and the strug-gle to get China to where it is now, but things are changing."

I question him directly and ask whether he is still searching for his identity.

"Not any longer." Again, that smile. "China has changed me and moulded me considerably, good and bad, personally and professionally. It has been a part of me for so long and I am nothing but thankful for it. My faith has grown and that too has shaped and helped me develop. But above all, China helped me grow up."

FACING WEST

Wrapped up in her almost ankle-length padded coat, Mrs Tara Li huddles into her seat. The winter wind is in the wrong direction and the only seats we can get are by the door. It keeps blowing open. Other customers and our erstwhile patron seem oblivious to our plight, so after a few pitiful efforts of ineffectual complaining we are forced to huddle into our corner and hope that the conversation will warm us up.

Tara was born in 1969 in Beijing and has never moved. She is a product of 'the movement' as she was at Peking University in 1989, the year of Tiananmen Square.

"That was in my second year at Peking University. I was reading psychology. I wasn't involved."

Everyone I meet who was in Beijing at that time tells me the same thing, either way.

"It really affected my job prospects when I left. It was difficult to get a job. No institutions would take students from Peking University at that time. Also, psychology was a new and unusual degree and people were suspicious. They didn't know what to do with me. I had hoped to go into a hospital job but they gave the job I had applied for to a disabled person. They said they needed to balance the workforce."

She looks directly at me as she speaks and I feel this is a time to adopt the Chinese approach and read between the lines. The reader must do so too, as I would like my visa renewed.

"I had no job. In those days, graduates were allocated jobs by the government. You went where you were allocated. If they said you had to be a secretary, then you went to be a secretary, no matter how good a degree you had. At that time the authorities looked at your university, your degree, your record, your family, everything. Then they decided where you'd work. Also 65% of your salary would go back to the company for 'costs' and you were left with the rest to live on. The university threatened to send me to a middle school to be the Communist Youth League leader. Can you imagine!? Me?! Do that job?! I said, 'No!' They didn't like it!"

Again, she looks directly at me. Impassive features leaving me to draw my own conclusions.

"I see."

"I had relatives in the US – my mother's sister. They saw an advert for a French company who produced interior decoration materials, curtains and the like, who wanted people in Beijing. I applied."

So, it took an advert in the US for a French company, looking for someone in China, for Tara to get a job almost around the corner from where she lived?

"Yes. I got the chance to go for the interview. I was up against people with doctorates and sales management degrees. The French guy asked me what I could do. I said I'd just graduated from the best university in China. I was not the best but I was a good student. If I had got in through the hard entrance exams and then graduated, I felt I could learn very fast and do well at whatever they gave me."

She laughs at the sheer audacity of it, the arrogance of youth.

"He gave me a chance. It was very poor pay but the manager of the showroom was leaving soon and she liked me. She taught me everything I needed to know about how to sell the products. I had to remember a lot. But I'd been a good student so it was ok. Many of the managers at the French company were foreigners so I was really lucky to get the job."

"Could you speak French?"

"Of course not! But I spoke English and, of course, I am Chinese so I knew how to use Chinese psychology."

That direct look again. More between the lines? I get confused sometimes.

"After my three months' probation I got a contract as a sales manager. The job wasn't the greatest challenge for me, although I made many friends. In 1993, after a couple of years at it, I quit."

If the reader has dipped into a few of these Notes already, this will be a familiar comment from many people.

"Why?"

"Really, it was down to my family. My mother thought I'd become a stranger to them. In those days, a senior professor at a school would have earned ¥200/month (£20.00). I was earning five times that and I was getting commission on top. I didn't have time to spend the money. Also, I really didn't know how much money I was earning. But I was working very hard. I had to get up very early and, with entertaining clients in the evenings, I would often not be home until 23.00. My family never saw me."

"It must have been tough for both of you."

"My mother said I was more like a Westerner than Chinese. I wore a smart suit every day and smart shoes. Not good. I was under a lot of pressure. Also, in my heart, I felt I had lost touch with my friends and with myself, so I decided to leave. I was so busy making money from morning to night that I couldn't reconcile my outer and my inner self."

She pauses for a long time, clearly reliving those feelings.

"I was lost."

So?

"I quit and stayed at home for three months and read books. Then my mother said, 'get a normal job'. Friends introduced me to a national, state-owned, company and I got a job as a secretary. My mother was happy that I'd got a suitable 'woman's job'."

"Were you happy?" I ask.

"I was not a good typist! During my lunch break, I would go out and spend money. My colleagues thought I was strange. I was only earning ¥400 (£40.00) a month but I was spending ten times that much. I tried to change a lot but it was so boring!"

"So what did you do? Quit again?"

"I tried to quit. I went to the department head but he said perhaps I could do a different job. The company was in the scientific instrument business. Import and export. They were setting up a new department to deal with exporting. They realized

I could do something else and they said that they were patient enough for me to learn and to try this different job. I said I would, but they had to give me the chance to choose my team and the products myself!"

The direct look again, but this time a self-conscious smile flickers across her face as she recalls the attitude of determination and confidence of her youth. It hasn't seemed to dissipate much over the years, from my perspective.

"There weren't many competitors and a few senior advisors helped us find some really good products. We sold measuring devices, scientific instruments and the like, with customers in the power industry as well as tobacco companies and others which needed accurate measures for their processes. We sold online and were very successful. However, I was under more and more stress again. There were no real policies to work to. We were governed by the ideas from the big boss."

This is an all too familiar story to me from across China. Hierarchies are everything in Chinese companies. Friends joke that in some businesses, the CEO decides the colour of the toilet rolls. Actually, I have never seen any colour other than white, but I get what they mean. Corporate structures are nothing like the layered and delegated authorities of the classic Western business. In China, there are two types of people in a company: the workers and the bosses. The leaders decide everything, and the workers do as they are directed. Within some layers of authority there is scope for independent thought, but outside the strict boundaries the direction is top-down. It is changing, but slowly.

"We were also earning too much money!"

"In whose opinion?" I ask.

"That's what the finance department felt. In the beginning, the company took 70% of the revenues and we got 30% to split between us. But after the first year they told us that we were only going to get 10%. At first we thought this was terrible but we did the maths on the projections and realized we were still going to make a lot of money so we said ok. hen, at the end of the year, we had a huge quarrel with finance. They'd added in so many extra costs and would not tell us what many of them were. Also, in 1996, there were many more competitors, overseas companies and many within China. There were more resellers and more high pressure on us to compete."

Tara is retelling the history of China's late 1990s manufacturing boom. Her words reflect the realities of living through China's 'opening up' to international competition. When 'Made in China' really took off. Her business felt this acutely.

"It became harder and harder to find products and to compete. Also, our competitors were not as 'clean' as us."

The direct look. I know what she means.

"As a state-owned enterprise we couldn't compete on 'financial support' to deals. I found it just too difficult to sell our products and to solve everything myself. It was then that I attended an exhibition to sell our products. It was quiet and I took the chance to walk around the other exhibitors.

"I stumbled on a stand from the Seattle MBA programme. The next day, I applied and during the week of the exhibition I sat the entrance exam. I didn't score well because my written English wasn't as good. The Dean gave me a chance, though, so I became one of the first group of MBA students at Seattle University in Beijing. It was really interesting as they flew in US professors every two months to lecture. I was working at the same time and it was tough doing a part-time course. For many nights I just stayed in the office all night as the internet links were better there. I didn't sleep, just worked during the day and studied at night."

This amazing commitment to self-improvement is a characteristic of the Chinese that runs deep into history. In my personal opinion, it is an ethic which many Westerns would do well to note and learn from.

"The learning was very different to the Chinese way. We could, and were expected to, challenge the professors. That's not the way in China. I became even more influenced by Western thinking and approaches. My classmates were high-level people from business. It was a stimulating and excellent experience. It was what I really wanted to do."

"So how did that affect your work and your career?"

"It was also then that I looked deep into my heart to really think about how I felt and what I wanted to do. I knew a little about human resources and decided this could be combined with my psychology degree as well. I decided to tell my boss that I wanted a change. He said ok!"

"How did you know where to start, what to do, how to make a difference?"

"It wasn't easy to start with, mainly as HR was under the government's control and I had to operate according to government rules and approaches. I couldn't use the theory I'd just learned. The government forbade it! So I quit."

A recurring theme here.

"Where did you go?"

"I went to work for Legend Computers, the forerunner of Lenovo. I was called up by a head hunter who said they wanted someone who had a psychology degree and HR experience. The job seemed made for me. Unfortunately, as a government worker, I had an apartment with my job and I lost that when I left. It was a really big decision to move. Also, in those days, it was a very strange company, at least in my eyes. Before every meeting everyone had to stand and sing the company song and repeat the names of the founders. It was like a cult. I didn't like it. It seemed like the old days in China when everyone had to recite the mantra of allegiance to Chairman Mao. They said they wanted to promote me but since I was 'having problems', I was visibly not participating in the singing, they wanted me to sit a 'cultural exam'. I didn't. So I left."

"To go where?"

"I joined a joint venture company between Legend and a software business. I had to move locations again, as Legend was in the north west of Beijing but the new company was in the centre. So I moved and bought an apartment for my parents. But it just wasn't to be. After two years the government changed the rules and the business folded and I was out."

Tara moved to a Hong Kong business selling fashion wear. The HQ was in Hong Kong and she joined at a time when they were opening new stores. She managed the opening of 42 stores across Beijing alone, responsible for HR but pretty much as the general manager. She struggled, as many mainlanders still do, to explain the Chinese approach to 'foreigners'. The word 'foreigner' is applied broadly to all non-mainland Chinese, including those from Hong Kong. The city might often be mistaken as being 'Chinese' but it is far from it. Language, culture and history are fundamentally different and attitudes clash at many times. Then SARS struck.

The airborne and sometimes fatal disease of SARS (Severe Acute Respiratory Syndrome) hit many countries and businesses very hard. For Tara, it was catastrophic as the Hong Kong business simply cut off the mainland entity and scrapped it in response. It was a time of bitterness for Tara and the team who were willing to work for nothing until the epidemic subsided, but the Hong Kong owners were adamant and closed everything.

In one of the more telling remarks I have heard in China about Hong Kong, Tara's view should be a wakeup call to any business trying to make the Hong Kong linkage to the mainland.

"I decided to leave too. My staff and I couldn't understand the Hong Kong attitude. We didn't like the way they just cynically cut us loose. The Hong Kong attitude was too Western!"

She stayed at home during SARS. It says much for the fortitude, not only of Tara, but of so many Chinese people who suffer setbacks to bounce back or endure what most Western-ers would find life-changing and catastrophic. The epidemic officially lasted from November 2002 to July 2003, but the ef-fects were felt for many months later in border controls and heat sensors at all airports across Asia until official eradication in January 2004. To lose a job for more than a year would be unthinkable in the West but it is almost no big deal in China where the family and strong savings ethic cushion individuals from the worst life can throw at them.

Tara eventually secured a job with DuPont.

"They were a wonderful business. So many of my MBA case studies had been on DuPont. It was just great to be there and experience it for myself. It was my dream job. They were sell-ing the business and I was to be there to manage all the HR issues in Beijing through the process. They really cared about their employees and, between 2003 and 2008, I had a really great time. DuPont sold to Koch and I did the transition as everyone moved over. I was responsible for all of it. It was after the DuPont business was bought by Koch that I realized that US companies were very different. DuPont had, what seemed to me, a very European approach and style – Koch did not. In five years, they gave no salary increases at all. The sense was, 'if you don't like it here, go somewhere else'. Everything had to be approved by headquarters; we had no discussion or discretion at all. They had a high staff turnover."

Tara and I discuss her experiences of the differences be-tween a European and a US corporate business. Her overall impression, and that of many Chinese people I have met, is not wholly favourable so far as US corporate culture is concerned. There is a generally held view among the Chinese that many US businesses are too aggressive, too sales-focused and don't care about their people. While this is a stereotypical perception, it does seem to be embedded in the minds of many Chinese peo-ple. In addition, there is a common perception, probably not always a reality, that US businesses set aside Chinese culture in favour of the 'American way' being the only way. Needless to say, this goes down very badly with the Chinese, who expect respect and cultural sensitivity from their overseas employers.

Tara is quite emphatic. Cultural sensitivity wins every time.

Tara left her US employers with no regret and moved to an Italian company where she stayed until the business decided to relocate to Shanghai. She didn't want to leave her elderly parents and, by now, she was married with two young children. The potential wrench would have been too great so she opted to stay in Beijing and leave the business. There were struggles with the Italians during her time there and she recalls a few moments when she had to stand up to Italian male egos. But overall, she found herself enjoying the on-going, and now long association, with non-Chinese corporate life.

"It was clear to me, looking back, that I was really always leaning West. It was interesting to find that Westerners might not have expected this tiny Chinese woman to be so tough but we got on fine in the end. The fact that I am Chinese has never held me back in a Western company, they didn't care if I was married, or had kids. In fact, DuPont let me take my daughter to work for the few times when our nanny was ill or we didn't have help."

Tara explains to me, throughout our discussions, that labour law in China is quite different from that in the West.

"It is a good deal easier to fire someone in the US or in the UK than it is in China. Certainly, if that someone is underperforming and pregnant. The documentary proof required to sever contracts is enormous and no more so than around pregnancy."

The now repealed focus on one child, and the importance of family and that child is ingrained in the Chinese psyche. It can take up to two years to sever relations with certain employees and the burden of proof has to be agreed and signed for by the employee if the individual is a pregnant woman. The regulations also differ in substance and in interpretation across China, province by province, city by city and sometimes court by court, and even judge by judge. The lesson here is get the right advice in HR and ensure it is localized.

Tara also reflects that, "Foreign companies find it a lot more difficult to shut up shop and disappear. Local companies can close and/or disappear quite easily, leaving the staff floundering in their wake. Foreign companies, with brand reputations to uphold, find it much more stressful and difficult to manage underperformance and dismissals. If a Chinese company wants to close a branch, it can do it inside two weeks. For a foreign company it can take up to two years!"

By now we both feel that, despite the warmth of our coffee, our feet have resisted the cold long enough and it is time to call it a day. As we part, I reflect on the conversation. Tara introduced herself to me as 'Mrs Tara Li', a Western introduction and a Western style of address, for a Westernized and essentially Western experienced professional. It was of little surprise for me to learn that she had married an Englishman, in fact a Yorkshireman (known for their straight-talking and sometimes rude directness).

Just before I wrote these lines I spoke to Tara to find she had been battling breast cancer for over a year. She is now in the last stages of the disease and knows she has little time left. Her only thoughts are for her children and the stability of the family after she has gone. The stoicism and straightforwardness has not left her but her love of all things Western has given way to a desperate hope in Chinese medicine to overcome what Western medicine cannot. Unfortunately, leaning West or being Chinese can't stop the inevitable.

Tara sadly died shortly before this book was published.

THE
CHINESE-
AMERICAN

She looks like any other professional Chinese woman as she bustles through the door. Joyce Chao orders her latte in flawless Mandarin, her strong Asian features fooling the serving staff as much as they do pretty well everyone else in the place apart from me, but then I know her. Once she has sat down, I have her usual friendly greeting, in flawless English.

"You eaten yet?"

It's mid-afternoon but it's a common Chinese greeting. Food is important and the lack of it has been a Chinese curse for centuries. It's why you really never see rice left in a bowl at meal times. The greeting also defines underlying politeness and thoughtfulness, which permeates all relationships here, personal and professional. She visibly relaxes when I smile and nod.

Sipping her latte, Joyce looks every bit the businesswoman she is, but there is a critical difference from the others bent over work papers around us. Joyce is Chinese-American.

"It doesn't matter where I grew up, or what colour my passport is, because I look Chinese," she says. "I have Chinese blood and heritage. Being Chinese is in my core. I jokingly tell my friends I am now half Beijinger since I've been here for over 12 years. However, the Chinese in me comes out with an American touch and delivery. It can be a bit direct and to the point sometimes but this is why I feel I can add value. My mainly US clients want clarity and certainty. In a culture where communication is subtle and passive, I provide a balance and that's where I hope I offer value and why I get paid."

Joyce is second generation Chinese from the US. She grew up there with American schooling and a rich corporate work experience. In 2003, a keen interest in learning more about her own Chinese culture and language prompted her to respond to an education management job advertisement based in Beijing. She got it, moved and has been here ever since.

She's had to adjust and adapt over the years, but she's retained her US openness and candour. She has a big heart and a warm, effervescent and endearing personality. Since arriving in Beijing more than a decade ago, she has managed to combine her personal style of fast talking and passionate delivery with a deep attention to the details of the cultural differences and idiosyncrasies of the 'Chinese way'. The result is a dual language and dual culture expert advisor.

Having worked with a variety of UK and US businesses operating in China, Joyce has a very well developed sense of what works and what doesn't. She's seen all shapes and sizes of business try and succeed, as well as fail, in their efforts to enter China and/or position themselves here.

"In such a fast-developing economy with many changes and challenges, I can't say there is a definitively right way of doing things here but there are certainly wrong ways. Time and again I see advice and good intentions fall by the wayside. The negative impact is not often immediate but time will tell. My role as an advisor is to offer ideas and solutions, and I don't hold back informing clients of the risks. However, at the end of the day, the decisions of how to do business in China belong to the client. The core of any strategy and advice that I offer is to aim to build up the relationship base and not to do anything that might tear it down."

"Doesn't it frustrate you when you see things happen that you have tried to guard against?" I ask.

"Sure it does. But I am older and wiser now. I've come to understand the simple fact that China's big, with a long history of over 5,000 years. Yes, there are other civilizations with many years of history, but none so colourful and fragmented in the past 60 years as China's. Certainly, nothing comparable to the miraculous transformation of the past decade seen here. The frustration is not always 'I told you so ...' It's that modern China is a big but constantly moving target. What I experienced in 1987, my first trip to Beijing, is vastly different from what my best friend's first trip was like in 2007. And it's just the amazing ways and speed of things. I'd like to say it is bewilderment more than frustration."

Joyce is a bundle of energy as we talk. She's constantly multi-tasking on her smartphone, email and, of course, the ubiquitous WeChat. She seems to know everyone and everyone knows Joyce. She is a 'do it now' person, arranging connections, making meetings. She works quickly, knowing that in China if you don't seize the moment, it's gone.

"You know, I have been so fortunate. My parents' generation experienced a revolution which was gritty and horrid, but in the past 12 years I've had the privilege of experiencing a different revolution in China – one of technology and economics. It's humbling and it's what drives me. My parents' and grandparents' generations paved the way for me to do what I can do in China."

"So what do you actually do?"

"Coming to China mid-career and possessing a developed knowledge of both sides of the ocean, I suppose you could best describe me as a cultural guide and, at times, 'fixer'. It's my business to use my sort of chameleon role to know how to get things done in building the international bridge in China. I've many Chinese friends from all over the world who I've helped and who can help me when I call on them. Relationships are important anywhere in the world but they are vital here. It's not a chore to keep up with these either. These people are my friends as well as good long-standing acquaintances. I enjoy spending time with them and we all help each other whenever we can. That's how it is here. That's what relationships (guanxi) are all about."

"As a Chinese-American, does that have an effect on how people see you?"

"If I don't open my mouth, no one can tell the difference," Joyce says with a wink.

"I've opinions and solutions that I hold back at times. It's not what the Chinese are used to, not from a woman, and one who looks Chinese. But people are very accommodating and gracious. They'll hear me out, because I'm a foreigner, but I'm caught in the middle sometimes. People here expect me to understand the Chinese approach of decision-making and my overseas clients want results. At times the locals default to 'you don't understand what we mean because you didn't grow up here ...'"

She shrugs her shoulders with a feigned look of confusion. Her phone vibrates continuously and she flips out a few more WeChats as we pause.

"Because I've always been involved in education and in writing as a profession I'm often asked to write or review English speeches or materials for some of my Chinese contacts. There's never any talk of money or getting paid for such 'favours'. It's part of relationship building and people tend to understand it is part of the 'favour bank' between friends and friends of friends. The Chinese have an amazing ability to weigh up and balance the right level of reciprocal favours between each other. When I explain this to clients, they often balk at the expectation that they are to do something for nothing. Many simply refuse. That's when the trouble starts. Remember what I said about relationships earlier?"

"How could I forget?" Joyce delivers her messages so you don't forget them easily.

"Back home in the West, we often help friends move, offer them lifts in our cars and the like. We don't expect payment. So, what's the big deal? Is it because some businesses really see China more as a client, than as a friend?"

Ignoring the deeper philosophical or socio-political point for a moment, she nevertheless leaves a pause long enough for it to sink in before she continues.

"I try to help whenever I can. The rule is 'don't promise something you can't deliver'. Sometimes you just have to help. It's the right thing to do because even though there are many shiny high-rise buildings all over the cities of China, it's still a developing country. Among other things it's still trying to catch up from the lost generation resulting from the Cultural Revolution. Occasionally you feel you are being taken for granted but that's a very Western perspective. From the Chinese point of view, they will not see it like that and would be very offended if they thought you believed it."

Where Joyce seems to excel is in the highly ambiguous area of 'reading between the lines' of meaning, actions and words of the Chinese.

On a related note, I believe that there's a remarkable similarity between the British and the Chinese. There used to be a joke about the so called 'Whitehall Mandarins' of British government never being clear about what they meant. The British are often known for being opaque and for the use of euphemisms. The Chinese excel in this art. Reading between the lines of what is said to understand what is actually meant requires a very good cultural translator, as well as linguistic interpreter. Joyce is both.

"Something different, and what might be hard for Westerners to understand, is that Chinese, both as a language and as a culture, is all about context, symbols and layers of meaning. We love lucky numbers: seven and eight. And nine means longevity. Also, just don't think about using the number four in lifts, signage, seating, anything. In Chinese, four is too close to the character for death. References to historical characters, old sayings and proverbs, as well as odd plays on words and even Chinese characters or political figures will only result in the Chinese actually understanding the meaning of a comment. To them, it is second nature. Even to me, and certainly to my clients, it can seem unfathomable and the subject of significant confusion."

So how to survive this complexity?

"Basically accept it. And get a good Chinese strategist, one that has the perspective and modern history knowledge. It's the fact for all cultures; outsiders will never be able to make full sense of it. Having someone around to help keep you straight, and away from the cultural landmines, is always useful."

She smiles at me knowingly.

"I've been seeing more and more that international businesses and organizations go out and recruit for China without asking necessary questions of applicants. They probably don't appreciate that the Chinese have a set of very specific views on other cultures. They've not been exposed to the multicultural and cosmopolitan cities of the West or the complexity of businesses that cross borders. It's a mistake for Western businesses here to employ people just because they look or sound Chinese. It might seem silly but I still see global brands employing Cantonese speakers from Hong Kong or South East Asia. Unfortunately, mainland Chinese don't see Hong Kong as the vibrant global city we do. There's deep suspicion of Hong Kongers, not to mention that Cantonese might sound the same to the untutored ear but it's not the same language as 'Putonghua', the mainland language."

Joyce will not discuss the other prejudices against the Japanese, Singaporeans, and regrettably, minorities within China. However, a brief look at Chinese history will educate you to the long-standing mistrust and concerns that plague current Chinese thinking. 'The rape of Nanjing' and the long Sino-Chinese war, as well as the opium wars and other struggles with everyone from the British to the Dutch, are worth being aware of.

"Something else here that always confuses clients is the total lack of diaries," adds Joyce.

A change in topic is probably called for – I've mentioned this elsewhere. But Joyce elaborates.

"It's CFD, Chinese Fire Drill. Everything seems to be last minute, fast and furious, well-managed but all in a massive hurry. That's why you have to seize the moment and do everything straightaway. The whole place, most businesses and pretty well everyone's private life is managed on an 'Are you in

Beijing? Are you free tonight, tomorrow, the day after?' basis. Trying to arrange schedules for overseas visitors who expect everything mapped out in advance and set in an organized diary is a nightmare. It's a very big education process for Westerners. No matter how many times I tell them, they still don't believe it. Even the VIPs may not have a diary. They have to keep time somehow but in China they simply can't plan much time in advance."

Doesn't this make it all a little difficult to do things, even like book flights and hotels?

"Hotels are easy, there's so much spare capacity here, getting a room is never a problem. The flights are also often all booked at the last moment, except for some of the international ones which usually need a bit of forward planning. However, after that it's a free for all. Within very strict Chinese guidelines of course. If you're senior, you will get a meeting with most people. If you're not, then don't count on getting a meeting at all, certainly not above your own level of seniority, unless you are accompanying someone more senior. This goes right to the top and the hierarchy of who should be seen and for how long and where is played out at intergovernmental as well as corporate level."

I have personally gotten used to arriving in China after a break or business trip with no diary plan at all from one week to the next. I know that after a few WeChats or emails my diary will fill with the people I need to see and those who want to see me. It's a bizarre experience at first but after a while you get used to it. Many people arriving for the first time, or even after a few visits, fail to appreciate the complexity of the Chinese way of working, particularly the total lack of diaries.

"I've known really senior guys arrive at the airport not knowing which hotel they are staying at, who will be picking them up, whether they have a dinner to go to straightaway or what the agenda is for the next day. I mean, they do have a general idea and with a few specific end goals, but never the specifics. These are the best people at getting things done in China. They are the old hands (with a high level of tolerance for the unknown) who know that by the time the aircraft gets to the gate they will be met, greeted, transported, fed and watered in the right way and with the right people. It can go wrong sometimes, but equally the Chinese will pull out all the stops to ensure the senior visitor, as well as the local leader, does not lose face.

"It can be incredibly frustrating and you can't always be certain of the seniority of everyone around the meeting or dinner table – but people can mobilize very quickly. I've known flights to be changed and schedules dropped and or rescheduled, even using double bookings and two dinners to attend in an evening, being arranged so that the right 'face' can be shown and the right people have been met and spoken to. It really is almost an art form of organizational logistics. It's quite impressive!"

Joyce is in her element now. This is her life and she makes her living from managing the complexity and ambiguity of Chinese etiquette and hierarchical management, all in the interests of getting things done and continuing to build that international bridge.

I ask, "With so many Chinese people studying overseas and English levels increasing, is there still a role for your type of service? The cultural bridge and interpreter?"

"Definitely yes – and even more so. People like me, we come with experience, insights and perspective. Many only see a part of the culture they enter. Chinese students only get the academic experience plus some work time. They might know the US or British culture as a consumer but do they really know enough about what Americans or British people think? On the other hand, foreigners come to China, learn the language and love the cuisine, but do they have Chinese friends from all walks of life and know enough about how the Chinese think? A more key question is do they care enough to try to know?

"While I say this, I also know that advisors with my background have a limited window. It's a matter of time. The Chinese have passed the stage where they were the hungry recipients of international business thinking. In any event, most senior leaders here are well-travelled, speak almost perfect English and have read more management books than you have. Many have overseas degrees and overseas expertise is a lot easier to obtain. They no longer need advice. They are now the consumers as well as the business owners of the emerging global market. Goods and services might be created elsewhere in the world but they are now sold, usually through joint venture partnerships, to the millions of Chinese who have cash now. It's moved from 'made in' to 'sold in' China."

This is a recurring theme in almost every discussion I've ever had here personally. Businesses now need to arrive in China with quite a different mindset from a few years ago.

"There is so much opportunity here. From education and healthcare, specifically care of older people, to handmade chocolates and high-street fashion. The top end gift market, from wines to handbags and watches, has been hit by the anti-graft purge of the government and everyone actually applauds this initiative. However, there remains so much that can be done, and to go for, in specialty markets and many others too!"

Joyce should know. It's where she works and is very successful.

THE TRAVEL
BLOGGER

In the bowels of the China World Trade Centre at Guomao, the Central Business District of Beijing, lies a labyrinth of high class shops, restaurants and eateries. The café we meet in is another recent and quite possibly short-lived establishment with eye-watering prices and impossibly small portions.

Han Jiang is a travel blogger. With over 280,000 followers, he was recently awarded the accolade of being one of the top 10 travel bloggers in China for his 'lostinbeijing' site. We sit in an atmosphere of affected service and 'Beautiful People'. Han is a cool dude in a flat cap. Where I come from in Yorkshire in the UK, only farmers and I wear flat caps to protect our heads – but here in Beijing it's a mark of sophistication and worldliness. Han is intensely affable and likeable. He has the typical air of someone who has hit the headlines but still can't quite work out why.

"I'm just an ordinary guy who likes to travel and write stuff."

Han was born in a small town some 70 km north of Harbin, the capital city of Heilongjiang in north east China, in the 1970s. When I ask him how many brothers and sisters he has, he just grins.

"A lot! My parents had a lot of kids. I'm the youngest and I was born when they were 40 years old. I went to primary, middle and secondary school in my home town and then read mechanical design at Harbin University. I graduated in 1993 and then worked in a factory for three years. I hated it so went back to university for another three years to do my masters from 1996–1999. That second degree was a bit tough, as I had to fund it all myself. It was just when the Windows system came out, so I worked it all out then taught high school students how to use it at weekends to get the money I needed to live!"

At the age of 27 Han was in Beijing trying to find work. He had a dream to travel but the average factory wage was about ¥300–¥500 (£30–£50) a month and that was never going to fuel his desires.

"The economy in northern China at that time was terrible and even now it's not great. That's why I came to Beijing. There is opportunity here. It's the capital and it has heating in winter!"

He grins again.

"I learned to speak English because I thought I'd be able to get a job with a foreign company and maybe travel abroad on the back of that. The first job I got was with a state-owned company. It was a research institute but I decided to leave after a year. I managed to get a job as a salesman with an overseas information technology company. I stayed for five years but it was hard. I was exhausted and my hair fell out!"

Han is completely bald and I'm not sure whether he blames this on the Western company, the stress or his DNA.

"I managed to travel a lot when I was with that company. All across China, usually during the National Day holiday in October, as well as Spring Festival and the other holidays. I went to Tibet and really liked it there. It gave me the travel bug. It is so beautiful there. I travelled to many of the places I had always dreamed of going to in China. It was great. My most favourite place is Tibet and I did the Mt Kangrinboqe (Mt Kailash) trail right around the holy mountain. I am so proud of that accomplishment."

The mountain is regarded as sacred by the Tibetans and to circle the mountain is a pilgrimage of the highest level. The area is the source of some of the greatest rivers in Asia including the Indus, Brahmaputra and the Karnali. The circumambulation is 52 km and said to bring great fortune to and cleanse all the sins of those who accomplish it.

"After the IT company, I went to work for a US company in the totally different area of procurement. I did it for four years but I really couldn't do it for longer than that. The big upside was during that time I went to 20 countries. Then I decided to just go travelling and blog!"

Another big grin.

"It was just the right time in China. Around 2009/10 there were not many smartphones in China but there was a hunger for more knowledge about the world outside China. Everyone was on their computers. In 2009 I managed to get a five year travel visa to Australia and I blogged about it. Lots of my friends asked me how I had managed to get one so I wrote about how to do it. Suddenly it was not just my friends who were asking me about travel but many more people through my blog. It was right then that the Chinese started to travel abroad more and I was lucky to be there at the start of the boom."

Han doesn't just write about the usual places or the usual things to do, but enriches his blog with tips on culture, language, music festivals and cool and different hotels, bars and eateries.

"I believe it's better to travel by your heart."

Which means?

"Follow the unusual paths, go to places others don't, get into the culture and experience the reality of the places you visit. I went to India and to the Festival of Durga. It got so much coverage and hits on the site, but that wasn't why I went – I was just really interested in it. I try to find interesting stories, talk to local people, find out facts about local history. I also try to make a clear connection between where I go and the Chinese people to make it accessible and readable. As a child I was very curious and I've held on to that curiosity all my life. I think it's good, things happen when you are curious. I wanted to be an actor or an artist when I was young. I think it was that creative edge in me that has made me want to travel and experience other places and peoples. Once I stayed in an old people's resort in the UK. One elderly lady asked why I was there with all these old people. I said I was just curious about what it is like to be an elderly person in the UK. She was surprised that some young Chinese guy was interested."

Is this sort of travel just for young people then?

"I think you have all your life to make money but when you are older you have the money but not the energy; when you are young you have the energy but not the money! My blog focuses on the places that are free and where you just need energy and enthusiasm, not always the money. I try to introduce the street food, the history the landscapes. These things don't cost a lot to experience and see."

Who do you write for?

"Me really."

Big grin.

"Well, I guess I have to admit I try to make it accessible to as wide an audience as I can. I don't have an age group or particular profile I focus on. I just write. I also try to do a bit of planning before I leave, to find out if there are any festivals I can go to, or interesting things happening in that place or that country at that time. I go to the more out-of-the-way places. Once I got an email from an old guy who follows me. He said he couldn't travel due to ill health so he travels through me, which is great. Many bloggers just post photographs but I write too, and I try to get under the skin of the place. I try and stay in one place for a week or ten days if I can. That means I can get past the superficial and have the time to stop and look, watch the people and the life and ask questions, go further away from the tourist places. That is where the real life is."

Han loves to be as authentic as possible in his travels – he is not the typical tourist and encourages others to follow his lead. He completed his first book after travelling to six or seven countries, which included countries across northern Europe, Israel and South East Asia. He is contemplating a second one. He is now courted by travel companies and country agencies, so usually travels for free and is often paid too. Writing for magazines and other organizations seems to generate enough funds to live on. Latin America remains on his hit list. However, he is at pains to point out that he has enough money and admits to being a Buddhist, needing just the basics for his life. There is no mention of a wife or even a girlfriend, so I assume he is entirely free of ties and happy with his lot.

"I hated the office politics of business. I just wanted to be free of all that, to do my own thing. I love my way of life. I am free and have no worries about eating and living. I can write, arrange where I go and when I go, and share my experiences. It's a good life. Many of my old classmates are rich now and they tell me I did the wrong thing but I think they are the ones that went the wrong way. I believe that if you have a dream, you should follow it or your life will be gone and you will have missed it. I love doing what I want, choosing where to go and then going there on my own, as a free spirit. I'd love to feel I can influence the next generation of Chinese tourists through my writings to explore more when travelling, to search out the culture, the history, the authentic food and traditions. Not just the shopping!"

As we finish Han bemoans the smog in Beijing.

"I'm going to get a flight back to Harbin, right now," he announces, "the air here – it's just too bad for me. It's not healthy."

Always travelling.

BREAKING WITH TRADITION

Celine, as she prefers to be known, is a confident and self-assured young woman. Born in Beijing in 1983, she has recently returned from two years in the UK where she completed a Masters in International Management at Royal Holloway College in London. She is a highly articulate woman who speaks perfect English with only the hint of a Chinese accent. She has returned to get married. Her work now is in advertising account management at a media company and her husband works for an overseas education company. They are the quintessential urbanites of China, members of the new emerging middle class of the country with a powerful blend of language, international outlook, education and money.

"I am very fortunate as I have worked in the media industry since I graduated," she says, "first in Tencent (the hugely successful competitor to Alibaba) as an advertising executive and in business development for two years in Beijing. After that, I spent almost six years in a start-up advertising company in a similar role before working for Vogue China for almost three years. Then I went to London."

Why did she return to China?

"When I was in London, I came home a few times for family reunions and, of course, at Chinese New Year. It was at one of these events that I met my husband. We were both at a casual dinner of family friends. Then both parents agreed to meet and we started what became a long-distance relationship. After a year, I then decided to come back and we were married recently."

Celine is proud to be a Beijinger, born and brought up in the city where she now lives.

"Beijing now is not what it used to be. The pace has visibly increased. But this is an important city on the world stage now. Shanghai is probably more visibly international but Beijing is the place of political power and decision making. Some people really feel that Beijing is home. They feel they belong to Beijing. We are proud of our city as it has some of the best education establishments and hospitals in China and they are of a world class standard."

So, what does she see happening in the next few years?

"I guess I might have a baby in the next three years, maybe then I will be self-employed so I can look after the baby and spend more time with it. I want to set up a Chinese-UK business."

Doing what? I am curious.

Her reply is enthusiastic and clearly articulated.

"Education is the future of China, the Chinese and Chinese children. I want to set up summer schools for Chinese children to be in the UK. I want to have an education company focused on cultural exchanges. My husband and I discussed the idea and he is more experienced in this so he can advise me."

The idea unfolds and is as disarmingly simple as it is astute.

"When I was in the UK, I worked on a similar project so I was able to work with a number of UK schools. I think there is a market ready at both ends. Here in China many parents have money and want their children to be exposed to the international stage and the UK, where there are schools with the facilities and financial needs to provide the services we could use in the long summer holidays. My husband will build the China business. I think it is a brave idea. We are going to give it a try and see if we can succeed."

Here again is that unstoppable and raw enthusiasm that you find so often in China. The attitude is, "Why not?", "Let's try ..." and "We can do it". The idea seems logical and an interesting and saleable one which UK schools could well buy into.

"My husband is a very traditional Chinese man. He likes history, Chinese opera, poetry and calligraphy. I am very satisfied with how our relationship is developing. I am particularly happy about the equality in our marriage. It is a democratic marriage. We can discuss anything and talk a lot about our future, where we will live, what we will do."

This is indeed a little more unusual than the old traditional way of Chinese marriage. Celine's comments say more than the words alone. The fact that she is saying these things suggests something different, something surprising to many other Chinese marriages.

This is the new style of marriage where the woman is empowered and equal. Not tied to the children, tradition and the kitchen sink.

"The role of women in China is changing. More and more husbands are taking roles in the home as more and more women take wider responsibilities at work. It used to be that women should have a baby, look after the home and prepare food while being a good daughter and, specifically, a good daughter-in-law. Now, it is more like Western society. In bigger cities, such as Beijing and Shanghai, many women choose to be at home, they are not forced to by social norms. It is a choice, not an expected role."

The story of women's rights and empowerment is a recurring theme, which seems to have lost its old taboo. Stories of women being held back and prevented from having a wider role come flooding in across history in China and certainly there remain places where the role of women remains at best ambiguous and at worst home- and baby-bound.

"I know there are places such as in the south of China, such as in Guangdong, where men are at the top and women are at the bottom. I have heard of villages where women are not even allowed to sit at the same table to have food with the men."

I'm not sure of how much of this is true, but who am I to argue? China is an enormous country, full of diversity and differences. It's quite possible that such practices exist. However, in Beijing the picture is quite different among those whom I speak to. There is a strong and growing number of women's empowerment groups which are well-attended and supported. They are led by Chinese women for Chinese women, from groups struggling to raise issues around domestic violence, another taboo subject in many cultures and no less so in China, to self-help business groups encouraging and mentoring women to take the lead in the work environment.

"Work has changed women's lifestyles and life position in China. Financial independence has been the catalyst for women's empowerment and freedom from the past."

Indeed it has and so it should, in the eyes of many, including me.

chapter 22

THE CLASSICAL IMPRESARIO

It's an unusual setting for a discussion about China. Wray Armstrong and I are sitting, sipping gin and tonic in the refined surroundings of the aptly named Gin Palace bar in the Strand Palace Hotel which is neatly placed at 372 The Strand, London. We have been trying to arrange a meeting for some time and finally our diaries coincided – not in Beijing but 8,000 km to the west in the UK. The Strand Palace is a well loved, though somewhat faded, icon of the London theatre world.

"We used to call it the Stranded Palace," Wray smiles through the gloomy but strangely welcoming space that has started to fill up with 'early doors' drinkers. "It was always the place the orchestras were billeted for the London concerts."

Wray is a soft spoken Canadian with an encyclopedic knowledge of the global classical music scene and a bewildering array of people, places and pieces fall in a torrent of musical notations which I can barely grasp. As a young man Wray grew up in a small town in the province of Saskatchewan in Canada but always dreamed of moving away.

"My grandfather was one of the pioneers who first opened up that part of Canada. Pioneering is in my familiy blood, so it came as no real surprise when I moved first to Toronto, then London and finally out to China. I was just following the Armstrong line of adventurers. Back in 1978 I joined the Toronto Symphony Orchestra. At that time they had just had a successful tour from China and I worked on a project to bring a Peking opera and acrobatics team to Canada. It was my first real taste of China and I was fascinated."

In 1991 Wray moved to London and met a young Chinese conductor called Yu Long with whom he worked for a year or so. Yu Long is now one of the most famous conductors in China, known as China's Herbet von Karajan, and widely acclaimed as one of the most influential people in the Chinese classical music scene.

"Long told me that he was going back to China to set up a classical music festival in Beijing. I was lucky enough to go to China in 1996 to attend his very first festival which was to become the now famous Beijing Festival. Everyone I knew in the arts felt China was going to be big but no one knew just what was going to happen and no one knew about China. The business I was working for at that time was involved in the Beijing Olympics and between 1998 and 2008 I was heavily involved. Then on 7 August 2008, during the first week of the Olympics, we staged the 'Divas in Beijing' concerts, including the Great Hall of the People as a major venue."

It was a spectacular success with world famous stars and packed houses. Wray agreed to stay on to set up a representative office for the business based in the prestigious Oriental Plaza office and shopping mall complex in the very heart of Beijing.

"I really thought it was amazing and decided to leave and set up my own arts management business with a China office. I was terribly naive and started out in Hong Kong. This was not only very expensive but also a long way from Beijing and the centre of the Chinese classical music scene of the time. I had a backer but we soon started to run out of money. So I moved to Shanghai."

Two years later in 2011, after some moderate success, Wray was back in Beijing.

"I worked as a consultant to the Tianjin Grand Theatre. Contact lists are everything in this business and after 40 years in the trade I knew, and know, a lot of people. In those times people didn't know what was fake or real. There was even a 'fake' Vienna Orchestra which came to Beijing between 2005 and 2008! Well meaning officials from the culture ministries around China would sponsor random projects and invite orchestras which had the right sounding name but were cheap. They got what they paid for."

Wray shakes his mop of grey hair and laughs.

"It was chaos. We have to charge a fee, then there are the air fares for the players and staff, and in country transport costs and maestro fees, let alone all the incidentals that surround things like stages and sets. It's an expensive undertaking to move a top orchestra and the top musicians around the world. Subsidized orchestras can get 'gigs', but fully operating and commercially run orchestras, the best in the world, are very expensive. It is not a level playing field but broadly you get what you pay for and for many in China, price was a key thing and everyone wanted a 'deal' or a bargain. They compromised on price and rarely got the best.

"All the pioneering spirit from my grandfather came in very useful at that time. It was like the Wild West in China arts then. All the cities started to compete for the biggest and grandest concert halls. Across China there are now 35 halls. Supported by the provincial government for maybe the first year of operating, they can afford the fees associated with bringing a famous orchestra or soloist to the venue, but then they run out of money fast."

Wray recounts how cities all over China, such as Xi'an, home to the world famous Terracotta Warriors, decide that they are going to hold a big concert but they don't have the right venue, so they build one. When a city hits a certain size in China, then there is a trigger for it to have a national library, a national opera house and a national concert hall.

"For example, in Changsha, the capital of Hunan Province, there is a logic to it having these facilities as it grows and becomes more prosperous. Civic pride exists in China as much as anywhere else in the world. We agreed to help them host a fantastic concert at the top of the international scale. We have to plan at least a year in advance and we knew they had the money and agreement to build the main concert hall so moved ahead. When it came to the time of the concert we found that the new hall wasn't finished so we ended up playing to packed houses, but in the old, much less grand, hall."

Wray explains the way the concert scene is managed and run in China.

"Basically we leave all the ticket sales and the profits from them to the owner of the hall. We charge a fee and ensure that all the costs for the staging are covered. We tell the owners that we don't want empty houses but they can keep all the money. In all the years I have been organizing concerts in China I have never been disappointed and everywhere has always been full! No one wants to lose face!"

However, it is not always a smooth ride and Wray has me laughing out loud at some of his stories.

"Orchestras rent their instruments in country and that can be a challenge. We have had harps without pedals, no double basses, harp strings missing and pianos out of tune! We have to sort it all out, often at the last minute. We are the swan on top of the water, but underneath we are always paddling like crazy!"

I ask, "Are the arts important in China?"

"Of course. The arts, including music, are deep in the culture of the Chinese. Western classical music has been enjoyed by millions for many years. There is huge support from the government at a national, local and provincial level.

"The people want it too and concerts across China are always full. New orchestras and choirs are emerging all the time. It is a bit chaotic but it's all there. Parents are also pushing their children towards classical music, across all instruments and, of course, vocal styles.

"It's not just popular culture either – Western classical music is big in China. Parents know it makes a difference if their kids are musical. A study done in the United States showed that children who are good at music are good all rounders and perform at an above average level in everything from maths to college entry exams. This is to the extent that five good students may be competing for a place, then the one who is good at music will get it. The last figures I saw show that in China there are over 60 million school age children currently learning either the violin or the piano."

As ever, the numbers in China are staggering.

"While there used to be just a handful of orchestras in China, all based in the major cities such as Beijing and Shanghai, now there are over 70 major ones and I'd say that about 25 can actually play, but some are really dreadful!" Wray smiles broadly. He has a well developed sense of humour, borne out of working around China for many years and of having to find ways around the most bizarre of musically-related problems.

"Everyone has the right to play in the people's national concert hall. Many cities you have never even heard of have fully developed orchestras. Across China there are thousands of instrumentalists who trained abroad and are now back teaching and coaching the next generation of musicians. This is only going to grow and grow now. The Chinese have an amazing ability to apply themselves to learning an individual skill such as a musical instrument too. I predict we will see more and more world class musicians emerging from China over the next few years."

And Wray will be there to represent them. As what many would call an impresario, Wray is the organizing genius behind most of the big international classical concerts in the Chinese music world. He knows all the players, both the musical and the political ones.

I first met Wray at a mutual friend's dinner party and then at one of his concerts, which turned out to be inside the grounds of the Forbidden Palace in the centre of Beijing. It was showcasing a young and quite exceptional Eastern European pianist. The place was packed and Wray had important guests to entertain. He was a master of charm and persuasion. At the end of the concert he bent close to me to whisper that the rather benign gentleman in the crushed suit was a ministerial level influencer who had just given his blessing to a new round of concerts. He was clearly pleased.

Wray's comments on the undoubted strength of the Chinese to excel as individuals opens another thought. I muse that this is both a blessing and a curse for many. The power of individualism and the collective support of family drive every Chinese person to compete and win personally. However, this also holds back on the building of teams. We have seen this more recently in the difficulties China has experienced on the field with soccer and other team games where the skill of the individual player must bow to the team to win matches and tournaments. Single stars don't make a team yet single stars are what society is conditioned to create.

Wray returns to the subject of his youth.

"I was born in 1950 and grew up where I was born, a place called Prince Albert, 200 miles in the middle of nowhere in central Saskatchewan in Canada. My grandmother was a teacher at the local school. She had 35 kids in the class and taught classical piano. We had a big family and I had eleven brothers and sisters so we were never short of someone to play with. My mother was a pianist too and my father played the accordion and was in the local dance band. Music was always a big part of my life. There was a community dance every six weeks followed by a midnight supper. I had a very happy childhood and I learned to play both the banjo and the saxophone. I was a good linguist and studied linguistics at Saskatoon University before going on to do translation for the government, French to English and back again. I hated it and did a fair bit of singing in a local choir to keep myself sane. I asked the choirmaster if he knew how I could get a job in music. He suggested I apply for a job as an apprentice in arts management and I never looked back. A year later I got a job with the Toronto Symphony Orchestra and I was hooked."

Wray stayed at the orchestra for the next twelve years, eventually serving as the managing director for the last five until 1990.

"Toronto is a great city and the orchestra was good, but we were only the 'warm up' for the New York series and they needed to move up a notch. In the late 1980s the financial recession hit us and it was tough. I decided to move on and was lucky to be offered a job by a major organization who managed and represented artists at the highest level in London. I wasn't really good enough for the Toronto job. I was too young and too inexperienced, as well as a bit too vain. It was the right time to move on."

After a while in London, where Wray met Yu Long, he moved to China.

"In China most of the funding for the concert halls comes from the government on the back of real estate developer money. There is a building wave of enthusiasm and money in culture and the arts so I feel that what I am doing in China now is the culmination of a rising tide in my industry. We are signing more and more artists on to our books. It's been very hard and a long and rocky road, but I am really feeling a change now. We are one of the few organizations on the ground in China who can make things happen. None of the big promoters have anyone there and they now know they need to be. That's where we come in. It's been seven hard years but now the money is flowing in."

Wray sinks back into the plush soft furnishings of the London hotel bar and sighs a sigh of a satisfied man. For a while I have been transported from the wide open plains of central Canada to the back stage mayhem of a Chinese classical concert. Somehow it all seems to make sense. As the country emerges from its recent turbulent past, it is clear that at all levels there is a growing interest in culture and the old Chinese values of calligraphy, painting, music, dance and the wider arts. These have been supported from the top of the political world in China and the people are also getting behind the programme of reenergizing China's cultural, as well as economic, power. As the numbers of middle class Chinese grow in affluence and disposable income, so too is there an increase in the money flowing into the arts, as much as it is into other aspects of life. Classical music and, specifically, Western classical music, is seen as worth investigating and experiencing. At the concerts I have been to there are as many enthusiastic young audience members as there are older, clearly more wealthy ones. All sit spellbound at the music as 'the phone police' literally shine a light on transgressors who are rude enough to try to film or photograph proceedings. At the end the artists are mobbed like film stars by adoring fans seeking signatures and selfies.

It's not what a Western audience would do and is very Chinese, with more green tea than alcohol consumed at the intervals, but I can personally agree with Wray that the Chinese love the sound of Western classical scores and are digging deeper into their pockets to support them.

CHAPTER
23

CREATIVE FRIENDS

Sitting in the quiet breakfast area of one of Beijing's better hotels, the China World Hotel in Guomao area, we swap WeChat messages as my guest dodges traffic. There are two types of time in China: on time and China time. With traffic and other distractions people never worry too much about the odd few minutes here and there. Indeed, people are so used to it that flexibility is almost infinite and patience is too. It is impossible to function in any city in China of any size without being super flexible due to the traffic. Recently, it was reported that despite the feelings of many, Beijing is not the worst place for traffic congestion and delays, nor is Shanghai. Even worse are the rapidly expanding cities such as Harbin (Heilongjiang Province) and Jinan (Shandong).

Li Mingxia, or Sophie, as she prefers to be known, is a bundle of energetic creativity. Business-like and professional, she is well dressed in a mix of Chinese and Western fashion. Working in the world of media and, specifically, magazines Sophie is a long way from her accounting degree gained at Taiyuan University in Shanxi Province. Born in a small village 30 km West of Taiyuan her parents are farmers, her mother is a housewife and her father often worked away when she was young to earn money to support his growing family. So she was brought up in a very traditional Chinese way. However, Sophie felt there was something missing in the life seemingly mapped out for her in a traditional rural farming village.

"I looked at my mother and thought to myself that I didn't want that life. She married young and had children young. My father was out working and she was at home. I decided that I wanted to go out and earn money and be independent. I came to Beijing in 2002 to study English and managed to find work with an English language magazine the following year. It was the only one in Beijing at that time, having started in 1996, and I was lucky to get a job working for the chief editor, who was British. I became his personal assistant. At that time the Chinese market was very strong and a lot of people wanted to advertise in the magazine but it didn't last. Soon after I joined there were lots of internal problems and I decided to leave and work for a rival magazine which was set up by the founders' sister. It was a bilingual magazine as she really believed that they could attract more Chinese readers, as well as English ones. It was ok for a while but the market moved so fast that it was very tough."

Sophie found the explosion of online media soon pushed the business she worked for into difficulties. She worked as the assistant editor but, despite a good product, the magazine failed and folded in 2009.

"It was a really good experience for me. I learned so much. I attended all the big creative and fashion events in Beijing, the big hotels, fancy restaurants and bars. I was also able to get to know about other parts of China and other countries too. I travelled widely. It was a good time. However, new media and the need to move online was so strong, with everyone on WeChat, there were enormous frustrations and challenges. I could see I needed to recreate myself in order to survive. I was being left behind in a market which was moving so fast that even those in it couldn't respond quickly enough!"

Sophie decided to start her own business. With two other colleagues she set up and worked together to publish a fashion magazine.

"We took a look at the Western approach to fashion. It was very interesting and we did well to start with. We hired Western designers and foreign editors but we didn't last long as a printed magazine unfortunately. We also had an online version on We-Chat and that is all we have left now. We have one person full time on WeChat and all the others are part time. Now we have four WeChat groups of creative and fashion-based people all sharing information, their business ideas, activities and events. We are a start-up company and we don't make much money. We create and run fashion and style events. The groups are growing and we are expanding all the time, but we need an investor to help us move to the next stage. However, it's difficult to find one. The groups we moderate are bilingual and quite international. It is a creative network with music, arts, design, fashion and style bloggers. We call it Creative Friends."

We eat breakfast slowly, lingering over our Western-style food and coffee, along with Chinese porridge and dim sum. We wield chopsticks, chatting through the mouthfuls.

"I live a portfolio existence."

Sophie delicately picks her way across her plate.

"I'm always having to look for ways of making money. I have had to totally reinvent myself. I have a lot of contacts and am trying to leverage them as much as possible. I have a partner who is French and lives in Singapore. We are collaborating on some creative projects which are focused on culture and innovation. We both have the same goal; we want to make more connections between the West and China. I have lots of ideas and I really want to do something for women."

I have written elsewhere in this book about women in China. There is real and positive change in many businesses but, away from the cities and the few high-profile role models, there remain many challenges in a seemingly never ending search for equality and empowerment. Sophie is another of the many women I have met who have a desire to do anything they can to help others in breaking away from the many inequalities and stereotypes which still exist.

"Chinese women, and particularly mothers, need to be better educated. It is not just about going to school to get the government posts. We need to help women to genuinely learn more. They have no real training to be parents but the expectations on them are huge. They are expected to devote themselves to being a housewife and a mother. They are not expected to have their own lives. I've seen a lot in my life and experienced so much. I really want Chinese women to have a better lifestyle and a better quality of life."

Sophie is frustrated that so many women have so little opportunity to expand their horizons. She worries that things are moving so fast in media and technology that it is impossible for anyone to keep up, let alone creative women, often with a child, but searching for an outlet for their skills.

"WeChat groups are so popular but what about tomorrow and the next day, and the next? How can I or anyone who is over the age of 20 cope with these changes, it's so confusing and frustrating. There are so many possibilities. I really am frustrated. I want to build a platform for the creative industry, creative women particularly, and the people who I know need to be able to connect better, with each other and with customers. I'd like to build an App, an online platform which can do this job. We are only allowed 500 people on each WeChat group. The system will not allow any more than that at a time unless you have a business account. We have four groups already which we call Creative Friends and now need to start another, so I can see the demand for this ability to connect as a really valuable one. I just can't make much money from it!"

So how does Sophie survive the everyday costs of life, with a low and often zero income?

"I make some money by running a few events, but I bought a house a few years ago in one of the growing suburbs to the east of Beijing. I bought one and then sold it and bought another, a bigger one. I made a bit of money. It's a good investment."

Sophie, like so many middle-class Chinese, is into real estate.

"When I first started work with the magazine I actually lived in a hotel apartment as part of my job. I was living rent free, for about eight years. That really helped me to save money so I could buy that first apartment. Now I rent a small place in Guomao."

Guomao is not the cheapest place to live in Beijing. It is almost in the very centre of the city's Central Business District and just over the road from the main headquarters of China Central Television (CCTV).

"It is really hard to make money from new technologies. Young people don't accept things and don't accept the old way, the traditional way of things. They think they can make money by developing some new application and then get an investor to scale it up. Some are successful but so many burn. My older sister has worked as a college school teacher all her life. It's a stable job. But some of us want something different, despite the challenges; we are not all like my sister. We have to strive harder and accept that there are consequences from our active choice to reject the stability and safety of study, qualifications, government job, husband, children, and then feeling we have no life."

Sophie fixes me with a purposeful stare across the bi-cultural breakfast table.

"We Chinese can adapt more than many people if we have to. We are used to being flexible and having to cope with change. Europeans are not like us. I have been to Europe many times over the years and I've noticed that Europeans are quite stubborn, quite conservative. Really I believe that China is a more exciting place to be. China is moving very fast and I'm experiencing the change that China is experiencing."

She stops eating and settles into her subject.

"We don't complain, we Chinese – we take responsibility. We have no unions or welfare state to support us like Westerners do. We have to look after ourselves. The Chinese way is to get support from family, so we strive to work hard and this need to be self-sufficient makes us very strong willed."

I nod. I had stopped eating some time ago, transfixed by the energy and determination of this woman.

"Even when we face problems we know our family is always there for us. Our parents provide the mental support and emotional backing, as well as access to our wider family who will never let us down. I was lucky to have other things to do to support me when I started out here in Beijing. I also feel China is becoming more tolerant and women can really now have their own careers and be personally independent – we are more able to live our own lives in our own way."

Sophie is single. By choice.

THE FRUIT
MAN

The telephone line to north east Australia is poor. It is a bad line.

Actually, it's not supposed to be like this. I had arranged the interview some time ago but we had not managed to meet before Chinese New Year. Lu Pin Shen's departure on a cruise with his parents around New Zealand and Australia for the Chinese New Year intervened on my somewhat tight editor schedule.

"They may never get the chance to go again so I wanted to really make this a special trip," he told me.

So here we are. Me ensconced in my seat against the wall in the coffee shop and Lu Pin Shen (or Sing as he prefers to be known as) in a hotel bedroom, somewhere not far from Cairns in Australia. We both have free internet so we decide we can use the free phone facility provided by WeChat. I suppose we could use the free video link system but the phone seems to be the best option for intermittent and low-strength internet signals at both ends. An amazing piece of technology and so simple to use.

"How is the weather there?"

I tell him not to be too smug; he knows full well that Beijing is freezing at this time of the year. Clearly Cairns is not.

Sing is technically a Hong Kong resident, although he was born in Xi'an in 1968; his mother is from Sichuan and his father Shanghai. They are both retired now but were among the early trade investors in Hong Kong and clearly didn't do too badly. Despite all this, Sing lives in Beijing where he has a house, when he has time to visit the city.

"I was lucky enough to be able to study in the US. I went to Vanderbilt University in Tennessee, then moved back and worked for my parents for a bit. However, in 2000 I set up a hi-tech company in the US, which did ok. I ran that until 2005/6 and then sold it. I didn't make a lot of money but it was a good experience and I made a bit. I started to look for opportunities back in China and by pure chance I got into raspberries."

"You did what?"

"Raspberries. I know, it does sound a bit strange."

"Yes."

I'd thought it was a bad line but Sing is deadly serious.

"Most of my friends were into hi-tech or were in finance. I know from my own experiences that hi-tech is about all or nothing. You either do really well and you make money or you lose it. I realized that no one was into agriculture. I became fascinated by it as a business opportunity, after a while. If you spend money in agriculture, unlike hi-tech, you won't lose everything even if the weather is bad. China has 1.3 billion people and there is a fundamental foundation in agriculture. It just needs to be modernized."

Sing is right. Even though there is an inexorable shift from the rural economy to the increased urbanization of China, it still needs to feed itself. The agricultural system remains largely archaic, despite the significant reforms which have taken place over the past 30 years. It is still dogged mainly by family plots serving themselves or local markets. Highly commercialized farming does take place, of course, but there is significant room for improvement.

"The need is there but not a lot of money is put into agriculture. I realized that it was not quite as easy as I had thought, but it's not an impossible task. There's a lot of potential. You are dealing with a very broad cross section of people, including some of the poorest in society. Also, believe me, dealing with local village officials is not easy. The internet is a lot easier to deal with than soil and plants and farmers but I decided to get into raspberries as an entry point in agriculture. People in China don't know what raspberries are. They are a new fruit here. Given all my experience over the past few years, and I've had a few failures, I am the raspberry expert now."

Soft fruit is sold all over China, as in any country. But, according to Sing, the common strawberry, for example, was only introduced to China in the late 1980s – blueberries didn't make an appearance until 2000.

"You just don't see raspberries at all. One primary reason is there is limited know-how as it is a complicated fruit to grow to a high quality and high yield. In the UK, the fruit is common but not in China. I believe that in the next five to ten years, the raspberry will be as common and as successful as the strawberry and blueberry have been. I want to be the one that does that!"'

Sing has a very clear perspective on his primary target group. His target audience is the health-conscious middle classes of China. Specifically, he sees his first target as the sprawling metropolis of Shanghai.

"Maybe 5% of the Chinese population know about raspberries, possibly even less. However, foreigners know about them and they are familiar with them, so I know that's a ready market. Also, Chinese people who have been abroad will be aware of the raspberry. There is a market there. Of course, the biggest market is the ordinary citizen. I have been working with resellers and wholesalers. These guys are always looking for new fruit. Many have tried raspberries but have failed because the varieties that have been available have been of low quality and of low yield."

Sing and I discuss what I find to be a fascinating marketing problem. Since the traditional raspberry growing season is very short, only three months, it is in the public awareness for a short while and then disappears again. Hence, each year this presents the wholesalers and the sellers with a struggle to reintroduce and relaunch this strange fruit anew. Needless to say, many have just given up. Sing has an interesting solution to this constant need for reintroduction.

"Do it once."

I'm convinced I lost him on the line. "Do what?"

"Do it once. Launch them, then just keep producing them 24/7 and 365 days a year."

After a number of experimental and I sensed, quite expensive, false starts over the past eight years, Sing has now identified the solution to the supply and awareness problem for this humble red super fruit.

Greenhouses.

"The biggest problem has been the consistency of the quality of the fruit. There is a huge health-conscious marketplace out there among the emerging middle classes of China. These people are worried about their, often only, child. They want the best for them and fruit is a big thing on their agenda. But it has to be fresh and good quality, ideally organically grown. The raspberry needs proper growing conditions, just enough water and just enough sun. I have approached the whole thing from a scientific point of view. I've applied the tools and techniques I learned in the hi-tech environment to raspberries. The main thing is to control the environment. Greenhouses help you do that.

"A friend of mine in the UK who is a grower told me something funny. He said raspberries are like women. They are special, they need a lot of effort, but if you put the effort in then they will repay it and you will be treated well. But if you don't put the right amount of effort in, you will have big trouble."

Sing chortles down the phone at me. I remain studiously and respectfully silent. He tells me that he has been trying to grow raspberries in a few different places since 2006. He started in Hunan Province in the middle of China to the south of the Xiang River but was not successful.

"Unfortunately it was just too far away from anywhere. The suppliers were not there and though labour was cheap, pretty well everything else from the foam boxes to the packaging had to be shipped in at great expense."

Transportation costs were just one of a series of small individual problems that eventually made him give it up and move back into China.

"I have learned my lessons from previous experimenting. We have now found the perfect place in Yinchuan city, Xinjin county in Ningxia Province. It's in the west of China but it has a dry climate, transport links are excellent and I have located a very good site with excellent access to the airport. The sun is bright and the air is clear. It has a very good climate. With the greenhouses overcoming the problems of the wind in the area, we have a year round growing season. I know the sun can be strong there but, by using the greenhouses efficiently, we can control most of the adverse aspects of the weather and take full advantage of the good clean air and great soil."

This part of China is not unfamiliar with growing small red fruit. It is the centre of goji berry production in China. The goji, sometimes known as the wolfberry, is renowned in China for its medicinal properties. So the area certainly has the pedigree from that perspective. Sing also tells me that it is the centre of an increasing amount of Chinese wine production with French, Australian and German growers planting vines here.

Sing tells me he is returning to China after his long holiday with his parents to start building the greenhouses.

"What is the size of the facility you are building?"

"We will build in stages. The first stage is aiming at around 500kg a day. Once we get the quality right at that level then we will shift the production up to 5,000kg a day."

Sing delivers the numbers in such a neutral and straightforward manner that at first I miss the sheer size of production he is envisioning.

"We know from our planning that the Shanghai market alone can support around 500kg a day through the wholesalers and markets we have researched there. We will be investing around ¥20.0 million (£2.0million) to set up and get started. From a distributor perspective, I know a lot of people who have grown strawberries and been successful. They have tried raspberries, liked them, but haven't managed to get it right on the quality and supply side. They are willing to give us a try. There are others who are still doing lower-quality raspberries and making money, so we know they will be interested once we can prove the quality."

Sing expects to employ around 100 people at the facility to start with, including management, administration, farming and picking.

"Everyone will be full time from the very start. That is unusual in the soft fruit market, which is seasonal. The problem is that the pickers are seasonal migrants so I have to compete with other producers of berries, wine and the like. We will have to fight for the labour. But we have a distinct advantage over everyone else."

Sing explains that most pickers work for three months, learn how to pick properly to a high quality, non-squashed, standard and then leave after the season's crop is finished. The next year the growers have to start all over again with new pickers, so quality never really improves. Sing's strategy of offering full-time, year-round employment means that he can train the pickers and then retain them to pick at the high quality he needs to penetrate the market. It is a simple, and hopefully a competitive, strategy which should make him money and keep it rolling in around the year. Solid long-term employment will be attractive as well; though he may lose the migrants, he should, he hopes, attract local pickers.

"We will even be able to afford to train people for six months, as long as they stay. Labour costs are increasing in China, but for this type of labour it is at least ten times cheaper than in Australia and about seven times cheaper than the US, even though they are using migrant Mexican labour."

"What about the supply side?" I ask.

"Well, what I learned in Hunan comes in here. Locally in Yinchuan city, I can source everything I need, from packaging, foam boxes, soil care, glass and repair materials, everything. I have been very careful about everything. Location has been critical and the soil type and composition has been essential. I have paid a good deal of money to get the right research done and to get the right agricultural advice. I know this scientific approach will pay me back. I have tried to apply all I learned in the hi-tech world to this seemingly low-tech agricultural production facility. However, it is anything but low-tech. To get the right outputs I have put a lot into the right inputs."

Sing has gone to extraordinary lengths to employ the right people too. He has a German facility manager who lives locally.

"He is very precise in his approach. I need that type of almost scientific approach and precision of attitude to make this a success. I know he will be able to overcome many of the problems of growing raspberries in China."

Do you worry about competitors setting up and stealing your ideas and market share?

"It is very difficult for someone to do so. On the surface, what we are doing looks simple, but this is a scientific and hi-tech approach, so it would be very difficult to copy. It is also very expensive to set up properly so I think we have a head start on our competitors, which they will struggle to match or catch."

Sing expects to be in production soon, by the next growing season.

"We will be aiming for the best quality produce all year round. This will allow us to be on the shelves all the time, not just for three months. We want to build distribution and market share, as well as sustainable long-term brand awareness simply by being there when others are not!"

"What brand are you using, a Chinese or international one?" I ask.

"Actually, we don't have one at the moment but I hope to have a Chinese name alongside an international one so we can get the best of both worlds! The positioning is very important as we specifically want to target the middle classes with an eye to their, or their families, health."

"Will you just be Mr Raspberry or do you have ambitions for more than just raspberries?"

"I think this is a process. I believe that raspberries are a good entry point. If they are successful, I may move into strawberries, blueberries, all at the top end of the quality spectrum. Also, there is significant opportunity from moving into related products such as yoghurts, flavoured milk, ice cream and other areas."

Sing expects to be in production soon. If you are reading this and you are in China, look out for the raspberries. There is a pretty good chance if you find good ones they'll be Sing's!

THE ONLINE ENTREPRENEUR

Juan Xiao (her English name is Betty, though I prefer her Chinese name which means 'little' or 'little one') has the broadest and most beguiling of smiles. She lights up the room with it. Her eyes smile, her mouth smiles, her whole body smiles. Born in 1982, she is a product of a new generation in China, the always on, digitally savvy, internet generation. Born and bred in Beijing, she sees herself very much a Beijinger.

"Beijing is my home town," she says. "I love this place. All my family and relatives are here and all my friends. I know it is not a good place to live because of the pollution but I still like the city. It is losing some of its charm and, as a local, I sometimes feel that we are losing our dignity and the workers are so rude and everyone is always rushing around with no care for others. It is such a shame. I feel a bit sad that it is changing and becoming less friendly and more impersonal. However, around Spring Festival most of the workers have gone back to their home towns and Beijing is left to the Beijingers, the locals, and it is lovely then. That's when I really feel it is home. The real Beijing is full of the history of our country. It is where the last emperor was, it is where most of the famous Chinese cultural sites are and there are many good things here. However, it is also a city fuelled and serviced by immigrants from all over China. Sometimes that detracts from the real Beijing but we have to accept it."

She smiles again. This time it is a smile full of wistful sadness, perhaps surprising for a young and successful woman who you might feel would relish the variety and complexity of a vibrant and diverse city. But no. She is already nostalgic for her days at school. Such is the speed of change in China and, specifically, Beijing that even the young can be nostalgic about their recent past. Like many young unmarried women, Xiao lives at home. Parents will be hopeful for marriage, but I sense a determination to buck those immediate expectations in favour of entrepreneurialism.

"I went to Ritan Middle School. Then the Beijing Technology in Business University where I studied journalism. I stayed here. Now I am a Taobao entrepreneur."

Taobao has been an extraordinary success in China since it was founded in 2003. It is owned by Alibaba, which in turn set Wall Street alight in 2014 with the biggest IPO in history at $25bn in September 2014. Taobao features nearly a billion products and is one of the top 20 most visited websites in the world. It is a little like eBay, with all the bells and whistles you could imagine on top. This is not the place to explain the intricacies of Taobao, but suffice to know that fortunes are made on it every day in China as ordinary people use it to buy and sell pretty much everything. Xiao is a classic user and her story serves as an example of how it has touched and changed the lives of many young Chinese people.

"I was really lucky after I left university as I worked for Wall Street English, a well-known English school in China. I worked there for five years from 2006, and in 2011 I went to New Zealand on a working holiday. I saw many interesting things and found some very interesting products there. I thought that my friends would like to hear about these products such as Mānuka honey, health products, special make up and milk powder."

She posted her views on the products online, on WeChat, the ubiquitous Chinese cross between Facebook and Twitter with video and voice communications and soon to come electronic payment thrown in. It's a common thing now for all the younger Chinese and most of the older middle class ones too. Many of her friends asked her to buy some products for them and send them back to China. So, she did.

"I don't want to earn a lot of money. I want a different lifestyle from many of my friends who are always so stressed and busy, bound to their work. People started asking me to send products and then they posted on WeChat that the products were good. Then more people, who I didn't know and who were just reading about the products, started to make contact and asked me to ship products to them too."

Starting small, Xiao now has more than 400 regular customers across China for these specialist New Zealand products.

"The quality is very good and I get great reviews online, so it seems people want to buy more and more."

She smiles at me. A modest but clearly very proud smile. It is heart-melting and speaks of Xiao's warm and honest approach, which seems both to emanate from and permeate the products she sells, as well as the style in which she does it.

"I decided I did not want to work in Beijing. It is polluted and the subway is so crowded. It is mayhem at rush hour and people rush to work and spend a long time doing it and getting home, for what? A bit more money. I didn't want that. It is easy to trade products and I can manage my time well during the day so it leaves me with time to go out, to talk to people, to do interviews!"

That melting smile again. This is a very determined young woman and her smile belies the determination and focus her actions show. She has limited ambition for the business and it seems something of a means to an end to allow her to do something extraordinary.

"I want to go to a poor area of China and teach poor children; maybe Sichuan Province, in Xi Chang city. I have a friend who did that and spent three months there. She found it very rewarding and I want to do something similar. Maybe to teach the children English."

This is unusual in a China populated by so many that are money-hungry, status- and face-seeking. Xiao's quiet and determined comment intrigues me but she does not elaborate on when she believes this dream will be realized.

"I get up early in the morning and call New Zealand to book and order products from my suppliers. I know exactly how long it takes to get the products to Beijing. I have to manage things carefully and guess thoughtfully about the or-der pipeline and likely sales timetable so I do not order too lit-tle or too much. I package products in the afternoon and then send them all off. Many customers are friends, but more and more they are friends of friends and I just can't let any of them down. It is important that they can rely on me, so they trust me, trust the products, come back for more and tell others so my business grows."

The simplicity of her approach and focus on great prod-ucts, delivered on time at a sensible price, would be the envy of many larger businesses. Unsurprisingly, people pay on time and regularly re-order.

Simple business models work.

"Taobao is a good chance for me to set up on my own. For less than ¥20,000 (£2,200) I was able to get everything set up and started. If I work efficiently and carefully, I can earn up to ¥50,000 (£5,500) a month, which is just enough."

The subject turns to women and the role of women in so-ciety, and sparks the standard question all young unmarried women are asked across China every day. "When will you get married?" Many have the answer ready, that they are dating and hopeful, or engaged and planning or marrying soon. Xiao has none of these answers and avoids answering altogether.

"Women in this city are much more independent. Work changes everything. If you work and have money you have in-dependence and self-determination, you don't need a husband. They can tie you down to social norms. I know a friend who asked her husband for money to go travelling and he said no! So she got a job and started travelling! She was right to do it. He had no right to tie her down. As women become more con-fident and self-orientated and independent then they become more empowered and have a voice. This is very important."

The subject is one we chat about more and Xiao is clear-ly passionate about the importance of women in society and the home as equals. Her perspective is increasingly common among young women and there is a growing movement of women's empowerment, not only in Beijing, but across many of the major Chinese cities. It is still, however, a little discussed or encouraged subject in the lower tier cities and rural communities where tradition seeps through the fabric of family and history. However, China is changing quickly and I believe the shift is more and more clear as the old formalities of family and rural life give way to the spread of urbanization and the lifting of millions of Chinese people, first out of poverty and then into the emerging middle classes with money and ambition in equal measure.

CHAPTER

26

THE DIPLOMAT AND TWO BASKETS OF PINEAPPLES

I was unusually early. Beijing traffic can never be so unpredictable as when there are foreign dignitaries visiting. Usually it's impenetrably slow moving and even though the roads aren't closed as often as they used to be, allowing the speedy and uninterrupted passage of the big black limos, we do sometimes get rolling road closures and the occasional diversion. But not today. I had time on my hands so wandered around the gardens so carefully laid out amongst the high rise blocks of the now fashionable Jinsong area of east Beijing. Within easy reach of one of Beijing's largest and most fashionable public spaces, these neat towers house a mixture of government officials and middle-class families away from the usual unceasing roar of the capital's traffic.

Li Zhi comes down from his apartment to greet me.

"Welcome, welcome! No smog today!"

If you ever thought talking about the weather was a specifically British phenomena, think again. It is nearly as ubiquitous a small talk subject in Beijing as in Bradford, Bedford or Beaconsfield. Some say the bad weather kills thousands every year in and around the capital from respiratory diseases. You can taste it on a bad day and it undoubtedly stops Beijing from otherwise being one of the world's most liveable cities.

We bemoan the continued problems of bad air and my recent difficulty in acquiring air filters as we ascend the unusually well-lit lift to Li Zhi's well-appointed apartment.

Li Zhi lives with his wife, 17-month-old son and *ayi* in a spacious (for Beijing) upper floor apartment. The *ayi* (translated as 'aunt' or 'mother's sister' and pronounced 'ai-eee') or nursemaid has a special place in Chinese middle-class families and no self-respecting working family would be without one. Often from poorer parts of the city, or even the surrounding region, many *ayi's* live in as a permanent home help. Something of a cross between nanny, cook, cleaner and general help, the *ayi* is an indispensable part of many young families' lives, releasing the parents to work or spend time on other activities, such as the care of elderly parents.

We sit quietly, as their son is asleep in the next room with the *ayi*. Li Zhi's wife prepares tea and then sits down quietly. Tea is served and we pass pleasantries and gifts. We don't take our coats off. The heating isn't turned on each year until 15th November and the early November freeze across northern China has everyone quietly cold and grumbly.

Li Zhi is happy to talk. "I was born in Anhui (安徽) Province and went to school there too. Then later I went to study science and technology as my degree at Wuhan (武汉) University and graduated in 1998. At the end of it all, I sat the government office entrance exams and passed. I spent the next 13 years in the government foreign affairs office, working mainly in the neighbouring countries to China. I never dreamed I would end up as a diplomat. At that time the Ministry used to collect students from all over China and many different degree courses. I was the only one from my college. They even sent me to Hong Kong for two years at one point. It was amazing.

"My parents were teachers in the local middle school and my two brothers are a teacher and a worker in the courts of justice. I was taught well and studied hard so was top of the class at middle school. My parents were very proud that I was good at studying and I was rewarded by being seen as one of the best in my subjects in the country. I became one of the youngest division chiefs in the foreign ministry."

Li Zhi became one of the few global travellers in the government of the day. Among other places, he spent time in the US, Germany and most of the Asian neighbours. However, as he recounts, the diplomatic life has its sacrifices.

"The life of a diplomat is seldom understood by others. I found that it was impossible to either be with my parents as much as I wanted or to start a family. It's a choice, to serve the country or to have a family. To truly serve the country you have to give up family. It's difficult for wives to give up their jobs and it's a fact that children's education suffers. As China develops it is the role of all diplomats to work hard and tirelessly to help keep pace with the speed of the change."

Li Zhi found the time in foreign affairs exciting as well as exacting, but after 13 years wanted to have another type of challenge, in business.

He left the Ministry to work for a state-owned enterprise but also an important think-tank of China. He was there for three years as a consultant. The company worked in many areas, from transportation, oil, gas, energy generally, military weapons and high technology.

"I really got to expand my contacts in the world of business and after those three years as a consultant I really felt I also understood the state owned enterprise business model. I worked in all sorts of the areas they worked in. It was a fascinating time."

"The Chinese government is very wealthy and it spends a lot of money on experts to support the state-owned enterprises in their efforts to modernize and become more efficient. Of course, these businesses are state-owned so there are some disadvantages with the system. There is a tight structure and, of course, they belong to the government so they are not so flexible as non-state owned organizations but they are really trying very hard to develop and expand. Also the government encourages people working in state-owned enterprises to go out and try to set up businesses. So I left."

Li Zhi joined Beijing Forever Technology, a high tech company supplying the energy businesses in China.

"The business was established 16 years ago and I knew the founder back then. We became friends and when the business went public on the Shenzhen exchange a couple of years ago, the founder asked me to join. With all my experience in foreign affairs he felt I could help in their development. The business went from nothing to over 700 people and a multi-billion yuan business quite quickly. It had no privileges. It just grew, like China has grown."

Since Li Zhi joined two years ago, the business has developed significantly overseas with interests in East Africa, South East Asia and also Eastern Europe. He has grown the business and actively recruited skilled staff to work with him. He is clearly enjoying himself and his new found entrepreneurial edge. He works in Beijing, the headquarters of the business, which acts as the main central agency. Ten years ago the industry was in its infancy in the country. It struggled to meet the seemingly insatiable demand for power as China grew.

"When I worked in government I felt like I was a small cog in a gigantic machine. I'm now in a place which is much freer and a really good experience. I've been so lucky. Now I have much more flexibility for family and it has totally met my expectations for me to regain some control in my life. I am the decision maker for my department. We really work as a team and we have no rules and constraints except those we impose on ourselves as a business. We can develop everything ourselves. Forever used to be a software company but now we are an 'InternetPlus' business, internet plus technology, internet plus energy. China is at a good point in our history and it's good for our company."

As he pauses for another round of tea, I reflect on the phenomena of InternetPlus, a government mantra developed by Premier Li Keqiang in March 2015 in his Government Work Report of that year. It became a shorthand, along with the word 'innovation' for government and wider private sector initiatives to integrate technology and such areas as mobile internet, cloud computing, big data and the Internet Of Things to support China's growth. The result of this government-sponsored and blessed exultation has been an explosion of initiatives and businesses across China to exploit the new relaxation of rules around all the internet can offer.

The series of initiatives, and guiding principles defined by President Xi Jinping and Premier Li Keqiang, set the tone for China's outbound business expansion and international diplomatic moves. One Belt One Road (一带一路) is an essential element of these and is a revitalization of the old trading routes or 'silk roads' of antiquity. The 'belt' is to the north and west across the old overland routes which used to transport silk, porcelain and fine goods out of China to the West through what is now Eastern Europe and the former Confederation of Independent States (CIS) of Russia. Initiated as far back as the days of the Venetian merchant traveller Marco Polo in the early 1300s, who is reputed to be the first European ever to see China, the 'belt' encompasses the land routes through to Pakistan to the south, Kazakhstan in the north and Iran and Iraq in the west. The 'road' is the maritime route to the south of India via the planned deep-water port at Colombo in Sri Lanka and then round to the east of Africa. China has been using this trade route since the days of Admiral Zheng He, the explorer, mariner and diplomat of the early Ming dynasty in the late 1300s.

"The One Belt One Road initiative of President Xi is allowing us to develop technologies and opportunities in countries along the routes. We are really busy in these places. We are able to introduce new technologies and also to bring learning and new ideas back to our business to develop and exploit inside China. Making it all work, through our engineering design and IT technology experience, is really exciting.

"Going out with infrastructure supported by government initiatives at the highest level is the first step for all business to benefit from the initiatives. Then we can move forward with information and new energy applications. Our company is key to this kind of work and I'm free to choose both domestic and international partners."

It is clear that Li Zhi is genuinely energized and enthused by the opportunities he feels the Chinese government are creating for him and his colleagues. His wife sits smiling and nodding at him.

More tea please.

"During the last 20 years, I have seen things really change in China and the international position has also changed. In a certain way we have a democratic environment with the opening up. The generations after the 1970s are a special group. In 1978 we had the start of the open-door policy and since that time we have people who have no real experience of the Cultural Revolution. There were no real limits imposed on my childhood at all compared with those generations of the 1980s and 1990s who have had to deal with the one-child policy, huge expectation changes in society, the impact of the internet and so much more."

This is a common theme and topic of conversation from those born in the 1970s in China.

"The 1970s generation are a more responsible generation, we live in a period of being moderately wealthy but not so well off that we care nothing of the hardships of our parents. Those difficult times are still there and close to us. We know more of the difficulties they had to endure, along with their brothers and sisters, our aunts and uncles, with whom we regularly speak and share time. We are just far more aware of the developments than subsequent generations."

The speed of change in China is so fast that many I speak with talk of 'generations' in terms of decades rather than lifetimes. The 1970s group are the post revolutionaries, the 1980s group the privileged one-child generation – some would say cosseted 'emperors' and 'empresses' – the 1990s group are the 'Millennials' and in the 2000s we have the 'always on', international, internet age.

"The West developed slowly. What took you 100 years to achieve, we have done in about 30. Of course, we have had some problems."

Indeed.

Li Zhi's wife, Ms Wang, has been sitting quietly attending to our tea so far. However, she now joins the conversation.

"My grandparents were in the Red Army and they both fought against the Japanese in the 1930s."

I am taken aback. I know I shouldn't be, but this simple statement spans the generations and brings me up sharply to the reality that is China. There is a rawness of memory so lightly covered by the present in China that to ignore it is to miss so much that explains the place, the people and the culture.

"My grandfather was a comrade in arms to Premier Li Keqiang's father. My hometown of Dingyuan (定远) county in Anhui Province is the same as Premier Li and my grandfather joined the liberation of Fengyang county just next to Dingyuan (凤阳) county in 1949. During the Cultural Revolution my grandfather recommended that the young Li Keqiang go to work in the villages of Fengyang county. He was there for 4 years and then went to Peking University. The rest is history!"

Another revelation.

"Fengyang County in Anhui province is a very famous place in China as it was the birthplace of the first emperor of the Ming dynasty (1368-1644). My grandfather was called Zhang Jiaguo and he was famous during the War against Japanese Aggression. He always taught me that you must not take anything from others but to always give whatever you could to help others. During the famine in the 1960s there was no food and no crops for many many people. People starved to death. But my grandfather had crops so he gave away food to others in the village. He saved many lives."

The 'Great Leap Forward', architected by Chairman Mao Zedong, resulted in the terrible famine of 1959–1961 across China and estimates vary of between 15–45 million people starving to death. Fengyang was no different, and in one famous village, Xiaogang (小岗村), later credited with being the birthplace of new capitalism in China, over 50% (67 people) of the total population of 120, died of starvation between 1958 and 1960.

Ms Wang's parents were PLA (People's Liberation Army) and had many siblings. Her mother was one of seven children.

"I was the only child, but I was not treated like a girl. My parents brought me up as a boy and treated me as a boy in my early years. However, I wanted to be a dancer and started learning to dance when I was 13 years old at the Anhui Provincial Arts Institute. I was quite good at it and the PLA Arts Institute wanted me to join them but I gave up the opportunity as my parents didn't want me to go to Beijing. They wanted me to stay at home and make my contribution to society in Chuzhou (滁州), our home town."

Chuzhou is a small city in eastern Anhui Province to the north west of Nanjing (南京) in east China. It has a long and rich history and was the home to one of the more famous poets in China, Ou Yang Xiu, of the mid Song dynasty (960–1279).

Ms Wang became a member of a local dance troupe and then toured with them all over China as a folk dancing, classical Chinese dance group. She was clear that it was not ballet dancing. This was never historically popular in China and was often branded as being a Western and imperialist import by many.

"It was a hard life travelling all the time, and though I loved dancing, specifically Mongolian classical and traditional dance, it was tiring."

After three years on the road, Ms Wang returned home and then went to study economics management for a further three years. After that, her parents encouraged her to get a job 'suitable and stable for a girl', as a local government officer. She was only 21 years old.

"After 26 years I met Li Zhi agai. I moved to Beijing in 2014. I was 37."

There is a meaningful flicker and exchanged glance with her husband. There is an uncomfortable pause.

"You are clearly very happily married, I can see that," I venture.

Li Zhi leans gently back into the conversation.

"We were at primary school together, in the same class, classmates. When we went up to the fifth grade, she moved to Chuzhou. I caught up with her in the school playground as she was leaving and asked her if she would return and bring me a gift of fruit each spring and summer holiday. 'Please bring me fresh pineapple,' I said to her."

Ms Wang interjects, "There was no fruit in those times but I asked if I should bring back two pineapples? He said I should bring two baskets so we could share them with our classmates. I put this thought in my heart as I left. Pineapples were very expensive but I really wanted to buy them for him ... and for our classmates, of course, so I went to my father and asked him for ¥60 (£6.00). I said if he would give me the money to buy the pineapples, I would change from my mother's family name of Zhang (张) and to his family name of Wang (王)."

Normally girls keep their family name all their lives, unlike in the West, where the usual practice is to take the surname of the husband. Not so in China – so to do so is a big deal.

"My father gave me the money and I went to the market to buy pineapples. But I remember that I couldn't afford even one, and certainly not two baskets. However, I had promised my father that I would take his family name, so I did as I had said I would, even though I could not buy the pineapples as I had hoped. My mother was very angry with me! She beat me! But I had promised. So that was that."

"So what did you do with the ¥60?" I ask.

"I spent it on something else! I can't even remember what it was!" She giggles and her husband laughs too, reaching across the table to touch her gently.

Li Zhi turns to me.

"She was the prettiest girl in the class and I always remembered her as being so willing to help others, such a generous person. She was my dream girl and through all the years as I grew up and started working and then being successful, I always remembered her. She went to study dance and I went to become a diplomat. There were no mobile phones then, and not even telephones, so we lost contact, but I never forgot her. I kept trying to find her. When I had enough money and was a bit freer after leaving to work outside government, I searched for her even more and eventually I managed to find a contact number for her father. That was in 2012, it was so many years since we had seen each other but he remembered me and gave me her mobile phone number."

"He telephoned me." Ms Wang smiles at her husband. It is a wonderful smile. She loves him very much and that smile shows she had waited all her life for that call. "He asked if I remembered him? I said of course I did and said I knew he was calling about the two baskets of pineapples I owed him!"

"It was our destiny to be together. Destiny is something that can't be explained by science. It is something greater than we can understand. It was fate. Although both of us had been married before, those sweet memories of childhood had made a deep bond between us." Li Zhi was looking at me intensely.

I have nothing to offer in reply but a slow nod and a smile at them both.

Life in Beijing has not been too tough for the relatively newly-weds, and their son came along soon after marriage. They are wealthy enough from Li Zhi's job to afford the apartment and the *ayi*. They believe it is best for Ms Wang to stay and bring up their son and they have a wide circle of friends now. They are a little different as they have chosen to bring up their child themselves while so many couples both work and leave the care of their child to the grandparents. However, this is no ordinary couple.

We cover a lot of ground in our warm coats as we clutch our tea; from the U.S. election and Brexit, to the refugee crisis of Europe and the influence of religious extremism.

"The West and the East are transforming. It's very important that civilizations learn from and tolerate each other."

"Of course."

Our interview is brought to a close a short time later as the *ayi* brings the little boy through to his parents and, although she takes him outside to play, I have to leave all too soon.

I am, however, left with a lasting memory of Li Zhi affectionately stroking his son's hair and Ms Wang giving her sleepy toddler a cuddle, while whispering an unfamiliar word in his ear.

"不要哭小菠萝、我们爱你小菠萝" ("Don't cry little *boluo*, we love you little *boluo*.")

Boluo is the pet name or nickname they call their son.

Boluo is Chinese for pineapple.

THE WECHAT
MILLIONAIRE

Look up 'edutalent China' on any Western internet browser and you will find lots of references to education and talent management, but you may not find Sam Yang's business.

However, if you have the good fortune to be a WeChat user and can read Chinese, go to 'pdachina'. Specifically, if you are a recent parent suffering the joys of bringing up one or more of these 'alien creatures', you may find something interesting there. I wouldn't normally promote the business of anyone I interview, but I feel compelled to draw this small-but-perfectly-formed business to the attention of the world.

I am supposed to meet him at 09.00 but arrive a little early at 08.52. We had hoped to meet in my eponymous coffee shop but a change in both our schedules meant I had to forego my early morning coffee and make the journey out to him.

Sam Yang is already at his desk, though he later admits that he was still in bed at 08.00 am. There is the welcome smell of tea to greet me, as well as the warmth and unusually firm handshake of 'Sam'. This is unusual, as most Chinese people do not go in for the bone-crushing American grip or even the polite-but-firm British clinch. But Sam Yang is no ordinary Chinese man.

At first, we struggle through the complexities of the English language since I do not have my trusty translator with me this time. It was all a bit last minute sorting the interview, what with Chinese New Year only ten days away and many people already having left Beijing for their home towns and families. However, Sam finds the solution with 'Baidu Translate', the Chinese equivalent (one ought to say better version) of Google Translate.

"I was born in AnKang in Shanxi Province in 1970. I grew up in the country next to the famous Hanshui (Han River) in the shadow of Qinling (one of the most sacred and famous mountains in China). My only real memory of my childhood is hunger."

Not a bad opening remark to start our discussion. I am drawn in by the mystical images of a mist-shrouded mountain and the roaring mighty river next to which perches a small village, populated only by farmers scraping a meagre living from the poor soil. However, as with all dreams of romanticism, the reality was much harder to bear.

"Life was very hard, but we were happy," he says. "I was the eighth child of three older brothers and four older sisters. My eldest sister has a daughter who is the same age as me. It was normal in those days to have a big family. Especially as farmers. We struggled.

"I went back to my home village three years ago. Everyone had moved to the cities. There was almost no one left but the old and the very young. My school had many children when I was there, but when I visited there were only ten kids in the whole school. People want their children educated in the cities. It was very sad to see such a big change. I felt that I could have drawn some love and warmth from going back there, like I did when I was young. But I could not. There was almost no one there I knew. My feeling is that in another few years there will only be a few people left."

There is a long reflective pause, punctuated by the pouring of more tea.

"I went to college in 1990 in Xi'an. I attended Shanxi Normal University and read biology. I did this at school so had no real choice about what I had to do at college. I was there for four years and then stayed in Xi'an for another year working as a computer engineer."

I look at him quizzically, biology then a computer engineer?

"I liked it."

"Ok."

"I then went back to school. I had worked for a year and earned enough money to afford to pay for the next three years. I went to the south west Normal University in Chongqing. I did what I had always wanted to do, psychology, because I really believed it would make me a better human being. I was actually rather unhappy at Xi'an University. I felt like I was inferior. I felt that I was the poorest student in the college as I had come from such a poor village and had no money at all. I enjoyed the three years studying psychology, although I was a bit lonely studying this new subject. Then I came to Beijing."

I am still reeling from the openness and candid nature of his story. It was a bit brutal and it came almost faster than I could write, though the brief Baidu moments helped the flow of consciousness.

"Why Beijing? It's a terribly expensive place to come to without a job, isn't it?" I ask.

"I wanted to work here. It is everyone's dream to come to the big city from the farmlands. I was a country boy and this is the dream city. I lived in Tsinghua University, as it was the cheapest place I could find to stay and to eat. It was only ¥25 (£2.75) a night for the bed and I could eat in the university canteen for only ¥5 (£0.55) a day! I only had ¥300 (£33) in my pocket when I arrived in Beijing."

"How on earth did you survive? Have you been here ever since?"

"Yes. Of course, I needed to get a job pretty quickly but I had no idea how to get one. I didn't have a resumé, nothing. I didn't know where to go or what to do. So I started walking around and talking to people to see if I could find a job."

"And you found one before your money ran out?"

I am amazed at the sheer and total commitment of the man. He arrived without the means to go back. The ticket home would have burnt all his money and he would have gone back to nothing, with nothing. Perhaps that was the motivation to stay and make it work.

"Yes. I got a job ... (Baidu translate to the rescue) as a .... (try again) ... in a warehouse. I started work for a computer company on ¥300 (£33) a month. It was not much but I was so happy that I was living in the dream city and had a job. The company had a dormitory for its workers so I had somewhere to sleep too and plenty of new friends at work. We worked together and played together. There were ten of us in the dorm. I was very happy."

"So, you stayed there for a while?"

"Oh no. After a year I started my own company."

Another surprise. His comment is as matter of fact as discussing the weather in the UK. So, after being without a Yuan to his name only a year earlier, and a year after working in a computer warehouse, Sam was setting up a company?

"Yes. It was a computer software and ... (Baidu to the rescue) systems integration company. We have GE and Ericsson as our customers."

As I said at the start of this chapter, Sam Yang is no ordinary man. As we talk, it becomes clear that his previous year had opened up a good many doors for him. He had managed to land his job with a computer repair company which already had the contract for repairing computers for GE and Ericsson in China, specifically in Beijing.

"They sent all their computers to us and they trusted us. We got to know the guys very well personally. So myself and a few friends decided to set up our own business and take the customers with us. So we did."

I can't imagine how the old bosses would have felt when that sort of work walked out of the door with 20 employees, but I could guess.

"We developed the business slowly and carefully, but after eight years we had a business that had sales of over ¥1.0bn. (£110 million). Then I quit."

"What?" I really could not take it in. Why would this obviously very successful entrepreneur just stop it all and start again? Perhaps serial entrepreneurs in the West know why, but I have to admit being somewhat in awe of Sam.

"Well, I was the general manager of Beijing and my friend was the general manager of Shanghai. We had done really well but I wanted to do something else. It was 2002 and I quit."

"To do what?" I ask.

"I had two years of rest."

"You had a two-year rest?"

"Well, I had enough money and I wanted time to think about what I wanted to do for the rest of my life."

It turns out that Sam also got married in 2002. They met through a friend. She has her own business and is clearly a successful business entrepreneur in her own right.

"I stayed in Beijing. I had made money but it was still in a relatively small company. I liked the work for GE and Ericsson but I hadn't really learned about their business model, how they managed cash flow, how they made money. I had been a general manager but I had never really learned, or been taught, how to manage. I decided I wanted to go to a big company, but I realized I couldn't speak English and to work for an international company I needed English. I decided to learn English but I didn't want to go to school again but to learn on the job if I could. I prepared a resumé and started looking. I was fortunate to get a job at Wall Street English as a 'cost consultant' or salesperson. I spent four years there and did every course they offered so I was able to learn English, while rising to become the deputy centre manager in the Guomao area of Beijing. I had 40 people working for me at the end."

He pauses.

"But you quit?" I am getting the hang of his pauses.

"Yes. In 2007, I quit and went to New Oriental (the largest provider of private education services in China). I spent two years there and became a centre director."

"Then you quit?" I chip in during another tea brew.

"Yes. How did you know?"

"Lucky guess," I remark.

"I went to Disney English as a ..."

"Centre director?" I guess.

"Yes."

"How long before you quit?" I ask.

"Two years."

"And ..."

"I started my own company."

"This company?" I ask.

"Yes. I had spent ten years learning about this type of business and I decided that I had learned enough to start my own business on my own. I had learned about managing cash flow, about business modelling, about how to manage people. It was 2011. It was the right time to do it."

"So, it is now 2015. How has it been? How many employees do you have now?"

"It has been even better than I could have imagined. I am on my own. I worked out I don't need to employ anyone to run this business. I work about three days a week and spend the other four days with my young son. I believe I have finally achieved my dream of managing work and life together in the right balance. More importantly, I have a business which really helps people. Now I train fathers and mothers to be qualified parents."

"Interesting. How does that work?" I ask.

"I learned from Disney English. They had a programme aimed at parents with children between the ages of two and 12. During my time there, I was able to speak to and interview more than 6,000 families. I realized that people just don't prepare for their children and they end up encountering so many problems with them. Suddenly there is a baby; in China it is their only one and only chance to bring up a child. There is a big pressure on parents. Yet they are totally unprepared. They don't understand their child, they don't understand their husband, or their wife, how the baby will affect them and each other and their relationships."

As Sam outlines his business and the model that underpins it, I am captivated by its simplicity and strength. The expectations are high for parents, but the expertise is low. There are no ante-natal or post-natal classes to attend, society frowns on those who 'can't cope' and there is little or no support for such conditions as post-natal depression. Against this backdrop: enter Sam.

"Clearly, it is not all parents that are going to be my customers. It is those parents who know they have problems and understand that they need help. There is an emerging group of people who are waking up to the fact that they need to be better equipped to bring up their child. They have many problems. It is there that I see the chance for me to make money and to genuinely meet a need in society."

The market logic is compelling and the need clear, but how on earth does he get customers? There are tens of millions of families within an hour of his small office in Haidian, but how does he get to them?

"WeChat," he replies.

"I use WeChat to let people know about the courses I run and once people have been on them, I encourage them to use WeChat to tell their friends and to engage with this business and me, as much as they like to get the support they need."

"How do you get customers then?"

"At first I thought I would have to use the same techniques as Wall Street English and the other providers that I worked for. This was by using a call centre to use lists to get leads which I can then give free tasters to, and then to sell the bigger more expensive courses to them. But no! I realized I didn't need to do that. WeChat allows me to get to customers with no costs at all, and has changed my life!"

"How?"

"It's simple: 80% of my customers come from WeChat. It is just me in my company so once I had set up this office, I just needed to get a few people on the first course. I had confidence that I had sufficient expertise and experience and qualifications to make a difference to parents, so I knew the product was a good one. I just needed people to try it and I was convinced it would take off from there. It has!"

Sam explains his business model: for ¥3,300 (£360) you attend a three-day course on parenting. That's it. If you want, you can then take his four-day 'train the trainer' course for ¥12,800 (£1,400). That's it. Simple. The trained trainers repeat the course after a year for free and they can teach with Sam as an assistant on his course once in the year if they wish, for nothing. There is another potential step which Sam has chosen not to take yet, where the trainers may pay Sam a small consideration for each person they in turn train. In his plan this seems a way off for now. In any event, his business model clearly works as he proudly shows me his bank account on WeChat, which after only three months has a rather healthy positive look about it!

"I am even making money while I sleep." He beams at me.

"I have used all my psychology training and all my years learning the business models of other businesses to get to where I am. I know how to develop this business and I fully expect to be able to earn around ¥600,000 (£65,650) a month in the future. But it has taken ten years of my life to develop the model specifically. I have also learned that I do not need to manage people. It is a waste of time. I don't need to. I can outsource everything I need help with, from finance to marketing. I want to put all my time into researching and applying the psychology of parenting so I can help people be better parents."

The numbers are nothing short of astonishing. It is a simple model, with a simple proposition. It meets a clearly untapped market need in the growing market of increasingly empowered women and the wealthier middle classes of Beijing, and in time, further afield no doubt.

"I have six volunteers who work for me for free," he explains. "These women feel that the course has helped them so much. They have seen material improvements in their relationships with their child, as well as their husband. So they want to help me spread this knowledge and the course to as many parents as possible."

There is also something deeper we discuss.

"Many women have been hurt through their relationships with their husbands. This is a big problem in China. They have suffered and felt terrible personal pain. They tell me that the course has helped them feel warm in their hearts as a result. Over 50% of my students are referrals from those who have already attended my course and 90% are women, though I do get some fathers too. Women have such pressure on them in China. I want to give people hope and help them to feel positive about themselves."

This is clearly a significant untapped need in China. Does he think he can go further to help women deal with these pressures?

"No. I am really not qualified to do that. I know the limits of my course and I will not go further into psychological consulting. That is not my area and not the business opportunity for me. I don't have the competences to do that."

Has he applied the course to his own life?

"I think I am a good father. My wife tells me that since I started doing this work she has seen a very positive change in me."

I ask if she's been on the course.

"No! She runs her own business and is busy with that all the time and travelling on business. She doesn't want to do the course taught by me. I try my best to be a good father. He is still young. I work and teach for three days each week and the other four days I play with my son. Money is not so important to me now. I have enough money."

I ask him how he feels after all these years and doing what he is doing now?

"I believe that if you do valuable things for people then the money will come. I truly believe this and so far, I have been right. I really enjoy my job."

He smiles at me. It is a smile of a man who does what he loves, has found the peace and place that he craved from the early 'inferior' university years. We share a final cup of tea.

"I am living my dream. Many people in China can't."

He is right, and he is lucky – self-made lucky.

READING BETWEEN THE LINES

I am early. My meetings for the day had finished and rather than go back to my apartment, I decide to walk over to the restaurant where I'm to meet Ray and his wife. It is crowded so I sit outside on one of the plastic stools ubiquitous in good Chinese eateries. The stools are a big clue to a place's standards and quality. It doesn't matter what the seating quality is but how many there are. If they are already occupied, these are the sure-fire clues for the standard of the food. If you can get a seat easily at around 18.00, consider somewhere else. This should be peak time and the best places are standing room only outside. Very few restaurants operate a booking system and if you are going anywhere good, then your best bet is to get there early or be prepared to wait.

I am coerced onto a table at around 19.15. I guess they would rather have me inside looking like I was going to eat, rather than outside looking like a hungry stray. Ray and his wife arrive at 19.25.

After the introductions Ray orders the food. This might seem odd to the average Westerner as I was given but a perfunctory choice, but in China he who orders the food is the host, and often pays, though I always fight for the bill. More importantly, it is very common for Chinese of all ages, shapes, sizes and locations to want to show their hospitality and choosing the best dishes to suit the visitor is standard operating procedure. Needless to say, you are expected to eat at least most of the resulting dishes with relish and thanks, or suffer the resulting loss of face of your host and awkward, if not short, future relationship with them.

"I was born in 1985." Ray takes the reins of the conversation. "I spent nine years in the US and ended with a degree at the University of California IRVINE UCI. I went out to the US when I was 15. I am now with my mother's company which she set up in 1997. It's a waste disposal unit manufacturer and we export all over the world. I'm responsible for exports.

We have customers in China but also in Thailand, Japan and the US and Spain and are expanding all the time. We have offices in Beijing, Shanghai and Nanjing, as well as Shenzhen and Guangzhou."

Ray speaks perfect English. So too does his wife, who is, as he remarks, a little older than him, though I never find out more. "We are both 1980s," is as far as I get. His wife is the model demure, deferring, respectful and quiet Chinese spouse, until Ray makes any errors of opinion and she gently intervenes with her corrections.

I have floundered around for a while so far, trying to find a small strip of common and solid ground we can rest on for our conversation. We are already through the first few dishes and, delicious as they are, I am struggling to find a morsel of mutuality. They are clearly a little suspicious of me and my motivations for some reason. I have sometimes found this to be the case in older people, but rarely in those in their 30s. In instances such as these, there is always a story behind the reticence. I had been looking for a springboard for conversation and was now searching among the responsibilities of work and marriage for inspiration.

"We share common values," explains Ray, looking at his wife for confirmation. "The important thing is the contribution I can make to the family business. I know I get paid but it is much more important than that. The most important values are responsibility, integrity, kindness and friendship."

"... and dedication, hard work and optimism. They are important too," Ray's wife interjects in perfect English.

"Yes, of course. You are right," Ray touches her arm gently.

We chat about his hopes for the business and expansion plans, as well as the global links with Amazon he has personally forged. Ray is a bright and ambitious young man, though quietly and unassumingly so. His wife supports him in whispers and coded looks. Ray is being groomed in the family business and as such has a *de facto* seniority without title as the owner's son.

"We share the same values about marriage too."

"... and children?" I try a probe in that direction.

"Many Chinese parents concentrate on keeping their children healthy, strong and well fed, but they do not attend to educating their personality."

Ray's wife adds, "Chinese parents are not good at bringing up children. Nowadays, Chinese children are unstoppable. In our childhood elementary school, kids were well disciplined, but not now. The Chinese school system is failing children by not instilling the right levels of discipline and correctness."

"The one-child policy has made things difficult," adds Ray. "Nowadays, parents are too involved. There is one kid and they are obsessive about it, over protective and opinionated. They are exerting too much influence over the school and the teachers. They are creating little monsters. Irresponsible and arrogant spoilt kids who are free from the core Chinese values we believe in. Well-educated children will have better lives with better futures."

He is clearly passionate about the potential for their own children.

"Yes," she says. "We want our children to be brought up in a Western or a US way. Parents don't know when to say 'no' to their kids. Kids should be taught to be polite and obedient, not loud, rude and selfish."

Ray adds, "There are so many people who just focus on themselves and their own long-term benefits. These are the selfish minority of Chinese who give the country a bad name. But their children will not be brought up properly. We believe that it is our duty to have children who will be well-educated and uphold true Chinese values. When I was at UCI, I met lots of kids born in the late 1980s and I noticed that the new wealth does make a difference. The wealthy kids have a strong independent attitude, but they are much more arrogant than my generation. They seem to believe they are owed respect and privilege, not that they have to earn it all on their own."

His wife nods in agreement.

"My dream is that the nation will be a stronger state and that we can compete in the world on an equal footing. Society needs to turn down the heat a bit. We need to see a shift away from materialism and for people to concentrate on what they do and who they are in contributing to society. It's not just about making money."

There is a definite tone of hurt pride for his country.

"I am not able to disconnect the personal from business or from the success of my country. I really want us as a business to be able to compete in the US and be successful there, and I feel that's the same for our country. We can, as China, compete equally in the world and certainly with the US. The size of the country matters, both economically and physically, and we are a big country in both senses. It's like Coke and Pepsi. We have the potential to be the 'Pepsi' country, to take on the 'Coke' of the US. Then we can ensure there is a state of balance and harmony in the world which will mean that there will be no conflicts and world peace will prevail, brokered through the two most powerful nations on the planet."

He looks quietly defiant as he gently holds his wife's hand beneath the table for moral support. However, the time with them has been guarded and the topics discussed broadly superficial. At no time have I managed to get them to discuss their parents, their mutual history, how they met, their plans for the future or their thoughts or experiences from their school or university days other than a skim across the surface.

Ray has already paid for the meal from the app account on his new iPhone with a swift swipe of the screen on the till reader as he went to wash his hands after dinner. As I protest he dismisses my genuine offer with references to Chinese hospitality and values. I can pay next time he offers with predictability. I suspect I'll never get the opportunity of a return match. They have beaten me hands down in a flawless doubles partnership of politeness and I have singularly failed to gain almost any points of insight and understanding. As we depart with polite and superficial pleasantries, I am left feeling somewhat deflated and cheated of the possibilities we might have covered.

However, maybe I have learned more than I had initially thought. It is as much what is not said, as that which is, to unearth the real story in China. It's always dangerous to guess but the lack of reference to a father suggests a divorce somewhere. The long period in the US suggests some family connection but a complex and perhaps lonely childhood. As far as his marriage is concerned, the tight knit relationship is clearly built on mutual support, love and respect. He loves but also needs her. They played a perfect partnership, almost finishing each other's sentences at times. Rays wife's job had been unclear but her self-assured manner and confidence was enviable. I was never told her name. I suspect she either works in the same business or industry, both of which usually result in one or other of the couple having to resign. The avoidance of the question avoided an awkward answer. Together I suspected that they will support each other so he will make a success of the family business and make his parents proud. She will produce the perfect child, or two, and building on their good education, solid shared values and beliefs, they will be models of the new China.

chapter 29

YOUTH CULTURE

Mathew (Shao) Ma describes himself as a rich kid who "lost everything" and who now has "nothing to lose". He has the clothes and demeanour of a man on a mission to make a success of himself in the film industry. He certainly looks the part, of which he is proud. A small, mousey girl who he never introduces, but who seemed like a cross between adoring fan, girlfriend and executive assistant, accompanies him. She says almost nothing for three hours.

Born in Shandong in 1993, one of five children, he tells me with a wry smile that his parents had to have three girls before they got the boy they wanted. Him. Then had another boy just to make sure. He was born into a rich family who had created significant wealth from building real estate. Then, when Mathew was 16, his father lost everything.

"We had everything and then lost it all. I don't know what happened. Suddenly we had no money. What could I do? I decided to drop out of school and go and earn money to help my family. I went into the building trade. I just worked as hard as I could and earned about ¥1.0m (£100,000) by the time I was 17 years old!"

He is beaming from ear-to-ear with an impish grin that is impossible not to return. The phone rings and he passes it to his 'Girl Friday'. She wanders off to deal with it.

"I wanted more. I didn't think there was much more building work to be done in my home town, it had already been done. Well, I may have been wrong about that but I wanted to get into the service industry, less hard work manually and more using my brain. I decided to open my own restaurant and I had this idea that we could do something no one else had done – have a Chinese fast food place that was like McDonald's, but for Chinese food. We set up in Shenzhen. I had to learn how to create a business and, along with three other shareholders, all who were older than me, we had a go at it. Now I know that location is everything in retail, use of colour and design too. Unfortunately, we got it wrong and after six months it was still not making any money. I was 18 years old."

"Hao is coming." Girl Friday reports back.

It seems the call earlier was from Hao.

Mathew's parents told him to go back to college. So he did. But not just any college to learn an academic subject such as history, economics or business – he chose to become an actor.

"I am always questioning authority and teachers. It made me unpopular at school and at college but I decided to learn acting and spent a year as a model."

He rummages through his pockets and extracts a well-used wallet from which he draws a faded photograph of a muscular and tanned bodybuilder model. Himself at the age of 18.

"I've not got that body now," he muses.

He looks ruefully at the photograph before folding it carefully back into his wallet and secreting it away into his voluminous coat.

"Also, I found out that the restaurant business had grown to having more than 40 sites and was making a lot of money. I had had a 30% share of that when I left. It would have been worth a fortune, but now I had nothing."

The phone rings again and the unassuming mousey girl takes it away.

"I went to the Chinese Central Academy of Arts to learn acting."

This is probably one of the most famous acting schools in China, though how he got in seemed a little sketchy.

"People thought I was crazy. I wanted to be at the top of the film industry. I thought I wanted to be a director, so I spent the next six months learning everything I could about being a director. That's when I met Hao."

Hao is coming. He informs me again, via his Girl Friday.

"I produced my first film with Hao. We were at school together, it was ok, but not that great, but a good start."

He pulls out his laptop and sets about powering it up and searching for the film. He keeps talking at the same time. The film is actually rather good, short and shot with many different angles and clever camera work. Not that I know much about film, but the young actor at its heart seems pretty good to me.

"I decided I wanted to start a film company. You need a lot of government stuff to start a company."

I take it he means paperwork and licenses. The phone again. Hao, I guess, is being challenged with navigation.

"It was hard work to convince everyone that I could do it, but I managed to sort it out and was the youngest guy ever to set up a film company in China. I realized that I needed to be an owner of a film company, that it was best to own it rather than be an employee. Now six months later, I know how to make films. When I started, I had 40 workers, three months later I spent all the money. So it's just Hao and me now. But we've never given up. We've just signed the papers for a deal worth ¥2m (£218.9k). Not much, but it's a start I guess."

He pauses from the delivery of his verbal onslaught.

"You know, there is only one way for the poor to become rich in China. Go to the cities. That's the only thing to do. That's what we did. We want to produce more films, that's what we want to do."

The phone rings yet again. It's Hao.

"We will succeed, you know. Most people don't know how to run a company. They don't have the vision of the future. I'm 21 years old and I want to launch an initial public offering (IPO) in five years' time."

The prospect of Mathew at the helm of a listed corporation intrigues me, to say the least, but I remain silent for now.

"In 2015, I'm going to set up three companies: an agency, a publishing business and a film company, so I can do everything from top to bottom and control it all personally. How can I do that?"

The question has wandered across my mind, I must admit. Though it was dragging its feet as he delivers his waterfall of insight and ambition.

"I'll tell you. The market is more open now than it has ever been before. The opportunity for new films is enormous. We can't produce Western-style films due to our culture. But, there are a lot of Chinese film producers with great opportunities for new styles of films all the time."

He reels off a string of names, some of which I recognize, but most are a blur of Chinese, as unfamiliar as the language.

"I want to develop a TV show, I am working on it now. We have a real chance."

"Where is the money coming from?" I ask.

"What?"

"The money – where is it coming from. Who are the investors – TV shows are expensive aren't they?"

"Oh, yeah, the money. To get the money – I'll let you into a secret. To my workers, I say, I have the money. To the investors, I say, I have the workers. It's simple."

"Really?" I can't help but be a little bit sceptical, but this is China and strange things happen to young entrepreneurs with attitude and good ideas.

"I am unusual ..."

Hao arrives mid-sentence, bringing with him man hugs and high fives.

Hao is a reserved and thoughtful, somewhat introspective 22-year-old who has the honour of having two of China's most famous singers as his parents. We acquire a tea and a stool for him. He hunches into his designer white collarless shirt and expensive jacket and listens in.

"I'm unusual ..."

We restart where Mathew left off.

"I'm not afraid to try anything. Many people are afraid to fail. I'm not afraid to fail. We have nothing to lose. It's so easy.

When I have fear, then I just confront it."

He bangs the table and grabs the air with theatre, which would fit well in a Shakespearean masterpiece. He has learned his craft well.

"In ten years' time, I will be more successful. I want to have my companies, I want to learn fast and get known by the top people, use the friendships, use the good people around me. Attitude is essential and having future thinking. These are the attributes of good and successful people. Only I see my future. My day is listening to music, writing and thinking. I am thinking all the time. I have two projects right now, the TV programme, and another one. And the money comes in."

"Remind me about that part?" I ask again.

"Look. To get money you just need three things. First, you have to look the part, you need to look rich. Good clothes, good looks. Second, you have to look friendly. If you don't look friendly who is going to believe that you will do anything? And third, you have to look like you are hopeful and thinking about the future."

"So, remind me," I repeat. "How do you get the money you need to invest in the companies you have, to do the work you will do and gain the contracts you need?" I feel a bit of a dampener at this point and wonder if I am getting a little old for this type of thing.

"Like I said. Just three things. Think about the future, look friendly and be strong."

"What about the clothes and looking rich?"

"Yeah, that too, like I said. Three things!"

"Right."

"I want to do the traditional things but in a new way. There is also an important thing to do. When the company is successful, we have to give back – give back to invest in it to make it more successful. Not just take the money out. I think end-to-end all the time. If I see something, I challenge it and think why

245

is that like that and why can't we make it better? I am thinking like this all the time."

"Right."

I am left breathless by the onslaught of seemingly disconnected, possibly unfunded, but undoubtedly interesting ideas from Mathew, who is a young man in a hurry. Going somewhere. I rather feel he will hit lucky somehow, someday. Probably, or at least hopefully, before he burns too much of someone else's money.

Mathew magnanimously gives way to Hao and we chat about life as a young Chinese man with wealth and famous parents. It is hard going and the gulf of the age gap doesn't help. The conversation peters out in an unsatisfactory way.

Hao is a personable, beautiful, well-dressed young man with wealth and connections, as well as talent. So perhaps Mathew has already got some of his ingredients for success sorted, though I'm not sure which.

I am clearly unable to articulate the penetrating questions I have in my head and Hao is left floundering in a bog of Chinglish communications which leaves us agreeing to meet again sometime soon, with a good interpreter, preferably at least half my age. Mathew's interpretation seems a little more Mathew and a little less Hao so we part sworn friends and agree to have food together at some point. My offer to pay looks like much more of a sure run thing than some of the rest of the conversation, but I am tired. I invite Girl Friday as well, but it's unclear to me if she accepts or if Mathew does so on her behalf.

BOOKS IN THE RAFTERS

We negotiate the labyrinthine maze of intersecting roads between the refurbished factory buildings. This area used to be machine shops and fabrication units until relatively recently. Now it houses start-ups and burgeoning adolescent businesses in everything from film production and photography to design and technology. The driver is using a mixture of navigation app and shouted directions from the occasional security guard and passerby. We eventually draw up outside another refurbished building, sleek and smoked-glass windowed.

Mr Xuan Zhengyuan is the senior vice president of Beijing Shunya International Branding Consulting Co. Ltd and, as such, he is a busy man. A pleasant young receptionist asks us to wait in the minimalist vestibule for a few minutes before ushering us into a meeting room. The window is wide open but we sit in coats as the temperature outside is around a balmy 10 degrees.

"I'm 47 years old now. I graduated from Wuhan University of Technology in 1991, having been brought up in Anhui Province in a small town on the banks of the Yangtze River."

We are well into our conversation now. Pleasantries have passed and the window has been wrestled almost shut by a very persistent Mr Xuan.

"I remember going to university very well. My home was almost 500 kilometres upstream from Wuhan, but because of the river and the ferries I was able to go by boat to university. My classmates were very envious of me. While they may have had to take a train for up to 20 hours to get home, usually standing all the way and unable to take a rest, I had a cabin and could sleep or walk around the boat. It took 24 hours to go upstream against the current of the river to university, but only 18 hours to get home! Then at the end of 1990 the ferries stopped and there were only a few tourist boats from then on. But the infrastructure had improved a lot and there were bridges, highways and train lines built so it wasn't so bad or so hard to get around! However, those boat journeys were so wonderful. I will remember them all my life."

We have warmed the room with green tea in paper cups and the coats are off. It is a small meeting room, bare save for a functional laminate table and four plastic, though reasonably comfortable chairs. Functional and serviceable. For internal meetings. Clients rarely visit as most are serviced online or through direct visits. The whole office is a workable and workaday environment, full of large computer screens and youthful faces.

"After university I moved to Beijing. In those days the government decided where you should be assigned after graduating. Just three years later the government stopped the allocation system. I was allocated to a building materials company and given responsibilities for engineering and technical support. I was also given a Beijing *hukou* so this is where I stayed. The business gave us accommodation in a shared dormitory with three of us in the same room. That was good but the bad thing was that the dormitory was so far outside the city centre. It was an adventure to travel in! We were outside what is now the west fifth ring road at Shijingshan District."

"What was it like to arrive in Beijing as a young man, so far from home?"

"I was quite excited, but I hadn't thought about how much opportunity there was here. Young people now, they think of the opportunity. It is different now. When I arrived, I stayed in the factory most of the time. I worked a three-shift system for two years. When I'd finished the night shift, which was midnight until 08.00, then sometimes I went to Beijing on the bus. I went to the book store all day then back to the factory on the bus at about 18.00, had supper and slept for a while before going back to work. I didn't go to see the sights and the famous places, though I did go to the Forbidden City several times with friends, but I had always been interested in books. After four years of working in the factory I left."

In every culture, in every place in the world, people can remember the big days of history either globally or for their country. The first man on the moon, JF Kennedy being assassinated, Princess Diana's death, the collapse of the Berlin Wall. In China, for a certain generation, it is 9 September 1976.

"I remember it very well. I was in the first grade of primary school. My friends and I were out playing when suddenly an old woman shouted at us, 'Don't play any more! Stop! Chairman Mao has died.' I remember about a month later there was a memorial service in the afternoon. I saw many people crying. Even some of the staff in the school were crying openly. In the October of the same year, the Gang of Four fell. I remember that too. Very well."

The Gang of Four were a group of highly influential leaders of the Party in China at the end of Mao Zedong's long and tumultuous rule. They were blamed, rightly or wrongly, for many of the excesses associated with the end of the era of Mao. Within a month of his death, they were arrested, put on trial and removed from office.

We pause as he remembers. Then, with a shake of the head, the Cultural Revolution was consigned to history.

"In 1995 I moved jobs. A friend of mine introduced me to a German company called BMH, I think it was. They provided equipment to the cement industry and they had a representative office in Beijing, as well as some other locations across China. In those days any Chinese staff had to be recruited through special approved agencies. This was the system then. It was a really great experience working for that foreign company. It was a great education, a bit like a second degree. I was a sales engineer. It really opened my eyes to the world outside. However, there was a lot of tension with the German boss. We travelled around China together visiting clients. In those times hotels charged a different price for Chinese people compared to foreigners. It was much more expensive for him than for me. It made him so mad. He would get very cross and shout at the staff in the hotels. He said it was unfair. That they were discriminating against him and foreigners. I guess he was right! It was true. They were. But that's the way it was."

In many places that's the way it still is. In my travels around China I still get Chinese colleagues to book the hotels in advance if I can. One of the side benefits of the huge oversupply of hotel rooms across China, even in the major cities, is that you can arrive almost anywhere at any time of the night or day and still be sure to be able to get a room without an advance booking. However, I have been stung several times with a higher price as a foreigner if I am not a bit savvy with the booking and even big hotels will haggle. But, you almost never pay the asked price. Even the Chinese don't! Haggling is a way of life.

"It was also such a wonderful thing to be able to travel abroad too. I used to accompany customers to see the plant and machinery being manufactured in Germany. And in France. I travelled quite a bit."

"Do you remember your first time outside China?" I ask.

"Of course! We were going via Hong Kong to Hamburg. Hong Kong was so different to mainland China. It was so exciting. It was like taking a space ship to Mars. My first trip on an aircraft was with my German boss to Shenyang. We first took a flight from Beijing. I remember it well. It was only a day trip but it was so exciting. Very few people were doing business outside China at that time in the late 1990s. It was mainly government business and the only people allowed to travel outside the country were those on government delegations and the staff of foreign business representative offices."

Mr Xuan worked with the German company for four years then his life took a change of course. A friend told him of a magazine that needed a reporter who could write about the technology industry. He took the job at *Communication World* magazine in 1999 and stayed for three years.

"I really enjoyed it. I have always enjoyed writing. I was quite good at it. I was reporting about people, about companies and about industry trends. It was good. I did miss the international business though, and the overseas travel. I also missed the German style of working and the organized life I had. Then SARS hit so I quit my job."

SARS or 'Severe Acute Respiratory Syndrome' hit China hard in 2003 and the borders were effectively closed for over nine months, during which the epidemic raced across Asia. In particular, businesses closed and many overseas enterprises withdrew from mainland China altogether.

"I stayed at home for six months. Then a public relations company approached me. I'd known them from the days I had been a writer and journalist. To be honest I didn't really want to do the job, but after talking with the owner and learning a bit more about what they did and who they worked for, it did seem interesting so I joined."

"So, what's it like working in public relations in China at this time of technological change, the increased 'going out' and globalization of China?"

"This is a Chinese agency. We have over 300 staff and offices in Beijing, as well as Shanghai, Guanzhou, Shenzhen and Changsha. There is a significant difference between Western agencies and Chinese ones. The Chinese ones work much much harder and the clients are much much more demanding. We do work for some international organizations such as Mazda, HP and Baidu, but they are all the Chinese branches we work for. Only California Raisins are based outside China, in the US, of course. The Chinese clients can be terrible, tough and even aggressive. They think because they are paying what they feel is a lot of money, then they have the right to be like gods. They have no respect for the people working for them. Western clients are much politer."

I have the distinct impression that Western clients get broadly disproportionately better service as a result. Human beings all over the world respond better to being treated respectfully.

We return to those days he first came to Beijing. I ask him, "How has Beijing and China changed in the last 25 years?"

"It was all a lot more difficult than it is now. You couldn't rent an apartment then. You were in company accommodation, single sex dormitories with often quite a few colleagues. That's all changed now and there are so many places to rent and so many estate agencies. Also, the labour market back then was closed. There was a government allocation system for jobs back when I first started working. Now it's a totally free market. If you wanted to get a job and move from one place to another, you had to go to the agencies. Now there are many different channels for people to find jobs and move around."

Mr Xuan recalls the first time he wanted to leave the building materials company to which he had been allocated.

"I had to go to them to say I wanted to leave. I actually had to pay them a fine for leaving work. It was ¥5,000 (£500). It was a lot of money! Now labour law protects the employee and although there is a month's notice on either side of an employment contract, people never hold staff to it and you never get any money back! They just walk!"

We discuss the changing pattern of employees and the costs associated with attracting the right talent.

"Many young businesses of today have people born in the 1970s hiring those born in the 1990s. While the more established businesses offer a wide variety of benefits, such as more holidays and health insurance, the start-ups pay government required benefits at the minimum level, not just to avoid paying tax. It is also to put more cash into the kids' pockets. The youngsters don't think about tomorrow or insurance or anything like that. They just want the cash. They are all about the here and now and are totally egocentric. We are very good here with staff and do provide the right level of healthcare and housing allowances as well. However, we still get a high turnover. We also believe it is about the values of the business."

Mr Xuan has worked for this company for seven years now and fully intends to stay.

"I'm settled here now. I enjoy the work, I enjoy writing and reading and my accumulated experience and knowledge makes my career here a fulfilling one. I love to read widely and this interest in the world certainly helps me to deliver a better service to clients. I've changed from being involved in technology and science to the creative world. But I like it very much."

"So why this fascination with reading and with books?"

Mr Xuan sits back in his chair and a faraway look crosses his face.

"When I was maybe five or six years old my father showed me a map of the world and I was amazed. There was a huge place outside China. I was fixated by that map. In the early 1980s China was just opening up and there were more and more magazines and newspapers available. My father subscribed to a lot of different magazines and I read them too. He didn't have the chance to go to university. He just went to middle school but he could read and write. From there he was allocated to a factory as a worker. He was not an educated man but unlike most of his co-workers he read a lot and he wrote too. He encouraged me to do so as well. He was always sharing things that he had read about with my mother. Of course, I listened too. One thing he said really struck me. He once said that some man called Einstein believed that light was curved. He had no idea what that meant but he loved to read and think about what he had read."

An amazing man. "He must have been a great influence on you?" I ask.

"He passed away about eight years ago. He was a great guy. I particularly remember something from when I was 12 years old. We had a leak through a small hole in the roof of our house. My father was up in the rafters of the roof on a ladder with a patch of leather to fix the leak. To get to the roof itself he started to pass down books. There were so many books up in the rafters of the house. These were books from the 1950s and 1960s. At the front of each book he had placed his signature and the date that he had bought it. There were all sorts of books from literature as well as history and an old stamp collection from the early 1950s."

It is quiet in the bare meeting room but he isn't there any more.

We sit quietly while he is transported to that small family home of his youth on the banks of the Yangtze River. His father high above the small child, handing down dusty tome after tome to his patient and bemused wife.

"My father was a thinker, a critical thinker. He wouldn't have expressed it like that. He just didn't follow the others. Though he wasn't educated he was immensely influential on me.

"I missed him when he passed away."

There is a long, almost uncomfortable, pause.

"I still miss him."

We hold our breath in a moment of remembrance.

"He changed my life."

THE DENTIST AND THE DOG

The coffee shop is dark. Heavy dark wooden tables fill the space with heavy dark wooden chairs set on the dark wooden floors and hemmed in by dark wooden pillars. It's not helped that it is dark outside. The low-strung lighting casts pools of light and staff lurk behind the moody dark counter and the low light displays. The Korean-owned branded coffee chain has been featured in some of the Chinese and other design magazines for its bohemian style, plush velveteen chairs and chandeliers and art.

We meet in the outlet in the centre of the expat-centric area of Jingtai. However, though I may be branded as a philistine, it's a very poor attempt at modern and cool in my view. But then I didn't help things by trying to charge my ageing iPad and plunging half the place into impenetrable blackness by pulling a seemingly disconnected plug from what appeared to be a redundant socket. I wasn't popular but managed to re-establish illumination before I was going to be asked to leave. My smiles of helpless, hapless apology are accepted even as I stumble across the room, knocking over a chair and dislodging a lamp stand in the gloom. It says something that my guest has had to WeChat me from barely three metres away to reveal she is already there, thankfully unaware of my ineptitude so close by.

Amber is a dentist. She is now working in a private clinic in Beijing and she has what she describes as her dream job. But it wasn't always like that.

"I graduated from medical university in 2006. I didn't get a scholarship. It was five years of hard study and it was very stressful indeed.

"My parents lived and still live in a poor county five hours (by train and bus) from Beijing in Henan Province in the middle of eastern China and they thought being a dentist would be a good life, but it was hard. I was in Chengdu in Sichuan Province at the dental school and a long way from my home town and parents. I got my first job in Chengdu and was there for two and a half years. It's a great place if you are young and I enjoyed life and being out all the time. Being a long way from home did bother me though so I decided to move up to Beijing, which is only five hours from my home town. I came in 2009."

Amber hasn't eaten her dinner yet, despite us meeting at 7.30 pm. We have had a coffee and Amber orders cake and cream. In response to my dental cavity referencing question, she responds that she needs the sugar for energy and she still has an hours' journey back to her 'out of town' apartment. Despite the hours she works and the good job at probably the best private dental clinic in Beijing, she still can't afford to live in the central part of the city, such are the prices here.

We talk about her home town and what got her into dentistry. Would she, as a highly qualified professional, ever consider moving abroad where her skills and command of English would make her very sought after?

"No. I don't want to move or leave China. I love my country, my culture is here. When I was at school our history books were full of the history of the world. We learned about the whole of history. I know Western children don't learn about Chinese history in the same way we learn about Western history. Many Western people talk about China but they really know nothing about this country. We know more about the world and its geography than you do. We know a little about each culture but we do know about the world. The reform and opening up policy in China has been very good. You gave us movies and TV programmes and we learned about you, and we learned the English language. You guys didn't learn about China and you don't learn Chinese either. There is no language connection between us."

Amber returns to the differences between China and the West regularly during our conversations, sometimes preferring that I don't record what she says. However, her opinions are no different to many I have come across, often from older people, but increasingly from a younger generation.

"When I first came to Beijing I didn't really like what I was doing so I left dentistry to join a large multinational electronics company (selling dental products, as well as others). I worked in marketing for one and a half years. I learned a lot. It was a huge company globally with long processes. I enjoyed the work (there) in many ways. It taught me a lot and opened my eyes, including about private dentistry. However, I hated it so I carried on with practising dentistry rather than trying to sell products to dentists."

Amber tells me that she had, as some Chinese people have done, though it's fair to say not all, a very negative perception of Western management styles. I am occasionally beset by a tide of deep-seated resentment of the West which runs from the actions of the British and European soldiers in the sacking of the Old Summer Palace in Beijing in 1860 and the introduction of opium to China in the 1830s, through to the lack of respect and arrogance shown by Western management to Chinese employees even in today's business environment.

"At the multinational I was able to talk to some big organizations. It gave me an insight into commercial work. I realized that if I ever wanted to leave dentistry, then there was something else I could do. I was lucky to have had that job. It gave me a different type of confidence and a different perspective. I worked in a different part of the city than I do now and I made friends in that area. Although I now work ten hours a day and it takes me nearly one and a half hours to commute each way every day, I like it out there. I've lived in my apartment a long time so I like the area. I feel safe and comfortable there."

Amber left the Western corporate to join a private practice run by an American woman. Chinese nationals can't own their own clinics, medical or dental, in China so the only way to be involved in this area of expanding services in the country is to join a foreign-owned venture.

"It was very stressful! I became ill so I took a year off and helped a friend start a dental clinic but it failed. Then I went to a new hospital, this one, run by a very good dentist. It was really good, but he left after a while so I left too. However, they asked me to come back. Beijing United Family Hospital was the first private health hospital in China and is very expensive but very good."

The hospital opened in 1997 and is widely regarded as the most advanced healthcare provider in Beijing. It has the capacity to handle diagnosis and care for most illnesses, with staff from all around the world. It uses predominantly imported technologies and machinery of the highest quality.

"The hospital services the very wealthy and many foreigners with healthcare insurance. I've worked here for ten months. I have learned a lot from my job and it has made me stronger and better."

Amber's enthusiasm for her job and her city is contagious. She is clearly very happy with her dream job.

"I really like Beijing. Most young people come to Beijing, or Shanghai, Guangzhou or Shenzhen. You can meet people from all over China, so many different types of people come to these cities to seek their fortune. Beijing is the capital of China and it has the best arts, the best hospitals, the best education, everything. It may be a very old city in its history but it is very young in its feel and age of people. Of course, the traffic is terrible and it is too expensive, and becoming more expensive every day. The rents are going up but my pay is too. I am paid well and they want to keep the good doctors and staff. It really depends on what life you want. It's your choice how you decide to live. It's not about your pay. I'm not married so life is ok. It's a choice. Parents do give everything they can to their children but it is a choice to be married, to have children."

"Has dentistry changed in China along with the rest of the economy?" I ask.

"Of course. When I started, people only went to the dentist or the doctor if they had a problem and it was fairly serious.

Nowadays, more people go for check-ups. This is why private dentistry is doing well. More and more businessmen are wealthy and so the demand for periodontal, orthodontic and cosmetic dentistry is rising. The superstars are having their teeth done so it is regarded as acceptable and aspirational. Everyone pays attention to their health and the more money they have, the more attention they pay to it. Everyone wants to be healthy."

"But aren't teeth the last thing people pay attention to?"

"In most societies the teeth are the last thing people take care of and it's just the same in China. Different cities have different price levels but people need to be reassured that we are all the same and we are all trained to the same level. Unfortunately, while there are training schools across China, medical and dentistry, not all have the same standards. Across China it remains a bit variable. We need to be able to change this so wherever anyone receives care it is to the same high standard. Of course, prices are lower in other cities as the overheads are not the same in rental and in pay of staff so everything is relative. That is one thing in the West; you have the same standards everywhere you go. We have the same principles but the opportunity to practise varies across China. It depends on the resources available. It depends on the leader of the school as well. It is a shame, but some are more closed to new treatment approaches and the application of new research than others. We have different training levels, universities, colleges and schools, so training is at different levels depending on where people attain their qualification."

Amber remains sanguine. "The middle classes in any country have to work for a living. Depending on their standard of living, they can afford different things but certainly healthcare and dentistry are part of the list of requirements and it is a growing area. The better off can access better care, it's the same the world over, and it's about what you choose to spend your disposable income on."

I ask, "Would you at least like to see the world and experience directly what other cultures have to offer someone as skilled as you?"

"Yes, I'd like to travel for the experience and to understand better but I don't want to emigrate. I'm a traditional Chinese and want to stay in China."

Though I press her a little more she remains steadfast in her assertion that despite her seeming mobility and personal freedoms she would rather enjoy the benefits of Beijing than take a chance in some foreign land.

I comment that in the West being a dentist is widely acknowledged as being one of the more, if not most, stressful professions.

"Yes, the stress is very high. Patients' demands are very high. I can't guarantee that their teeth will be perfect, everyone's teeth and mouth is different and people respond in different ways to treatment. But they are paying a lot of money and they expect perfection! It's the same as Western dentists. We all experience the same levels of stress working with the teeth of wealthy and demanding patients."

So, what does the future hold? Amber is still relatively young. Marriage perhaps? She brushes this away.

"I have to look after my patients. My ambition is to open my own clinic. Not a big one, just small, perhaps in my home town. My parents are getting older and I have my duty to go back and look after them. My father is an engineer and my mother also works. They are farmers. My parents were very proud of me and even thought I might go overseas to study. People come to the cities, but why? It is my feeling that in my heart I want to go back to the country, to be in a small village, with a dog and a family."

"A dog and a family? In that order?" I ask.

"Yes, I have adopted a dog!" her face lights up. "He was thrown out by his owner as a young puppy. He's a collie dog and he is quite large, so I took him to the vet as his previous owner had broken two of his legs. I got them fixed. He was only about three months old when I found him. He is now with my parents in my home town and they love him so much! He really likes to run."

Amber comes alive as she talks about 'Chu Er', so called as she found him on the second day of the Spring Festival in China. The Chinese have a long history of a mixed relationship with dogs and the stories of eating dog continue to circulate in the West to a rising crescendo of revulsion and disbelief. However, widespread criticism has essentially eradicated the custom and, although it persists in certain places, there is a growing trend for keeping dogs as pets, certainly among the middle classes where pampered pooches are a regular feature in the parks and even malls of Beijing.

"We have a family tradition of keeping dogs and raising them as guard dogs. Even recently we had to protect our home from someone and Chu Er barked and chased them away. He is a smart dog."

Amber speaks with pride as she describes how the new acquisition has taken to his new life and owners like a duck to water. She clearly has great affection for Chu Er and I suspect he is also tugging her heart strings back to the village life she describes with such longing.

"I'm not a city girl. There is no freedom in the city. I know it is good and has the best in education and medicine and that's not very fair to those in the countryside but I can't change things. I can just go home and do what I can for my family and my village."

I suspect this will be somewhat sooner rather than later for Amber and Chu Er.

THE CHILDREN WHO NEVER CRY

It is a long way outside the centre of Beijing. A subway journey on one of the new lines then, in what seemed to be the middle of nowhere, at Houshayu (后沙峪地铁站) subway station, we take a taxi from a lonely station to a small village and then, having crisscrossed through the streets, are abandoned at a cross roads opposite the community central offices. I'm glad I have my local interpreter with me, without whom I would have been singularly unable to arrive, or escape.

Ms Deng Zhi Xin is waiting with suspicious eyes at the intersection, stamping her feet against the grey and cold November day. We walk silently up the back street to the metal door embedded into the imposing rust-flaking compound gate. The building within is somewhat run down and ramshackle. We enter by a small side door into an unlit cold, but clean, corridor. Ms Deng waves us into a spartan and cold room which is empty, save for a metal table and four plastic stools. On the opposite side of the corridor is another room from which emerges green tea in white plastic cups. The nearby toilet is a typical hole in the ground Chinese type but there is no flush, no paper, no soap and no towels. There is also no water in the taps.

We huddle under Ms Deng's uncomfortable gaze. Somewhere in the depths of the building a child was crying. Then silence envelops us.

"So. What are your questions?"

Taking a deep breath, I plunge into the unknown. This could be a very short meeting.

"Tell me about your life and how you came to be here?"

There is a long cold silence.

I smile encouragingly. My interpreter shuffles uncomfortably in her coat.

"I was born, raised and worked in Beijing. My parents came to Beijing after they graduated in 1962. My father was from Guangdong. My mother from Shanghai. They were both electrical engineers. I was born in 1969. I grew up in a village to the north east of Beijing. We lived near what is now the fourth ring road. Back then there were only two ring roads. We lived a long way outside the old Beijing of that time. It's called the 798 Art District now and is well known for being a real centre for the arts and design and the like."

Deep breath.

"Back then it was an area that many state-owned enterprises were based in. There were many plants and factories there then. Each plant employed around 10,000 people. The whole area was built with low rise houses, there were no buildings more than four stories high at that time. Everyone knew everyone else, colleagues and friends were always around. We never locked the doors. Also, all the parents and colleagues knew every child in the building. There were often about four people in each room and each room was about 3 metres by 4 metres in size. Each floor of each block had three apartments with two families and a bathroom, a kitchen and a bed each. At that time the work was very attractive to young people and everyone liked the work which was stable. You could also easily find a husband or a wife too."

Another deep breath.

"My parents both worked in the research institute in the factory. The research institute belonged to the Ministry of Industry and Information Technology of the People's Republic of China. It was a very happy time living there then and all the kids knew each other, so after school we could all play together safely. There were no iPads and no mobile phones then, no electronic games. My childhood was far better than the kids now. Today no one knows each other and apartment blocks are more like prisons with each family keeping to itself. Then in the late 1980s many things changed. People started businesses and the factories started to run down and close down.

"My daughter is lucky as she can play with her three friends, and their families all live in our compound. But generally, nowadays, it is difficult for kids to find and make friends in their own compound. Things have changed. When I was five years old I just went downstairs to play with friends. Now you have to follow your child everywhere in case something happens. Even now neighbours don't know each other, so if something were to happen you might not be able to find anyone to ask and people don't want to know and won't help.

"I went to Beijing Agricultural University and read economy management. I was there from 1987–1991. I was a happy and optimistic student. Most of the students were locals and after we graduated we were assigned to government jobs across Beijing. I was assigned to the National Tax Bureau and worked there from 1991–1994.

"Then I left and studied for two years to get my accounting qualifications. I then went on to work for one of the international accounting firms where I tried to sit more exams, but it was difficult to work and study. I eventually managed to qualify in accounting both under the English and the Chinese systems. I worked at that organization for eight years from 1996–2003, predominantly as an auditor."

There is almost no stopping her once she starts to talk. It seems cathartic to her and is almost like an unburdening. She got married in 1998, at the age of 29. Her husband was trained as a radar technician, "a very narrow job", and was assigned to work at the main Beijing airport as an air traffic controller. He has been there ever since and still works there now. They met, like most Chinese couples, through a friend introducing them. After they got married, they lived with his parents for a short time. In 2000 they moved to the Wangjing area of Beijing in the north west of the city. Five years later their daughter was born.

"Beijing has changed a lot since I was a child. The buildings are higher and higher, the residential areas larger and larger and material life better and better. When I was young we had to use tickets to buy special goods and services as they were rationed. Many things were in short supply. Before the Spring Festival each year all the kids collected the ration tickets and kept them ready to spend. It was very exciting and we all looked forward to it. Then, something as simple as a small bag of sunflower seeds was a treasure. Now even a big bag costs almost nothing. In many ways, there are too many things now, it's too easy."

During the early years of Ms Deng's life, Beijing changed little. Her middle school years up until university were characterized by slow growth and limited physical change around her, but after her university years of 1987–1991 it all changed. The speed of change in China accelerated and the economy started to expand rapidly. The catalyst of Deng Xiao Peng and the changes introduced by government catapulted the country forward.

"We moved to Canada in 2003."

Er. Right. I was surprised. I never managed to find out how they had got the requisite visas, as these are not easy to obtain even now and back then doubly so. Perhaps it was her husband's skills that opened the door but it isn't clear.

Canada was not a success. Despite being a skilled couple her husband failed to find a satisfactory role. Although they found Canada to be beautiful, it was too difficult for them to settle down. Living in Toronto and having travelled extensively in the country, they learned that her husband's father had contracted cancer so they returned to China late in 2004. With her international and local accounting qualifications, Eve (her English name emerged in Canada) found it easy to find employment and her husband went back to the airport. She worked for several different companies from 2004–2010.

"I got a job straightaway when I moved back to China, but in 2007 I had a phone call which changed my life. Since my daughter was born I had started, naturally, paying more and more attention to children in the street and the news, as well as stories on the internet. At that time, I was drawn to a website called www.yaolan.com. Yaolan (摇篮) means 'cradle' in Chinese. The website provides nursing knowledge to parents whose children are between 0–6 years old. There are many columns written for the website and one which is titled 'Helping'. I could not help myself – I clicked on the 'helping' link. I remember seeing a small title 'two-year-old girl needs your help'. I took a look and was very touched. I contacted the article writer and donated ¥1,000 (£100.00) to help her. Later, I followed up to find out what had happened to this little girl who was so ill and found out that there were so many children needing help. The children and their families were coming to Beijing from other cities and provinces asking for help in medical care. I was so astonished at the scale of the problem, so I started to raise money for these children and became a columnist on the website."

Eve became a regular blogger on the site and, as a result, became more and more well known. Quite soon she had her own section of the site under the pseudonym 'Loving Cradle'. She became a channel for many parents who needed help for their children, many of whom were either terminally ill or had life-threatening conditions.

"These children lived in faraway villages where access to care was limited, to say the least. The parents were inevitably poor and unable to pay for the care their children needed to stay alive. There is almost no access to specialist care in these places, so they need to come to Beijing, where the best hospitals and doctors are located."

Local media across China promoted the site and she became more and more well known as the route to care for many critically ill children.

"Of course, all these children had parents who loved them and were distraught at the thought of them dying through lack of access to the care which was needed. Then one day I got a call on my mobile phone from a volunteer group in Henan Province. They asked me if I could help children from welfare homes. I was very surprised. These children are orphans. The organization wasn't set up to help children like this."

Eve had a small group of mothers who were all involved in the Yaolan charity work.

"Shortly after I had received the call, a few of us sat down and discussed whether we could do anything. We thought helping such children was a distant dream. It was terrible for us. Now we knew about these children we felt we had to do something. There was no doubt that they would die without the right care, but when a child is in a welfare home they are subject to very different rules and laws. By being involved with children in a welfare home we would take on the legal responsibility for these children. There is no state aid or support, but if they are ill, get hurt or die while in your care, you are subject to punitive fines and a lot of trouble. It is a big risk. We didn't think we could afford to take any action. But we also decided that now we knew, we couldn't walk away. We decided to act despite the legal implications."

Eve and her friends worked quickly.

"Within three days I found an empty apartment in a compound near to where we lived and managed to persuade the owner to rent it to us at a low price. It had no furniture. We called the Henan group and told them we would take the child. They said there were four in desperate need of help. So we took all four."

Within a year there were 20 children crammed into the small apartment.

"We were just swamped. In the first three years we moved many times, each time to a slightly bigger place, always begging landlords for lower rents, and buying second-hand furniture. We just kept on growing. Now we have around 50 children."

"Where?" I ask.

"Here. Do you want to see?"

The sound of the briefly crying child becomes clear.

We walk slowly along the dimly lit corridor. Away from the few small rooms used for administrative purposes, there is an open entrance hall with a huge double staircase leading upstairs. The sides of the open stairs are strung with protective netting, secured to the banisters with rope and electrician's tie-wraps. We are not allowed upstairs to the dormitories, as Eve and her team have a strict protocol for all visitors.

In the wing beyond the entrance hall are working toilets. The water is turned off to prevent it freezing in the pipes from the cold. The building has no heating yet. The toilets strike me as odd at first, until I realize that everything is infant sized. Petite empty coat and shoe racks with tiny wooden stools line one wall. We are greeted by four or five very smiley staff leading or carrying small children. The rooms we see are jammed full. Pulling aside the heavy felt cloth which covers the doorways, keeping out the now bitter cold of a Beijing autumn, Eve reveals a floor strewn with play mats and children.

They are everywhere. Aged between two and five, they are lying on the floor, playing with toys from the cupboards packing the walls, sitting, cuddling helpers or simply walking around with a book or a toy. On seeing Eve many toddle over to greet her. Leaning over the old shoe cupboard which acts as a makeshift gate, Eve strokes the hair of a little girl who clings to her other arm silently.

"We are so lucky to have a good team here. Of course, we have to pay a lot to keep all this going and to pay them. We have to respect their skills. They are all trained and qualified kindergarten teachers."

At first Eve and her small group of friends had made personal donations but that was never going to be enough, so they relied and survived for a while on donations which came through the yaolan.com site. More and more donations poured in but even these were not enough, so the team started raising funds from other sources such as wealthy benefactors. After three years they no longer needed yaolan.com funds.

"The money now comes through word-of-mouth donations. We have only just moved to this place. We are starting all over again. It is 5,328sq metres, although we only use about 2,000 sq metres of it at the moment. We are paying the market rate for the rent, Chinese landlords aren't charities."

Or charitable.

"We have enough space for about 80 children and we feel that's going to be enough. But we've said that before!"

"What happened with the first four children?"

"Unfortunately, one of them died. He had a congenital heart condition. Neither we, nor the doctors, could save him. The other three all recovered and were adopted. Around 70% of the children arrive here only a few days old, the rest are between a month or so and six years. Around 70% are congenitally diseased and will simply die without the love and attention we give them. Some still do. Around 30% of the children have cerebral palsy, bone defects or joint problems. They are all very sick. We have a few children with harelips too."

The length of stay in the home depends on the nature of the child's condition and prospects. Eve hopes that all the children will be adopted once they have been treated, assessed, cured or their condition stabilized.

"Many families want to adopt a child; there are many couples who are childless in China. However, few will adopt a child with a problem, but there are some people. Those are the angels we want to give a home to for these children. Those special people find us. It's amazing. There is no welfare in China. Quite a number of foreigners are willing to adopt our children. There are Chinese people too though."

Eve tells me a story of a little boy walking along a beach at dusk, after a storm. "There are many fish washed up on the beach, many are still alive and fighting for water, trying to get back to sea. An old man watches the child pick up a fish and take it back to the sea. 'What are you doing? There are so many fish dying on the beach.' The little boy looks up at him. 'Yes there are. But the ones in my hands will be saved.'"

"We are that little boy. I am so tired from doing this task. It is so hard and all consuming. I have no idea how long I can keep doing this or how many more children we can save in the future. It is very difficult to run an organization like this, to encourage people to pay attention to children like these."

She gazes at me thoughtfully. They are the eyes of a tired and weary, but committed and determined woman.

"So many people have affection and love but don't know what to do with it. They see that so many people and so many children need help and love. It is overwhelming, so even the most compassionate people feel helpless and do nothing as a result. But we are all like that little boy, and even if we all do just a small thing, then it will change the world we live in for the better and more fish will be saved."

As we leave to join the waiting taxi, I can't help asking Eve a question which has bothered me throughout the visit. Except for that first sound of a child crying, the place is remarkably quiet. The children are clearly very happy but had almost never made a sound.

"Oh there's a simple reason for that."

Eve shuts the door of the taxi and leans through the open window to throw her final verbal grenade.

"These children are orphans and, as babies, most soon learned that they never got any attention by crying."

Tears well up in my eyes as we drive away.

THE DREAM-CHASER

"I come from a small place right up in the north east of China near the Russian border in Heilongjiang Province. I am a dream-chaser!"

Li Fang is a self-assured young woman in a hurry. She is squeezing my interview in between a busy set of meetings before she goes off filming again. She is a film producer now and appears very happy, but it wasn't always like this. She grew up in a typical small Chinese city and her parents were teachers at the local junior school. On the face of it, she was destined to a humble life, perhaps with a safe and secure local government job, marriage and a child. However, Fang's life was to take a series of amazing turns. The first began with a picture she saw as a little girl.

"I remember looking at a history book one day and one image I saw changed my life. It was the famous West Gate of PKU (Peking University). It is a beautiful gate, an Emperor's gate. A red gate. The picture captured me and I fell in love with the place. I wanted to know about it, its history and what it stood for. I dreamed of walking through those gates into university. I was 14 years old.

"I worked hard, really hard. I so wanted to walk through those gates. I wanted to try for that university, even though it is the best and most difficult to get into in the whole of China. When I finally was able to fill in that application form, to go to university, I was only one of a few to be able to apply from my school. Everyone had to put down their preferred choices of university, in order of desire: first choice, second choice and third. I just put one university name on my form. PKU.

"You needed a specific score from school for university places. I was the last one to get into PKU from the whole of Heilongjiang Province. I was lucky. My grade was exactly on line for the entry requirements. It was my fate. I had been chosen!

"It was the best time of my life! I studied in the business school. PKU encourages students to chase their dreams, to seek freedom of expression and to love our country. It was a big shock to me. Back in my home town I was the best student in my school, but at PKU I was at the bottom! Everyone was so much cleverer than me. At PKU you can only run. You have to run fast all the time and work really hard or you will be left behind. I had always had strength in my life and I had learned to run academically from being very young with my teacher parents. That's my fate, to be passionate about my work and to be very diligent.

"I remember the day I walked through that red gate with my parents. I was very cool and calm, as I knew I had arrived. My dream had been fulfilled. Now I needed to make the most of it and I was determined to work hard. I didn't even miss my home town. I was so focused on studying. Of course, I went home in the holidays, but otherwise I just worked!"

Fang was hungry for experiences to help her studies and in her third year she managed to get a summer role as an intern with a large international electronics company: Siemens.

"I was really lucky as I searched on the job sites and found them, I really liked what I saw there so I called the local director. He said they were not recruiting interns at all, just full-time positions, so I was not wanted. However, not long after he had spoken to me, one of their employees broke a leg and could not get into work. They needed someone part time. He called me and offered me the job! I really believe that luck goes to those people that prepare. He also offered me a job after university but selling was not so appealing to me. I wanted a job in consulting or in an investment bank. I went to Boston Consulting Group (BCG) in Beijing. I worked really hard. I was a typical professional. It was hard!"

Then Fang's life was destined to change again.

"I became ill and had to go to hospital. It was one of the national hospitals and I remember it was very crowded. There were no beds available at all on the normal wards so they put me in a room where everyone around me had cancer. I remember one day I was talking to someone and then two days later they were dead. It really affected me and taught me that life is short and health is the most important thing. You should do what you love. I had never thought about that before. It really changed my life."

Fang had always dreamed of making a film and being a film producer, but had never followed this dream. Her time in hospital made her decide to give up her job and go to Wharton College in the US.

"I got in touch with them and said, 'I want to be a movie producer.' They admitted me."

Fang had researched film production courses in the US and decided to try Harvard and Wharton to get accepted for a two year MBA.

"Wharton accepted me but I only had enough savings to pay for one year. I then managed to get a loan from Citibank for the remaining funding through a school supported loan scheme programme. I was so happy. What really mattered to me with Wharton was that over 60% of the students were from outside the US. I really loved Wharton, it was so different from what I had ever been used to. However, I was surprised by the people that asked me about how I spent my leisure time. They said, 'So do you hang out with people in Chinatown when you are not studying?' It was such an old, shallow and superficial idea! It showed that they really knew nothing about China at all. There were 30 students in that class of 2008. I was working and learning with people from all over the world but they knew nothing about China. Why would I want to hang out with the Chinese? I knew about China and here was the opportunity to be with people from so many different cultures. I also wanted to show others about the real Chinese and talk about the reality of China. I didn't want to lecture them, just to help people better understand me as a Chinese person so I could help them understand China through me and my example."

Fang graduated in 2010 and tried to get a job in Hollywood, but the US was in recession and there were few, if any, jobs. She returned to China, along with many other Chinese graduates in the post-2008 financial crisis years.

"Most people on the course left the US that year. The opportunities are actually better here in China. China is growing up and there are better jobs here now with domestic corporations such as Alibaba and Tencent, rather than with the big Western multinationals. I came back with my dream but the film industry in China was only just starting up in 2010, so I couldn't get a job. BCG was happy to take me back so I went there for a little while and then worked for Apple in Beijing. I worked in the regional operations group. It was a good experience to be in a real business and it really helped me develop my professional expertise from an operational and business perspective."

Fang worked for another three years before she saw that the Chinese film industry was starting to take off, with more production houses and support businesses starting up and being successful. She decided now was the time to try again for her dream to enter the film industry.

"I began to look for a job more seriously and a friend told me that Disney was setting up a new project with Disney TV, so I applied, got the job and worked there for a year. Then I met a director from the Beijing Film Academy. I set up a company myself and am working with him as a producer. I'm also doing some freelance consultancy work for a US company here in Beijing, so I can earn money. There's not much money around when you start up a business! I'm also writing scripts and am adapting a book for film. I've managed to get an investor. He read the script and invested a bit of money. It's a thriller set in Beijing. I'm hopeful."

"How about marriage?" I ask.

"Marriage is not for me unless I can really find someone with common interests and shared values."

I thought that was always the case, but in China, with the propensity to often treat marriage as a business transaction rather than an emotional commitment, it's not always so.

Silence.

"Have you thought of returning to the US, none withstanding the difficulty of visa application?"

"I don't want to go back."

"Oh. Ok. Why not?" I enquire.

"In so many ways, it is impossible to understand a culture, even if you live there. It depends on who you are with as to how much you understand it. It's easy to be superficial and it takes time to go deeper into a culture. You just don't have the time or capacity to know even more than a limited amount. In the US, I found that usually the middle classes seem to be quite open minded, but that's not the real US culture."

Silence.

She remains tight-lipped on her opinions on the US culture, though my suspicion is that while there were aspects she liked, overall she wasn't comfortable as an 'outsider' and a 'real Chinese'.

I flounder back to the conversational certainty of her dream. Film.

"There is more opportunity here in China in the film industry and, specifically, in Beijing. Shanghai is more about business, Beijing is more about culture and film is more about culture, so Beijing is where you need to be.

"Film people are less concerned about money. The industry is booming and China is developing its own suite of genres. Just five years ago there was no distinctive Chinese genre in film. Now it is developing, the product is getting better and better and there are more and more talented people in the industry. We aren't like Hollywood or the Korean market yet, but we are developing faster and I think better. We are starting to get our own style in comedy and even sci-fi.

We discuss the success of the Western films of recent times in China which have included *Star Wars*, *The Martian*, *Gravity*, *Warcraft*, and the like.

"It's interesting that Western films can make it in China but few Chinese films ever make it in the West. The fundamentally basic thing stopping it is culture. Film is such a culturally oriented product. Western culture has been understood in China for many years. We absorb it through everything, from our school language and history lessons, to TV and films. Eastern and, specifically, Chinese culture is simply not understood in the West. You never learn about our culture in your schools or in your daily lives.

"You've never heard of famous stories from here, such as *The Monkey King*, in the West. You've never absorbed stories like this, despite it being so much a part of our culture and history."

The Monkey King is a famous fable in China, which comes from one of the early Chinese classical novels: *The Journey to the West*. This first appeared in recorded print around 1592 and charts the progress of a legendary Tang dynasty Buddhist monk, Xuanzang or Tripitaka, who, on behalf of his monarch, goes on a search to achieve enlightenment and bring Buddhist learning back to eastern China. *The Monkey King* is one of the mythological disciples of the monk. Otherwise known as Sun Wukong, the monkey is an 'immortal' and endowed with amazing skills, which he uses to support the monk in his search for enlightenment. It is an amazing story and worth a read, even though it runs to over 100 chapters and is spread, somewhat randomly, over four books.

"It is such a shame that you Westerners don't want to understand the East."

Another long silence.

"So why do you want to produce a film?" I try again, this time with a little more success.

"I want to make a film of general value that I can present to the world about real China and what real China is actually like. China is now in a position where we can make really good movie products. However, film in China hasn't got deep enough yet, in my opinion. I really believe that as more and more Chinese people watch more and more films, they will start to develop a deeper and deeper appreciation for it. They will want films to go deeper and deeper, emotionally, psychologically and physically. I want to make a film that has that kind of depth."

"Is that your next dream?"

"Yes. I want to make a film that appeals to both Western and Eastern audiences. I want to produce a film that will be liked, no matter what location you watch it in. It will be made in China with an international feel. I hope I can communicate Eastern culture to the Western audience. We need to present China's ancient culture better, so I believe we need to do this through a joint production team: West and East together. Then we will be able to really make something that is the right mix and be successful."

Fang speaks with an enthusiasm and conviction of belief that is infectious. It has always amazed me how the Chinese are able to brush aside the immediate problems they might face and drive forward with seemingly impossible objectives against all the odds. I have learned to never underestimate the ability of such individuals where the average Westerner would collapse under the enormity of it all.

A PERSPECTIVE ON CHINESE FILM

Professor Huang Yingxia is Dean of the Graduate School of the Beijing Film Academy (BFA), the only film academy in China and the largest in Asia. He is waiting for me. A wiry and intense man with a shock of black hair, he has lived through, and significantly influenced, the changing face of the Chinese film industry.

China is now the world's fastest-growing film market, with a feature film being released into this enormous market at a rate of nearly two a day. Box office receipts in 2014 ran to ¥29.6bn ($4.83bn) which made it the second-largest film market after the US, globally. The industry began in 1896 and the first Chinese film, *The Battle of Dingjunshan*, was made in 1905.

Professor Huang explains, "I was born in 1959 and was at primary school in western Beijing during the Cultural Revolution. I remember that the school had no glass in the windows and no desks or chairs to start with. We had to bring our own stool from home to sit on. The blackboard was a painted section of the wall which the teacher used chopsticks to scratch lessons on. It was primitive, and I distinctly remember the very first thing we learned was how to say, "Long live Chairman Mao." It's a very strong memory from my first day as a naive seven-year-old child at primary school. I remember those days were difficult and there were different groups of people fighting each other in the fields and surrounding area".

Professor Huang is there. His eyes grip mine in an intensity of memory, which holds the attention like a vice.

"I remember we had to put newspaper over the windows and then a felt and cotton curtain in winter to keep out the cold. Also, in the winter, we had no electricity so school started and ended with the light. I thought that was normal life. There were about 40 or maybe 50 children in the class. Then around Grade 5, I recollect they put glass in the windows but there were still no lights and no electricity in the school."

While this sounds harsh, I have spoken to many Chinese people of this generation who remember just the same and worse conditions in the schools they attended. Some had endured rooms lacking doors and sometimes schools were almost outside as semi-covered structures stuck on the end of otherwise unprepossessing buildings, housing a local machine tool shed, barn or shop.

"We had a stove in the winter to help us keep warm," continues Professor Huang. "Each child had to take turns to go in early to set up the stove in the winter so the room was at least a little less cold when class started. In our third year we were given a desk and a chair, though they were not new.

"Middle school was a dream by comparison. We had electric lights and glass in the windows. I also vividly remember that the classroom had a proper blackboard. It felt like a real school."

Professor Huang's father was a coal miner working in the local pit while his mother worked in the personnel department at the mine.

"My father was responsible for the pit mine shaft lift. It was a very important job."

There then followed a day remembered by all of Professor Huang's generation, with a vividness that is both compelling and telling.

"It was in the second year of my high school: 9 September 1976. We were all called into the playground at the sudden order of the principal. There were loud speakers around the square and a solemn announcement of the death of Chairman Mao. We all cried. It was a very genuine outpouring of real emotion. I remember that moment very well. I remain astonished, looking back, that everyone felt like that."

The reality at the grass roots of society was an outpouring as heartfelt and shocking as those that touched the hearts of Americans at the assassination of J F Kennedy and the British the day Princess Diana died.

"The year 1977 was when enrolment was announced for university entrance examinations. We were delighted. We all worked hard to pass the exams. The score required was 265 for those at high school and 310 for those of us at middle school. I got 307. So I failed! I had to wait another year to try again and then in 1978 I passed. I was entered into the Beijing Film Academy (the BFA). My entrance into the world of film was entirely accidental. I heard that the BFA would take students for the very first time. I played the violin at the time and my tutors said it was a good idea to try to get into something artistic! I listened to them and became one of the first intakes to the academy of the post-Cultural Revolution generation."

Huang fell into the sound recording department and has been there ever since. He rose to become Head of Sound and then Dean. Save for a period, which began in 1982 with 'the nationwide despatch', the BFA has been Huang's life. The 'despatch' was the time when students from across China were sent to the provinces and the fields. As he then explained, it was a tortuous and difficult time, with luck and timing of the changes around the Cultural Revolution playing a critical role in his fortunes.

"Every province had a film studio for propaganda purposes. I was sent to Hunan Province and stayed there for six years, mainly filming. I was the sound man on the classic film of the time, *The Great Parade*. There were famous directors such as Wu Ziniu making films then. The films were shot without sound and then the soundtrack was added afterwards, with the censor's permission."

We discuss the role of the censor at the time and the undoubted strictures and constraints that were imposed. It was undoubtedly a difficult time in the nascent industry, but an exciting one too as it emerged from the dark days of the Cultural Revolution.

Huang was based in the county of Changshan and, as such, his *hukou* (or resident permit) was issued there, rather than in his home in Beijing. In those days, as now, once you were given a *hukou*, that was it. You were destined to remain where you were placed forever. It would determine your future and the future of your descendants, where they would have their education, get married and live.

"There was only one way to get back to Beijing and to the academy. I needed to be a graduate student back in Beijing and to get my *hukou* 're-despatched'. I really struggled but managed to do it and in 1978, I was re-despatched to Beijing. So there I was, back at the BFA."

Huang's story is unusual, his timing could be said to be perfect, or maybe just incredibly lucky. That's because 1986 was the first year that students were allowed to graduate from, as opposed to just finish, their studies and be sent home, or to a pre-determined role. In 1988, the sound department of BFA was allowed to graduate students and he was therefore in the right place at the right time to do so. He became one of the first generation of students to be classed as true, certified graduates.

"I didn't know when the authorities at the academy would be allowed to issue graduation certificates. But I guessed it would be soon, so I just gambled on being lucky and prepared hard. I started to learn English and hung around film crews in the hope of being noticed. We first filmed without syncing sound into the process. Before the Revolution there had been sound syncing, but it all stopped during the Revolution, as the censors would review the scripts and we would dub in the appropriate dialogue and sound effects later. It wasn't until 1985 that we were allowed to film and sound-sync simultaneously. There was a big debate at the time around how film and sound should be filmed in reality. Of course, the film teams believed we should film and sync sound to be real, but the censors didn't agree for many years. Even after the Cultural Revolution, scripts were reviewed and approved before we could film and develop material 'in reality.'"

The change brought on a revolution in filming. During the Cultural Revolution, there were no films imported into China, so the developments of Hollywood and Western film techniques never touched the Chinese industry.

"To be honest, we had no idea about how to do sync sound. We just had no experience. Gradually, real sound was reintroduced to film tracks. The first ever film to have this was made in 1988 by Yie Shan. It was called *Wild Mountain*. It was awarded the Golden Cock Award. It was a defining moment in Chinese film-making."

Huang eventually rose to become the Dean of the Graduate School at BFA. He continued to learn English and, in 1996, he had his first chance to go to America.

"In the March and April of that year I was using and browsing the internet. It was early days and I actually got through to the West. I had an old desktop and a telephone modem beside it. I browsed the University of Southern California (USC) and saw an email address there. I just took a bet and sent an email to that address, totally out of the blue. I asked about their film curriculum."

To Huang's total astonishment he had a reply. It seemed that there then followed a series of halting and sporadic emails. Huang took a chance and asked if there would be any interest in USC either sending someone over to Beijing to deliver lectures about the US film industry or invite someone from the emerging Chinese industry, Huang, to go to the US. The take-up was almost immediate, it seems, and Huang was invited. He then had to get his boss to agree and raise the money to fund the visit. June that year found him flying to the US and meeting the person he had sent the speculative email to.

"It turned out that the guy I had emailed was the head of sound at USC. It was wonderful to be able to have the opportunity to meet him and to learn what was happening in the US industry. Better still, we were able to get him to come to

Beijing. He lectured for five days and we arranged two days sight-seeing as well."

It appeared that the visit was a great success and the relationship with USC has persisted ever since those early days. The head of sound at USC subsequently reported on the visit to the Dean and, in 1997, the Dean visited the BFA.

"She came and said that my language skills were good enough to lecture at USC. So I was able to spend a year there teaching students. The class was known as the '3/10' class and became a very famous production class in the history of the USC undergraduate school. I went with my wife and she undertook research on Chinese films, also at USC. Before the mid-1990s directors were from the fifth generation of Chinese film. They all grew up with the old traditions. We knew we couldn't just throw away the old ideas, but we had new ones of our own too."

Huang explains the 'generations' of Chinese film makers. He belonged to the famous 'sixth generation' which followed the generation who had pioneered, and created greater interest in, Chinese films abroad. There were films such as *Red Sorghum* (1987), *The Story of Qiu Ju* (1992) and *Farewell My Concubine* (1993).

"All films of the pre-1989 era were about the traditional emotions, family and the conflicts of the generations. After the mid-1990s, there was a new generation (sixth) of Chinese film, with a more Western feel to them. Films switched a lot to meet international cultures and tastes. The old generations' influence became less and less. Our generation has a culture to encourage people to be positive and to grow. We consider films to be an element to influence people's feelings. The government still wants all films to be a tool of propaganda about positive living, but it is also what the cinema goers are demanding, so both are in sync."

Chinese films are now winning awards. The recent Silver Bear Award at the 2014 Berlin International Film Festival was given to the Chinese-made film *Black Coal Thin Ice* and more are expected.

Huang explains why he believes the awards are now coming thick and fast.

"There has been a refocusing by directors on specific people and the individual, rather than the general story or a group of characters. This is becoming a more accepted approach as the big directors take a stand on this new style."

Huang is one of the most experienced professors on Chinese film today and he says that it is essential to be able to 'read society', to be able to bet on the next big wave of social consciousness, which will fuel successful and big box office hits. There is still rapid change in the economy, culture and emotional engagement of the people and this needs to be carefully and delicately anticipated.

"It is a very dynamic market. One day it is one thing and the next it is something else. This means that the film industry is very dynamic. Indeed, young students can be very successful if they hit the top of a cultural wave. However, you also see films crash and burn. There was a recent case where the predictions were for a ¥1.0 bn (£110m) box office hit but, on release, it only made around ¥0,5 bn (£50m), about 50% of the prediction. You don't make money when that happens!

"The industry has to guess the audience's taste even before they might actually have it. It is a nightmare for the industry and the investors."

It seems as if the small investors are being left behind as the larger, increasingly international ones, from the US, Hong Kong, Taiwan and even France, are taking a broader bet on a series of projects. They are also accepting low returns on some, in the hope of a windfall on others. There are signs of individuals, as well as institutions, backing Chinese film. Huang explains that some savvy investors are providing seed funding to student directors and small production houses to get an international award which will catapult them to fame. Then, on the back of the award, the next film from the director can gross huge returns on the back of a much lower, 'made you famous' contract. Here, the student or young director pretty well seems to sell their soul for the fame and gives up the returns to the investors. But then it is their choice and everyone wants to be famous in this industry. It is not populated by the shy, retiring types.

"So what is your prediction for the future of the Chinese film industry and cinema goers here?"

"When I look forward, I think there is still room to make money. The 3D technology and new sound systems will bring new techniques and also new audience experiences that will make money. There are big developments in sound, films like *Gravity* and *Interstellar* have been enormous successes in China, as well as globally. The Chinese don't make sci-fi movies and they have stolen some share here. Comedy will certainly work well into the future in my mind. The retrospective theme film will also be successful. Talking about when people were growing up, the sky was blue and the grass was green. This will continue to touch the hearts of the Chinese cinema goer and a large segment of the population. So millions will flock to watch these sorts of stories and millions will be made on the back of them.

"In the past, movies were used for the propaganda and educative purposes of the government. Now they are more for entertainment. Now they have layers and the shots must be more complex, the films are more technically difficult and creative. The demand of the audience is much more complex, much more open-minded. Of course, the stories have some significance, to teach the people something of a moral lesson, but they have to entertain first. The changes in the industry are a metaphor of China and have been a mirror of the changes in China."

Huang's life mirrors that of both the Chinese film industry and China's recent history. The story of film has changed dramatically in China, as has Huang's life. I feel that I have been the recipient of one of the best ever lectures on the history of the Chinese film industry. I am sure there are millions of words written on the subject, but to hear it first-hand, from the mouth of one of the most celebrated leaders in the industry, has been an education and a privilege.

OF HEROES AND LEGENDS

It is a better part of Beijing. The tower block complex is cleaner and better kept than many I have visited and all the lifts work. High above eastern Beijing, the clean and spacious duplex apartment has been converted into a high tech, high spec office and entertainment space. White is the dominant colour, from the walls and ceilings to the tight designer T-shirt through which Zou Guojun's fitness oozes.

While smiling smart young things tap away at keyboards in the adjoining connected space, we sit in comfortable silence as tea is brought and poured. All is calm and serene.

Zou Guojun has worked hard to get here to the 35th floor of a smart Beijing suburb. One of five children of a poor farming couple from Jianli (湖北监利), his story is nothing short of remarkable. Through cultivating an innate talent, he has managed to rise through the ranks of the martial arts, or Wushu (武术), to become a master, seven times Chinese champion and three times international free combat champion. His nickname was 'The Fastest Leg in Asia' for his prowess at kickboxing. He is the main coach for the national free combat team of China and runs a very successful organization, Hero Legends, founded in 2007, which runs enormous Wushu competitions and contests all over Asia. Wushu is everything – all the martial arts of China wrapped into a full contact and explosive power sport. It is also a beautiful and elegant spectacle when performed in its art form. Guojun's wife, Wang Yin Ping, is a world class practitioner of this aspect of Wushu and travels extensively to perform exhibitions and displays. She sits demurely to one side, quietly listening to her husband.

Completing the sofa sitting group is Liang Mang, one of the better known Chinese lyricists and songwriters. He is also the award-winning friend and muse to Guojun. Liang Mang sports a designer T-shirt with the face of a well-known Western rock star he recently bought in New York while visiting his daughter who is at college there.

"I was lucky." Guojun is quietly spoken but every word is delivered with a precision and power which holds your attention like a vice. "In my generation of the 1970s so many from the rural areas came to Beijing to have a new career. Many thousands came but most had to return to their farms. It was a time when most people's direction in life was fixed, they could not break out from their destiny. The people of the 70s are the middle power of China. Because of our time we all came of age for the Olympics of 2008.

"The Rio Olympics were interesting for China. We had proved ourselves in 2008. We didn't need to do so in 2012 or 2016. The government invested heavily before 2008, our success was well planned and executed. For 2012 and 2016, the British government invested and you saw the results. After Rio, we needed to invest again in gymnastics. Although we are a huge country we are weak in real gymnastics. We may be big but we have limited gymnastic skills. I was chosen to go to university because of my skill."

The line is delivered woven into his review of the prowess of his country's performance at the Rio Olympics.

"What skill?" I couldn't help myself. To interrupt is rude but there is a deeper story here. The conversation is allowed to shift to the personal.

Zou Guojun responds, "When I was young there was a famous film released in 1982 called *Shaolin Temple* (少林寺). All the kids watched it. We all wanted to be like the stars of that film, to escape our villages, to find a way out of poverty from the rural areas where we lived."

Shaolin Temple was a Hong Kong based film directed by Hsin Yen Chang and starring Jet Li. The iconic film holds up Kung Fu or Wushu as the ultimate fighting martial art but extols it as a force of good, not evil. It was set during the transition period between the Sui and Tang Dynasties.

"We all wanted to be like Jue Yuan (the fighting monk

played by Jet Li). We all wanted it but few could achieve the necessary levels of discipline to even come close. Many wished to be chosen – but were not – but I was chosen, because of my talent and efforts."

He pauses for a moment. In an instant we are all there, re-visiting the scene in the film when Jue Yuan stares up at the Abbot, unable to vow that he will not use Wushu to harm or murder. We too are transported in the film's flashback to the ancient time of the Sui dynasty and the start of Jue Yuan's story.

"All parents were full of hopes and dreams for their children to study, to go to university and have a career arranged by the government. My friends and I were the naughty boys though, not good workers. We thought Wushu would be our way to success, that by attending Wushu school we would be able to open up new possibilities and we believed it was possible to change your fate through Wushu. Many children studied out-side the Shaolin temple. At one time it was said that as many as 50,000 people were around Shaolin. It was very hard to do. Most gave up. I didn't.

"In 1986, before I did Wushu, I spent five years in a circus, working and playing with animals. My parents sent all of us, my three brothers and my sister, to Wushu school. They want-ed us to know how to handle ourselves and not to be mistreated in the village. My parents and my grandparents had been only children. They had seen 20 or 30 years of big change and dif-ficulty. At the home farm all they really wanted was to ensure that they could protect themselves and be good farmers. Then over time they became aware that their children and their lives could be changed through study and university. Many children were therefore encouraged to study and move from farming to university to change their lives.

"I saw the possibilities that education could offer and knew that I could not get what I needed from my parents. I had to do it for myself. My wife and I had somewhat similar experiences, she learned Wushu too, from the age of seven. So many different types of kids came to Wushu in so many different ways, rich and poor, from all over China."

Wang Yin Ping smiles gently, then breaks her silence.

"I had similar beginnings to my husband. I come from Shandong Province where I went to learn Wushu. I wasn't willing to be a farmer. I remember saying to my parents. I don't want to work like you are working! If I work like you, then truly I will grow up to be a farmer and I don't want that! I had seen the hard life of rural people and I wanted to find a way out. I saw that the Wushu way could allow me to escape and be more like the city scholars I saw. My family had had to move from Anhui, as my grandparents were landowners."

She pauses and looks through me. As her eyes refocus coldly on mine, I nod knowingly. The exchange is enough. She knows that I know. Of the Red Guard, the purges of Mao, the night murders, the beatings and 'normalization' of the capitalist bourgeois landowning classes in the Cultural Revolution.

"My mother was beaten by farmers."

She breaks into flawless English so there is no misunderstanding. My eyes never leave hers.

"I learned Wushu to protect my parents."

There is a very long silence. No one moves and our gaze doesn't falter until she is certain I have all the meaning she wants to convey.

"We are a traditional family," Zou Guojun gently intercedes.

"Mr Zou is ambitious," Wang Yin Ping smiles again.

" ... and my wife has good taste and knows how to look after our family," smiles Zou Guojun, melting the ice further.

"They are a typical middle-class family." Liang Mang completes the rehabilitation of the conversation. Everyone relaxes back into white leather.

Zou Guojun continues, "We have totally free choice and can go where we want and live where we want. Even though we may be rich or poor, primitive or developed. The important thing is nowadays we have the freedom to choose. We can be ourselves. We are strong enough to be ourselves and this is the most important thing."

I am uncertain if this monologue relates to themselves, the family or China. Maybe all three, I muse.

Zou Guojun performed well at Wushu school. His teachers saw in him something special. He was not only diligent and committed, but had also developed an increasing confidence which allowed him to grow quickly in the skills and disciplines required to make him a great Wushu practitioner. Before long he was admitted to the Wuhan Wushu college.

"There were not so many chances at the time and there were few resources available to the schools, so we had to really study hard to be successful. Very few people got into the college and many failed the course. I succeeded through hard work. The pass rate was only 1/10,000 and many kids failed. But, everyone had hope as the system was equal for all. If you worked hard and were the best, then you passed. If you didn't, then you went back to your farm! In those days, everyone had the same chance. Resources were limited and there were few choices available to better yourself. You could only change your destiny through effort and hard work, otherwise you had to resign yourself to your fate. So the goal was to get into university, then you would be allocated a job by the government and you would be set up for a good life."

This notion of destiny and fate runs deep in the Chinese psyche. There is a real sense that your life is determined by greater forces than you can control.

"Young people today have a totally different attitude."

I am brought back to the bright white room from my musings by Liang Mang.

"The younger generation is lucky. We've been through a lot and had a lot of difficulties to overcome. Now it has changed.

This generation is free to pursue what it wants to do. It has a more capitalistic attitude. They are working hard for their own goals which are very different than those of their parents. Their standards of success and opinions are very different from the past. Many are addicted to computer games and dream of being a game hero, not a Wushu hero. While it is good to be different, I am worried by this trend."

In China these differences are stark. The speed of change is so fast and so acute it is not just the grandparents who are bewildered, even young parents can't keep up with their own children's changing attitudes. These social changes, many of them driven from an emerging middle class with money and a willingness to spend it, are reshaping China. Some would say not for the better.

Liang Mang, a devout Buddhist, warms to the need for China to expand and reengage with its culture.

"Culture is very important, the arts, music, health, they are more and more important to China now. We have been building too many buildings, the economy is growing too fast. We must think more about our culture. When I was young, even now, I liked rock music. But we were not allowed to listen to it openly. We could be caught and punished for listening to Western rock music. It was regarded as unhealthy music. You could be caught by the police and there would be big trouble. In Beijing in the 1980s, if you were caught wearing jeans, then people, mobs of people, would catch you and cut the legs off the jeans you were wearing, in the street!"

It is becoming clear that Liang Mang was no ordinary student in those days. The late 1980s in China and, specifically, in Beijing were times of tumultuous change and political, as well as public, strife. While few people ever talk openly about the events of 1989, the student revolts and the scenes in Tiananmen Square played out before the world's media, here, though tangentially, those times are being spoken about.

"I grew up loving rock music and founded a rock band in Beijing. We can be very free with our lyrics and the government is now becoming much more open about music really. We want to express ourselves and talk freely about general politics when we perform live shows. But the government remains conservative and, though we can perform and use our lyrics to say what we think, we are still not allowed to do so or express these views through our music in the main mass media."

Herein lies a tension amongst the arts in China. On the one hand, there is clearly freedom of expression allowed and accepted in private shows and behind closed doors. However, mass media remains closely reviewed and the messages managed. Censorship is a way of life for the Chinese and most I know have a broadly cynical view of the mass media messages. However, they are also intensely proud of the ancient, as well as the newly emerging culture of music, dance and other arts across the country.

Liang Mang continues, "The new art in modern China is not strong enough. I am a little pessimistic about this. I believe that art is an important part of having a harmonious society. It is very important that art is still being created and that it is our own, new Chinese, art. I believe that music, painting, dance, literature and other forms are essential elements of a strong culture. I still see China is not a harmonious society. People spit in the streets, there is rudeness and arrogance everywhere. Some parents see this and are starting to discipline their children; they see it as a problem of youth. I don't agree. This is a problem of education. We still have a population of over 700 million farmers, that's over 50% of the population. Schooling is still basic in many places, despite all the progress. We have a long way to go!"

Liang Mang comes from an educated family. His father was a famous 'earth poet' of China. Back in 1989, Liang Shang Quann, Liang Mang's father, was arrested in Beijing for reading a poem in public during the college uprising. He had to write a long confession renouncing his actions and only narrowly escaped with his life by all accounts. Liang Mang recalls his father receiving visits from many people from all over the world, including Allen Ginsberg (1926–1997), the American poet best known for his poem Howl, in which he railed against American capitalism and conformity.

"I remember my father was always accompanied by two officials when he had overseas visitors. They were there to help manage the conversations and what my father was saying!"

From Liang Mang's smile I am pretty sure the officials had had a tough task managing the content of his poet father's skilful verbal dexterity.

Zou Guojun leans back into the conversation, gently nudging his friend into silence.

"This issue of manners and education is important. Two years ago I went to Hong Kong with a very successful businessman. He was talking very loudly all the time. I overheard our waitress say to another one, 'Is he from Taiwan?' He was really very loud and I know she thought he was ignorant and rude. But I said to her, 'Don't despise him. This is his first experience abroad. It's just his habit to be loud, it is not his character. He just doesn't know how to adjust his behaviour to the local custom. This doesn't make him a bad person.' She was a little embarrassed."

My own experience, travelling as I do frequently across the Hong Kong and mainland border, is that, broadly speaking, mainlanders are not welcomed by the Hong Kongese. This is nothing about the irritation of becoming part of the economic powerhouse of Greater China, on which their special status relies and depends, but a good deal more about the lack of manners that the Hong Kong population are so sensitive about in mainlanders.

Zou Guojun makes a very valid point. "You don't know what you don't know."

"People need to be more kind in these situations. The mainlanders such as my friend need a bit of time to know the difference between cultures. People need to have a little patience. I too, as a star and celebrity in China, have to live up to very high expectations and I often fall short. These expectations are the price we have to pay for fame. In Chinese we have a phrase for self-deprecation. We talk about *Zi Chao* (self-mock). It's important to be humble and know we all have to learn about each other and how we must respect the cultures of one another. I know Western people can't tell the difference between Chinese, Japanese and Korean. It's like we have to be excused for not telling the difference between Americans, British and Australians. Rural people in China are also different from the city people. To despise them is understandable but wrong."

The conversation explores the hopes and dreams of the differing cohorts of Chinese, from rich and poor, city dweller and farmer, government employees and entrepreneur. The China Dream, as espoused by President Xi in his early speeches upon taking up office, pervades the thinking of every Chinese person I have ever met. It enters our conversation with a predictability I have come to expect.

"We have all seen the changes here," Zou Guojun concedes. "The government continues to encourage people to let fair competition rule the markets and for all of us to pursue a freer approach. This country is worth loving. I am so very optimistic about China and our collective China Dream. Mr Liang Mang wrote a famous song about the China Dream. It has very practical lyrics about the realism of living in China, in a city, in an 80 square metre apartment, with a wife and the chance to travel."

Zou Guojun starts to sing and there is a collective soft and revered murmuring of the words from the adjoining sofas as Wang Yin Ping and Liang Mang smilingly join in. The words of the chorus are the most poignant for me.

"Stand a little higher.

You can touch the dream."

So many Chinese people are trying to do just that.

CHAPTER 36

MARRIAGE AND WOMEN'S EMPOWERMENT

Lanna Wu is unusual. She is from Inner Mongolia (内蒙古), from the steel-producing and polluting provincial capital city of Hohhot (呼和浩特). She speaks perfect English with a confidence and poise that makes you forget it is her second, if not third, language. She speaks Chinese and was also taught Mongol as a child. She was born in 1981. She is unmarried, by choice, and resolutely refusing to marry someone her parents think is suitable.

"I will find the person I want to marry for love, not for society."

Lanna moved to Beijing in 2000 to complete her first degree in English and International Trade. Then she went to the UK in 2004 and spent time with several UK companies, ending up as a project manager for the Greater London Authority.

"I wanted to do an MA, so attended the London School of Economics and got it in social policy and development. It took a year and then I worked for a consulting company for a year, looking at Asian strategies for business. I only had a postgraduate visa, so could only stay in the UK for two years, but I'm glad I did."

"Why did you come back to Beijing rather than go home?"

"My parents suggested that I work for the government back home, but I went home for a month and really didn't see myself working for government. There was also huge peer pressure. To get married, conform, fit in. It is a lot less in Beijing. But at home there is pressure from my parents and a wider pressure on them from the locals and friends. I came to Beijing and now work for the European Chamber of Commerce as a business manager. My role is in helping overseas companies lobby the Chinese government and to help them understand the Chinese market."

"What do you think is going to happen with overseas companies entering China?"

"It's going to be harder and harder for companies to enter China. The big companies are already quite localized. They know how to play by the rules. After 2008 (the global financial crisis), people think that China is the big market opportunity but costs are escalating here, so companies are changing their priorities. They are going to other Asian countries. I see the opportunities in China are for the Chinese corporates."

Lanna feels that the state-owned enterprises of China have the biggest chance to grow on the back of the expanding middle classes and the explosion of increased financial security many millions of Chinese now feel.

"Foreign-owned companies have two choices. They can wait and see what happens and grow with the market. Or they can work with existing companies in joint ventures. The market is going to be controlled here and people have to accept that is how it is. Overseas companies will lose patience and go elsewhere. They can't afford to wait forever. For consumer products, China is a market, not a production centre. They can make products elsewhere more cheaply now and then import."

Lanna is impressively knowledgeable and articulate about her work but I sense there is something else that drives this woman.

"What do you do when you are not working for money?"

Her face lights up, I've hit the right nerve.

"In my spare time I am the Chapter Leader of the Beijing branch of the Marco Polo Institute. It was founded by a group of French nationals and we have about 200 people. It provides a platform for young business people to learn more about China. We have regular presentations and share experiences. We publish an annual report and are a think tank, really. I knew the founder of the Beijing Chapter and he left Beijing to work overseas. He asked me to take over the role of leading the Beijing Chapter."

Lanna is a torrent of words and energy, unquestionably passionate about the work of the institute.

"My day job is the heavy stuff. I really think a lot about how I can contribute to making China a better place. I like the fact that the institute is about us all being equals in thinking together about problems and finding practical solutions. I really like the spirit of debate at the institute. I want to apply my knowledge to help society. No one wants to talk about social policy, but at Marco Polo we all share the debate to learn about the important issues facing us. I really want to be a public policy adviser and Marco Polo is really helping me better understand the issues."

I ask her if she can give me some example of the issues that she feels need addressing.

"There is no social pressure through work to get married. They don't care if I am married or not. However, a friend of mine who works at a large state-owned enterprise told me that she has been told that she can't be promoted as she is not married and so cannot be mature! I have friends who are married and many who are not. Most of the girls I know who are not married are working for foreign companies. Foreign companies not only allow you to be you, with no pressure on marriage or meeting the other social norms, but they also give good holidays."

The Chinese business approach to holidays is legendary. The Chinese are instructed when holidays are to be taken by the government. You are usually allowed five days plus one day a year. You have to make up the national holidays by working the following weekend usually.

"So many of my friends who work for the government or state-owned enterprises see no future in their work. They just turn up and show their face. The attitude of the bosses is parental. There is not much incentive to grow and develop."

"What about your parents? What do they think about your approach to life, not being married, working for a foreign business?"

"I am financially independent. I don't really let my parents have control of my life. They are ok with that now. My dad was ok from early on but my mum is still always on edge about it."

"About what?"

"She is trying to match-make for me all the time. She wants me to be happy, but I know what she really wants, which is for me to be stable, and to her, that means married with children. She is always finding eligible men. They have a good job, a *hukou*. She never considers if they have hobbies, what they are like as people. My mum says that doesn't matter. What matters is the stability. I tell her that I'm not on the shelf of a supermarket. Mum often cries when we speak or meet. She thought I was wrong to go to the UK. She said it was the worst thing I could ever have done but I know it was the best thing I could ever have done for me."

This topic is the central nerve of family discord and the spinal column of tradition in China. I have met young men and women who have felt forced to 'tick the box' and move on. Love is often not at the heart of marriage. Instead, it's the craving for stability that their parents have on their behalf in a society that has seen so little for so long. The increased number of divorces is said to be a product of recent changes in Chinese society and the battle of the generations, between tradition and a new culture of financial independence and increased choice for the young, emerging middle class.

Lanna is among a small, yet growing, minority of women who seek wider and greater empowerment.

"I am in control of me," she says. "For many people, marriage is about stability, being cared for when you are old as you will have children to do so but I want to find a partner who shares my beliefs and feelings. Many guys I meet are just partly looking for a box to be ticked. The social pressures are very significant. It is a competitive environment and marriage is on the 'to do' list."

She pauses, deep in thought for a moment, then plunges on into the thick of the subject.

"No one seems to think about the reality of marriage. I have many divorced friends. They married because they felt they had to and then became desperately unhappy. I see the struggle with many successful women I know. They feel they can't be a good wife, mother, daughter, worker, leader. There are those who have seen a wider perspective and have a husband who believes they are equals and shares the housework and the like. They are a different and empowered breed. They have a very different view.

"Even if you get married to a foreigner, you will still be subject, as a woman, to pressure from parents expecting children within a year and then for them to be fully involved in bringing up your children, not to mention actually living with you all the time to do so."

She looks at me to check I am not looking bemused or judging her in some way. I am doing neither. I have lived here too long and heard this story too often. It should be told.

"I face the same challenges as women across China. It's just that different people have different coping mechanisms. I am also a Chinese Mongolian. I am not Han (the majority race of China). I did try to learn the language but really failed. So, I am an outsider in Mongolia, as I speak Mandarin, and an outsider in the rest of China as I have a Mongolian face. I am in the middle."

"And how does that feel?" I ask.

"Some days it is good and I feel proud and some days it is bad and I feel frustrated. Beijing people are quite narrow-minded, as being born and growing up here means that they never really learned about anywhere else. Beijing is the centre of the world for them. They have the Beijing *hukou* and life is easier for them. When you are from outside, then you have to work harder to get what and where you want to be. It's not a problem for me. People choose jobs if they can get a *hukou* on the back of it but I believe that career choice should not to be made by the need for a *hukou*. I am relatively choosy to follow my own life choices. I believe that if I am capable, then I will be able to work out the problems and a way around them."

"Will you get married and have a baby?"

"Yes, I hope so. But for love, not for society. If I have a baby, then I will certainly have to send them for education to Inner Mongolia as that is where my *hukou* is, but I don't worry about that."

"And in five years' time? Where do you think you will be?"

"I want to be as happy then as I am right now. I like me and I want to be able to make choices on my own reasoning and views.

I really don't have a plan as such. I don't see my parents often and I want to build my life now so if I have to go and look after them in the future, I will have had a good life.

"I have a brother who is younger than me. He is 30 and lives not far from my parents so they see him often. That is good for them. I just can't go back too often with my job and my life choice. Every single woman in China suffers from the guilt of knowing they will have to look after their parents when they are older. Of course, I have to go home at Chinese New Year but there is lots of pressure then. A lot of my cousins are already married, so I am always in big trouble when I go home. I have to just sit and listen to everyone asking me why I am not married, when will I get married, am I seeing someone. I know it is their way of showing they care about me but it is very difficult. I don't care personally but, of course, I care about my parents and how they feel they are losing face to have an unmarried 30-something daughter. Every New Year I have to start the year with all the same questions. People only ask because it is the only common ground they can find with me since I am the outsider in almost every other respect. The older generation only ask me because they are concerned, they see it as a failure if you are not married, it is a social stigma."

"Aren't things changing as the new generation comes to terms with urbanization and increased affluence and choice?"

"I don't really see it. One generation is following the other. When I am home I have a role to play. Even my parents don't understand me. I have to play the role of contrite daughter who is struggling to marry. I have to play the role to shorten the distance between them and me. For me, I try not to see myself as Mongolian but rather as Lanna Wu."

She looks directly at me. A determined and defiant look. "I am me!" she declares.

I nod. What else can I do?

"Life is tough but it is tough for everyone. I see a lot of women who are still in a difficult position. Women struggle with the traditional role. I would love to see women stand up and push for more equality but I don't see that in so many of my married friends."

My heart goes out to her. She is quite emotional but she is incredibly strong-willed and determination is tight across her face. Pursed lips and a furrowed brow precede her final comments. Her voice is strong at first, but trembles as she continues.

She addresses me directly, "The longer you live in China as an educated woman," she says, fixing me in a gaze I am unable to break, "the more you realize you have no power. You feel powerless. People like me feel they can't do anything to break the situation. It is fundamentally always seen to be the government's problem, not a personal one. People say 'it's for the government to do this, it's for the government to do that' but I don't agree. It is for people to take personal responsibility to create and affect change. We have a disempowered population, but that's not the government's fault, that is the people themselves. They do not push for the change in society that they crave. China remains 100% male dominated. People do not want to engage as, ironically, they think it will make them even more powerless."

She slumps forward. She is exhausted by the emotion of it all. Her voice is weak now. She is weary and so am I. Time to stop this. What can I say? "Thank you," seems inane and flippant. This is a subject of such depth and emotion that I find myself personally unable to think straight about it.

Lanna has challenged my perceptions of China and of my own society, which at times seems little better in many ways in the area of women's empowerment.

She sighs and stands up, regaining her poise and self-belief as she does. "Thank you. It was a pleasure meeting you."

"Likewise," I mumble.

OF NAMES AND ANIMAL RIGHTS

The car park is one of those plush ones you get in only the best shopping malls and hotels. It has three basement levels and tyre squeaky polished painted floors. It is spotless. I don't usually get around Beijing by car but my translator has one and kindly picked me up this afternoon. We ascend the mahogany-lined lift to the rear lobby of the Beijing Legendale Hotel on the corner of Beidongdanjia (东单北大街) and JingbaojJie (金宝街) in the centre of the city. I remember walking into this hotel about five years ago, and walking straight out again when I saw the price of a cup of coffee.

Today is going to be expensive, I think, as we gather ourselves and our guest onto the central podium which seems to double as a viewing gallery of the rich and famous, as well as a place for afternoon tea.

Wen Bojun is wearing an enormous black semi-camouflage down jacket, a black T-shirt with a huge pink dinosaur emblazoned on the front, baggy trousers and expensive part-laced sneakers. Expensive sunglasses are pushed back on to his mass of black hair and he is wearing iPhone earphones which are permanently inserted, even when he is talking and or listening.

He is speaking into one of his phones, recording a WeChat message to a friend.

"Hello Mr Zhuang Da," he booms, as he pumps my small hand to a pulp in his enormous one.

I am rarely addressed by my Chinese name, but Wen Bojun is determined to get things off to a respectful start.

"How are you doing?" he broadcasts in English.

"Great to meet you!"

Wen Bojun is an instantly likeable, affable bear of a man. He gathers staff around him like bees to organize our table and my translator arranges coffee, tea and a three-tier cake stand which would not have looked out of place in the Ritz in London or the Waldorf Astoria in New York.

"What do you want to know about me then?" Wen Bojun is filming me on his phone as he speaks in English. I'm now wondering who is interviewing who.

"Well, I hear you have had an interesting life. You study handwriting and can tell people's characters from their names and you save stray animals? We could start anywhere really." I decide to get straight to the point. When I had been briefed on him in deciding if he was a suitable candidate for this book, he had seemed odd at best. The stories I'd heard of a self-made man, who has now devoted himself to being something of a one-man animal protection league, were intriguing but a little far-fetched to my mind, but he came recommended against the criteria I'd set so here we were.

Wen Bojun studies me for a moment through his phone then begins his story, recording as we go on, while sending We-Chats between breaths, slurps of tea and mouthfuls of cake.

"I was born in Beijing in March 1972. I'm a Pisces, blood group A."

This one phrase says a good deal; it categorizes him into a specific genre of Chinese, those who experienced certain events, as well as his being typically superstitious. The Chinese set great store by your star sign, the date and time of birth and your blood group.

Wen Bojun trundles on.

"We lived in the area just to the south of Tiananmen Square (天安门广场) in central Beijing. I was brought up and went to school here in Beijing. Then I studied tourism management at Beihang University (北京航空航天大学) for three years and went to Lincoln Business School in Auckland, New Zealand for a year. My parents had both moved to Beijing when they were young and my father was a very talented man who had studied politics and law. He was a wonderful man, a policeman, but he had a short life. He died in 1977. My mother killed him."

"What?!"

"My mother had the wrong name. It affected my father's life and shortened it. That can happen you know."

"Your mother murdered your father?"

"No, no, no. Her name was wrong. It brought him bad luck and a short life."

I was terribly confused now.

Wen Bojun is typing a response to a WeChat message and sends a voice message to another person in his other phone.

"Names are important. It depends on the number of strokes in a person's name. Certain numbers are bad, very bad. Some are good. You have a good name. Do you know you have the same number of strokes in your Chinese name as Mao Zedong?"

" ... and that's a good thing?"

Wen Bojun ignores me.

"I am a Buddhist so I want to help weak and helpless things. I help children. I have saved many children and changed their fate. I have given them better names to change their fortune. It is important to give children a good life."

I am now hopelessly confused

"Have you heard of Whitney Houston, Michael Jackson and Audrey Hepburn?"

I nod.

"Their Chinese names were bad names, and look what happened to them. All of their lives were cut short unnecessarily by their poor choice of names."

He is filming again.

"You understand?"

Not a word.

"Hmmm. Let me explain. Have you studied *Yi Jing* (易经) (The Book of Changes)?"

"I've read it – well most of it. I found it hard going to be honest."

"You did well. Most Chinese people never start it. But, you should know that it is very important indeed in China and to

Chinese culture. I have studied it at the feet of a master. Teacher Ding is over 80 years old and he has studied names since 1958. Master Ding worked at the China Academy of Social Sciences. He was then transferred to the Commission of Science, Technology and Industry for National Defence in Liaoning Province. He went to the courts, the jails, the hospitals, the morgues and the cemeteries of many unlucky people. Specifically, those who died young. He also collected 1,000 names of dead people and analysed everything he could about the circumstances of their lives and their deaths. He looked for a common thread. There was only one. The number of strokes of their chosen Chinese name, not even the name of their birth, but the one they used every day. He determined that there was an amazing correlation between the number of brush strokes in their Chinese name and their lives."

My expensive coffee goes cold. There is an unexpected chill in the air. Wen Bojun studies me intently through his phone.

"... so, your mother's poor name caused the death of your father?"

"No doubt about it. Her name was not good, so she effectively killed him too young. Teacher Ding changed my name too, and from then on I have had good luck."

"Right."

"When I was young I killed many dragonflies."

Wen Bojun looks mournfully at his hands then slaps them together hard. I nearly jump out of my skin.

"I was a cruel boy. I killed them. Sometimes I caught them and stuck them to a pole with pins. When I became a Buddhist, I felt I must make up for my cruelty to repay the dragonflies for my past."

"Okay."

I am beginning to want to end this conversation but my curiosity is too great.

"What about the poor animals?"

I am being filmed again.

"Well, after university I became a policeman in 1995 until I had to leave in 1997. Being a policeman was my first real job. I got the job as my brother was the district leader of Dongcheng Police Station."

"You have a brother?"

"No. I have a younger sister, same mother but a different father."

I avoided the obvious question as to the fate of the second husband. "But you just said you had a brother?"

"No, he was my brother, my friend – I called him older brother. I just called him on the phone and then went over and told him that I wanted to work with him. He was a nice guy and he helped me to get the job. He was a very famous policeman in Beijing. I can't say his name. His name was no good. He was my brother for five years. But his name was no good. In 2012, when I had understood about names, I told my brother that his name was bad and he should change it or he would go to jail. I could tell by studying his name. The next year he went to jail."

"Really?"

"Yes. For smuggling. He became involved in a big corruption scandal. I knew it would happen when he said he wouldn't change his name. He was the director of the customs office at the time and he was arrested. He was not directly involved, but he still went to jail. Bad name."

We pause for more WeChat videos, calls, messages, tea and cake.

"Before the police job, I was trained as a chef. I was trained by a famous teacher of chefs. He had prepared food for Chairman Mao. I got my chef certificate and my cousin in Shenyang (沈阳), who had moved to Auckland, suggested that I should emigrate and work in a Chinese restaurant over there. I had helped him with his visa application as he was a chef and the rules allowed a Chinese national to emigrate to New Zealand if they had a technical skill, like a chef. At that time, there were a lot of Chinese moving out there and there were quite a few Chinese restaurants, so the demand for skilled cooks was huge. I decided that it was a possibility, but I was only 24 years old and I wanted to look after my mother, so I didn't go."

"What made you leave the police?"

"Yes. That wasn't good. I always try to help friends and their friends, and it caused me a bit of a problem. A friend of mine asked me if I could introduce a friend of his to the Chief of Police. I said sure. I didn't realize that the guy was a crook and wanted to get the Chief of Police to intervene in some case against him. It was messy and my big brother said I would not get promoted so I left."

Through the lines, nods and grunts, it seemed that money had changed hands. It seemed the friend of the friend ended up in jail and the money disappeared, though it was all a little fuzzy. It also seemed like Wen Bojun became the scapegoat. In any event, he left the police and went to work at the government tourist travel agency CITS (China International Travel Service) in 1997.

"Most of the clients were from the government and the military. It was good money. It was all official business and I even arranged tickets for Mr Henry Kissinger."

Eventually competition came to the industry and with even some of the banks arranging flights through subsidiary companies and the rise of online tickets, the profits tumbled and he got out of the commission-based game in 2009, having made a decent amount of money.

"I started my own business in TV shopping with a friend. I invested the money and I sorted the contracts. My friend had a good business selling jade and the venture was quite a success until, at the age of 26, my friend died suddenly. He had a bad name."

"Maybe you should choose your friends more carefully," I suggest.

"I didn't know why at that time. It was only after I started studying names in 2012 that I really understood why this misfortune had befallen him. Now I have a business with a partner. We sell outbound travel insurance to the staff of Tsing Hua University, including the professors and the president of the University. But my real passion is saving stray animals."

"Oh. How does that work?"

Wen Bojun leans forward and shows me his phone. A few taps and I am watching some of the most horrific, gory and terrible videos of animal cruelty I have ever seen, not that I have ever seen many before.

"I have a big WeChat group of ordinary citizens, mainly in Beijing, but also all over China. We are trying to draw attention to the cruelty to these defenceless animals. There are many stray cats and dogs on the streets of many cities in China. Even here in Beijing. There are not only professional catchers who capture the dogs for certain restaurants, but even some corrupt policemen in Beijing who round up the strays and take them to dog homes. But in other cities we know that some corrupt police catch cats and dogs then sell them through middle men to make money. We know thieves are also stealing people's pets, killing them then selling to restaurants. In northern China, it is very cold so people eat dog. They believe that the meat is good for the prevention of getting cold and helps the body in the cold. It is barbaric in our minds."

We discuss the Royal Society for the Prevention of Cruelty to Animals (RSPCA) in the UK and other such charities as Battersea Dogs & Cats Home in London. Wen Bojun is amazed and deeply interested in obtaining more information. Within seconds the website is circulated to his group and replies of applause are returned quickly afterwards. This is a group in its infancy in China. As the increase in the interest in keeping animals as pets rises with the emerging middle classes, so too does the wave of revulsion against animal cruelty.

"My dream is that one day there will be animal protection legislation in China, but it will take a long time. There is no incentive for the government to act. They have many other priorities to enforce before they get to this one. At last year's National People's Congress in the Great Hall of the People here in Beijing, there was a segment where the government encouraged ordinary citizens to give a proposal before the Congress started. It was said that if a proposal got enough votes, then it would be considered by Congress for enactment. We mobilized so many people in 24 hours and an animal rights petition was placed before Congress. It had the most votes for any proposal. We were elated."

"And what was the result?" I ask, already knowing the inevitable answer.

"Nothing. It never got through. We were so disappointed and depressed. But we will keep up our campaign, we will push for the rights of animals and against animal cruelty in this country. I believe we will succeed eventually."

Seeing those videos, which still haunt me, I really hope so.

THE
LAWYER

Oliver Zhang is a product of the new China. Born in Hangzhou (杭州) and educated in China, in law, he spent two years in the UK at Nottingham, then Exeter University in postgraduate studies, before returning to China to work. Now in his 30s, Oliver is a successful lawyer in Beijing, having spent ten years in practice. But he has great ambitions to go further still.

During his time in the UK he fell in love.

"I fell in love across the political divide," he says wistfully. "My girlfriend was born in Taiwan from the Chiang Kai-shek side of politics. That meant we were always going to find life a struggle. I am from the mainland and she held a Republic of China passport. I remember when she had to go back to Taiwan and I saw her off on the aeroplane, I was speechless. We loved each other very much but we didn't know if we would ever see each other again because of the political differences between Taiwan and mainland China."

Soon after she left, Oliver returned to his home town of Hangzhou. They kept in touch.

"In those days (1990s) there was no international telephone link out of my home town so she used to phone me almost every day. We couldn't phone out but she could phone in."

They resolved to overcome the difficulties and marry.

"Her father was against it. He had fought against the communists during the civil war. He felt she was marrying the enemy. I remember listening to that call from him. She was so embarrassed."

They married.

Oliver now has two young daughters living with his wife in Taiwan. He has spent months away from them and expects to continue to do so for at least another year. Furthering his career has meant some five years in Shanghai and, more recently, five more in Beijing, now in an international law firm. He speaks perfect English, with an English accent, rather than the mid-Atlantic one common in English-speaking

Chinese, often educated in the US or by American/English teachers in China.

He worries about the education of his daughters and how to bring them up. "My wife and I talk about this all the time and I spend a little time each day considering my responsibilities. I think about how to support them in having an international perspective on China, proud to be both from Taiwan but also from the mainland. It is a challenge, but I am determined that they will be able to benefit from the developments of China. They are part of the new generation of hope for the future, when we will all be just Chinese, not Taiwanese or mainlanders."

There is another departure from the norm for Oliver and his wife. The young parents of today in China work, often away from home, like Oliver, or for long hours with long commuting into the cities where the work is. A daily slog of two hours in each direction is not uncommon in Beijing. As such, it is the grandparents of China who are bringing up the next generation. It is a situation Oliver and his wife do not feel is in the best interests of their children. His mother disagrees. "I need to help her, though it is our decision," he muses. "It is difficult for her to accept and I know she feels a little lost and without purpose, but we really feel that the girls must be brought up by their mother and father. Not only will this mean that my wife and girls must come to the mainland to live as soon as possible, but also that my mother must come to terms with our desires for our children."

This decision on their children is a joint one between Oliver and his wife, another departure from the old ways of being male-dominated.

"We speak every day and all our thinking is collaborative and joint. I miss them very much. But I know it will not be forever and we will have a good life together."

Oliver pauses for a long time.

"At the end of the day I am a southerner and that is also a consideration." In this short phrase lies another of the Chinese complexities. In a country, the size of Europe and more, it is inconceivable to most people that its diversity of geography can possibly be seen the same or treated the same. "It's like comparing the French with the English or the Italians with the Danes," says Oliver. "Here, we all share the same basic language, though many different dialects, but that's about it. The differences between the provinces and, specifically, the northerners and the southerners, are immense in culture, ways of doing business, attitude, style of acting and so many other things."

Oliver expects to go back to Shanghai to further his career and, in an ideal world, to return to his home town of Hangzhou.

"It's in my blood," he says. "I am proud to be from Hangzhou and I want the city to be successful and believe I can be part of, and contribute to, that success. At the end of the day, it is less than an hour on the high-speed train from Shanghai, which remains the international and commercial hub of China."

As Oliver is a lawyer, we discuss the changes in the profession in China. It is a very different system to elsewhere in the world and a complex web of evolving, as well as old, law.

"There will be more change," speculates Oliver. "I see more and more Chinese firms of lawyers working to collaborate with international firms. There is incredible consolidation in the profession and mergers are regularly announced. As more and more Chinese businesses look overseas, and international businesses expand in China, there will be a great opportunity for business development. His firm is already expanding and work is being done in Kazakhstan and other states on the borders of China, as well as across the Association of South East Asian Nations (ASEAN) region.

The professions – law and accounting, in particular – are relatively young, with many firms spawned from the government changes in the 1970s, when hitherto government departments across the land were cut loose to compete in the market economy. Also, the old ways of work being given to friends, through the time-honoured notion of *guanxi*, is changing. It has by no means gone away, but the next generation of law, tax and accounting professionals is forging new relationships based on quality of work and market reputation, rather than relationships and introductions alone.

"Clients are changing too," says Oliver. "They are looking at your credentials as a firm and as an individual, not just how well their boss knows your boss."

As this consummate professional discusses family, business and Beijing, there is a distinct flavour of change in the manner and words he uses. There is a palpable enthusiasm and optimism, as well as a willingness to embrace the differences and difficulties of China's turbulent past and to move on.

"I am excited about the future for China and I want my daughters to be part of it," he says. "I want to be part of it. Things move so fast here and there is so much opportunity. I know I need to be at the front of the charge, as those who are first will win long-term advantages. The West needs to understand that we are not going to wait around to get it 100% right first time. We will try and maybe fail, but failure itself will spur both myself and my country to greater things."

CHAPTER
39

THE CHEF

On the top floor of possibly the most expensive shopping mall in China there sits a suite of restaurants known, to those that need to know, for their stylish decor and high end cuisine. The customers are the high rollers of the country. The British owned coffee shop on the second floor of the mall is one of the best turned out in the world, occupied by the sofa slumped figures of expensively dressed businessmen from provinces all over China, variously barking into mobile phones or deep in contract papers and sales figures with customers or business colleagues. Elsewhere their fur draped wives, girlfriends and/or mistresses, and for some no doubt all three, shop.

The Beijing Kitchen is vying for them all.

As I am ushered into the post lunch clean and elegantly simple surroundings of light wood and leather, Ku Chi Fai rises to greet me from a table of his head chefs, seated in regulation black chef's shirts with gold embroidered logos and personalised names.

I've never met a celebrity chef face to face before and I'm slightly in awe as we take a seat in a quiet area away from staff soundlessly sweeping almost non-existent debris from every conceivable corner of the place. Along one wall there is a huge glass window exposing the efforts of the highest quality preparation to anyone who feels the inclination to examine the kitchen.

Ku Chi Fai, or 'Chef' as I can't help calling him, has sad eyes.

"I was born in 1963 in the District of Guangzhou in Southern China, just over the border from Hong Kong. My father worked in Hong Kong and I lived with my mother. He left before I was born to earn money there. Unfortunately my mother died when I was 14 and I went to live with my father in Hong Kong. At the age of 15 it was really hard to find a job. I had no qualifications, I could only really read and write and wasn't a learning type. I ended up in a restaurant as a basic low level kitchen apprentice learning to make dim sum.

A relative introduced me to the owner and he decided to get me working."

He was paid nothing and was given no holiday but he was fed. Hong Kong had strict child labour laws under the British who were still there at the time and there were high fines for those found to be employing child labour, so the establishment got round it by simply not paying him at all. Then at the age of 17 his father died.

"It was hard." Chef Ku smiled at me but his eyes held tears. "I was just so sad. To have my mother die when I was 14 had been such a blow and now my father. I had nothing in the world. I was fortunate not to go down the path of so many and descend into the mafia (the infamous Triads of Hong Kong) and every night I used to cry myself to sleep or wake in the night crying. No one was there to console me. Just me in my room, crying, falling asleep, waking, crying and falling asleep again."

"I learned in those days that there is no one who can help you except yourself. My relative in Hong Kong came to see me to console me but he couldn't. I know he was worried I would become a bad young man and get into the bad ways but I didn't. Somehow I also managed to avoid falling into a total depression. Then I went out and got a temporary motorcycle licence."

Chef Ku next recounted in gruesome and graphic detail the motorcycle accident which resulted in his left hand being all but severed from his forearm, the shattered left shoulder and the near death experience of the traffic disaster that almost ended any hope of ever walking let alone working, again. His body still displays the white scars of what must have been horrendous injuries.

There is an old Chinese saying that if you suffer severe adversity and almost die when you are young then you will be blessed for the rest of your life. Did Chef Ku believe this?

He looked steadily into my eyes.

"No."

"I see."

"It took me almost a year to recover. If I hadn't had been in Hong Kong and had the health care and support services they provided there then, I'd have died. I was in hospital for months and I realised that I needed a skill to survive the rest of my life. I also realised that success and good fortune only come if you are a kind person, if you have a grateful heart and you work very, very hard."

"Do you have religious beliefs? That's very close to the Buddhist belief?"

"No."

"Ah."

"When I finally recovered I decided I just had to work as hard as I could to develop the basic skill I had started to learn, that of a chef. I've been doing it for 38 years now. I managed to get a job and just worked as hard as I could and learned as much as I could every day. Even now I have a daily meeting with all my staff and remind them of the two elements of success, about being kind and grateful and to work as hard as they can."

Chef Ku managed to land a job at the bottom of the restaurant business but he was fortunate to do so at the famous Lei Gardens Hong Kong Restaurant group run by the charismatic S K Chan. Revered amongst not only the Hong Kong but possibly the global restaurant world Chan Shu Kit was, and remains, an inspiration to all his staff.

"Every day Chan Shu Kit had a meeting teaching all the staff about how to be a good person as well as how to cook and how to deal with the things life throws at you. I was so well trained every day, not just about cooking but about mental fitness and commitment. That's why I have such deep basic skills in the kitchen, they were ingrained in me every day. I learned how the raw materials grow, change and can be changed by the application of different techniques and approaches."

He worked for Lei Gardens for 14 years.

"It was like being in the Shaolin Temple of cooking, like being a dedicated monk learning the art of the Kung Fu of cooking. As the monks can deploy the different Kung Fu elements to different situations I learned to deploy the different use of ingredients and the subtle flavour changes of the seasons to master the palate of the eater."

As Chef Ku expounded the skills and knowledge he had accumulated I noticed we had magically been served with exquisite dim sum by reverential staff who seemed to materialise only for the second of plate placement thereafter evaporating to avoid disturbance.

The food was astonishing, and I broke the culinary lesson rather rudely to say so.

His sad eyes silently reproached me gently. He smiled understandingly and nodded. Of course it was good. It was the best in Beijing, in the north of China, in China, possibly in Asia. He said nothing and I mumbled my gratitude.

"It will help your flu."

How did he know I was recovering from a virulent and bed confining dose of Asian flu? I realised that this master of culinary Wushu knows all.

It did help.

"I finally left Lei Gardens in 2005 when a friend introduced me to the chance to work for the Ritz Carlton group in Osaka in Japan as the Executive Chef. I talked with the Lee Gardens boss and he said I should try it and branch out to do something new for me. He was so supportive and said for me to go but if I didn't like it I should return to the Lee Gardens and they would be glad to have me back."

How was Japan?

"I worked in the Osaka Ritz Carlton for four years. But the

Japanese people don't really know or understand what is good Chinese food and what is not. They tend only to order roast duck or bean curd or other basic dishes. I couldn't really express myself through those ordinary dishes. Any chef could cook them and I wanted to rise above just any chef."

Chef Ku yearned to return to China, not even to go back to Hong Kong. Through the Ritz Carlton Group in Asia he got to know that the Ritz Carlton in Beijing was looking for an Executive Chef. One of the absolute requirements that was being sought after was that any Executive Chef applying for the role must have worked at The Lei Gardens in Hong Kong. He took a flight from Osaka to Beijing for the interview and then prepared a meal for the owner and got the job.

"I worked at the Beijing Ritz Carlton for seven years until 2016. They were great years."

Did you cook for anyone interesting?

The names fell like confetti. Chinese and global celebrities, as well as the rich and famous included Henry Kissinger, Arnold Schwarzenegger, Jack Ma of Alibaba, Hilary Clinton, Nicolas Cage, Tony Blair, the top film directors of China and so the list goes on and on. He has prepared the birthday meal for the Kung Fu legend Jackie Chan for the last three years and many celebrities come back time and time again. Now they have shifted their allegiance to Chef Ku at his new venue, The Beijing Kitchen with its authentic approach to delivering outstanding Cantonese food.

"In 2016 I moved here to become the Executive Chef and also to join with the Chairman of the Hualin Restaurant Group as business partners. He owns the whole of the SKP Mall at Dawanglu in Beijing and the group are major property owners. We have a dream to get a Michelin Star."

I suppose every Chef must dream of such an accolade. What do you have to do to get one I wondered?

"Really it is very hard as you know but basically it's about consistency, creativity in the dishes, the highest quality of service and the quality of the environment. We will strive for this. In the meantime, since Hualin Group is nationwide, we will open in Xi'an in April 2018."

"Of course it is all about the staff. I never worry about people's experience really. It's their attitude that means the most to me. Without good hearts and being good, kind and humble people then they will not succeed here. No matter how skilled a chef is, if I don't feel he has a good heart, then I won't hire him."

Do you have any thoughts about another place elsewhere in the world perhaps, taking the top level of Chinese food to the world?

"I found that the Japanese don't really appreciate Chinese food and last year I went to Canada. The quality of ingredients is very high but it's not great Chinese food, a bit bland really."

I have to admit to being a bit of a foodie myself and we spend a happy time scouring the world for culinary opportunities for Chinese food appreciation. What about the UK?

"I went there and ate in China Town as well as some famous so-called Chinese restaurants. To be honest even they are not delivering true authentic Chinese food. I think the only place where there are enough people who might appreciate it as it should be would be in New York."

We work our way round the city for the best location and end up down around Lower Manhattan on the East Side.

"Yes. Definitely New York."

You read it here first. The Beijing Kitchen – New York. 2020 perhaps?

chapter 40

WANG
THE WISE

Outside in the street there is an impromptu vegetable market going on. There is a crowd of people, mostly older citizens, around a beaten up old van with its side sliding and rear lift doors open to the elements. I am early, but deliberately so, as the old *hutongs* of Beijing fascinate me. Although many were knocked down in the name of progress 20 years ago, the replacement housing still follows the old street patterns. Where further gentrification hasn't occurred, the 1950s and 1960s blocks of seemingly crumbling concrete house communities which haven't changed in generations. It is early November in Beijing and cabbage season.

They are everywhere; cabbages piled high in pickup trucks or old farmers' vans, spewing out of the sides as the doors are flung open to reveal the green delights inside. People are not just buying one or two, but ten, twenty, perhaps even more. Older men and women, wizened by age, turmoil and history battle for the most succulent prizes, haggle for the best price and scuttle away with their bags on wheels, buckets, back carriers or simple plastic bags. Cabbage is a special treat and a winter warmer. In the past it would have been buried in the family compound to emerge later in the depths of winter and provide much needed nourishment and comfort.

I am disturbed from my clandestine observation post behind a telegraph pole, and next to a street vendor's hot breakfast stall by my phone calling me to the now open tea shop.

Actually, this new tea shop has only just had its trade opening and there are still a few finishing touches being placed around by purposeful electricians and others.

It is not Mr Wang Minjie's own place, it is owned by his friend Mr Ji Dong, who I talked with in another chapter.

It is a place of serenity and calm. Beautiful pictures and art adorn the walls, including some photographs of fast disappearing Beijing taken by Mr Ji. White muslin curtains and light wooden tables and chairs complete this temple to tea.

We sit at a long wooden table in the central oval room surrounded by a zen like pebble garden and soft white lit ceiling.

Tea is honoured first and we sip from delicate china cups, savouring the hand-picked and exquisite dried leaves of white tea gathered personally by Mr Ji. It is a rare treat of indulgence.

"My parents came to Beijing after it was liberated from the Japanese in 1949."

Bump!

I am dumped unceremoniously into history.

"They were college teachers, nothing more, and I was born in 1967 into the second half of the Cultural Revolution. When I was a child, and because of my parents, we lived right inside the university. It was the Beijing University of Posts and Telecommunications (Beijing Youdian Daxue 北京邮电大学). It was the Cultural Revolution so the whole of society was in chaos. It was not a good atmosphere to study in as a child but because of my parents I was helped and encouraged to study well. I went to a good middle school in the heart of Beijing. I was very lucky. I was taught to have a good mental attitude. Many of my classmates were not so lucky and their parents didn't encourage them to study and progress. My way of thinking is quite different as a result. Through encouragement from my parents I ended up going to university in 1980. This was a time when China had its great opening up and the open-door policy heavily influenced me. I read lots of books and was open to lots of ideas, including Western ideas about the arts, history, literature and of Western and Chinese culture generally."

Mr Wang is an intellectual. A well-educated, quietly spoken man. Dressed in a traditional Chinese jacket and felt coat, he is composed and unhurried in manner and speech. He is a lover of traditional Chinese culture and an accomplished practitioner and teacher of the ancient Chinese musical instrument, the *Guqin* (古琴).

"The last 30 years in China have seen enormous change. Government policy changes almost every year. The Chinese people have changed too in their thoughts and ways of life. It is very dramatic. Westerners can't see it but the Chinese people feel these changes very deeply. When I was in middle school I read a lot. There was a lot of science fiction, books, movies, magazines. They talked of mobile phones and sleek fast electric cars, highways across the country and trains that went over 300 km an hour. Now, in my lifetime it's a reality."

Mr Wang sips tea and pauses. It is not a dramatic pause, there is no ulterior reason of effect he wishes to create. He simply stops to drink tea. All is calm. Time passes serenely, nodding at Mr Wang as it does.

"I have three observations about the situation."

We sit to attention respectfully in the presence of the sage.

"Firstly, I can see that China is on the correct path. Politics is conducted in the correct manner. Many different thoughts and talents are being used for the benefit of the people. The country now encourages people to follow their own thoughts and abilities."

A pause for tea.

"Secondly, the big changes China has experienced recently means that the Chinese people have enormous creative energy ready to be released if it can be encouraged by government."

Tea sipping.

"Thirdly, the special features of the Chinese culture have now been shown to the world. This is good."

There is no need for me to respond – these are facts. Mr Wang folds his hands in front of him. He smiles.

"I studied architecture at university between 1986 and 1990."

Oh. Tumultuous years in Beijing's centres of learning.

"As a university student, it was an interesting experience for us at that time."

Indeed it was, I think, but do not voice any of the crowded questions in my head of student revolt, Tiananmen Square, 'Tank Man', the Red Guard and the tumult and turmoil which followed.

"It was the early period of the open-door policy, Shenzhen city became the first Special Economic Zone and a lot of people were finding new ways of making money. Rock and Roll and popular music, as well as Western classical music was pouring into China. We knew about Michael Jackson, Madonna and other Western pop artists. So many new thoughts, new things, new opportunities were influencing university students. Government policies were behind these changes and the increase in the pace of change. After the Cold War, that was the strongest time for Western politics. That was when the US with Reagan and the UK with Lady Thatcher were really strong. After the Cold War, the Eastern European countries and the Soviet Union fell down, collapsed. Firstly, I was shocked by the speed of the fall, shocked by the huge changes. I was also disappointed that all my education of that time, of Chinese culture, of communist ideological teachings, which had been so deep within me, was shattered. When I found that everything was in chaos and turbulence, when I found that the socialist camp had seemed to collapse, I was depressed."

Tea and live, raw, compelling history.

"Unfortunately there was also rife and obvious corruption. It was obvious to everyone. So, on 4 June 1989 I wanted to go to the parade in Tiananmen. We students could feel the corruption. The media was full of it, my parents knew of it and told me of it. There was an atmosphere of corruption which pervaded the city. I hated it. We all did."

The room is electric; Mr Wang delicately and cleanly steps through the years of fog. His friend is watching him nervously. This is a delicate tightrope of political history.

"What could you do?" I asked. "You were just students."

Mr Wang fixes me with a calm gaze.

"It is not only the young people in China, but also those around the world, who have political opinions in turbulent times. On that day, 4 June, I did not go anywhere. I lived at home with my parents and they kept me there. They forbade me from going. Almost all the students joined the parade that day. I did not. So, my knowledge is the same as yours. I saw the same videos you saw on the news websites."

Calm eyes meet mine. No sign of anything but facts.

"After those times I started to think more deeply about politics. What is politics? What can politics do to affect a country? Then I read more and more about politics and about foreign politics and its effect on Western and other countries and their cultures. Little by little, the conclusion I came to is that the events of 4 June and the simple enthusiasm of the students was utilized by powers high above us for international reasons, political reasons. That event had far more political reasoning attached to it than we are aware of. It was not just about the students. The Cold War too. That had a political purpose not just towards China alone, but to all communist countries."

A pause for thought, for all of us in the room.

"Then I went to work at a construction company for a year after graduation."

Lesson over. Or so I thought.

"I was there for less than a year. I didn't like it. I went to work at the Yan Huang Art Museum (北京炎黄艺术馆) and worked there for almost six years. I organized many things at the museum as there were not many staff, so I got to do a lot of things. I was involved in everything from organizing exhibitions to warehouse management. The money was not good though and since it was at the time I needed to get married, I decided to go and earn some money as a salesman in Zhongguancun (中关村), (the Chinese equivalent to Silicon Valley).

I needed to get enough money together to get married so I sold machines for IBM and Siemens."

Having met his wife at the museum, he spent a short few years earning enough money for his marriage before the lure of the arts scene dragged him back to work at another art museum. He married in 1997 at the age of 30. Without much money the newly-wed couple lived with Mr Wang's parents to start with until they were able to move to a small one bedroom apartment provided to them by his wife's company, as she worked in a government office as an editor for a government magazine. They were lucky.

"I then managed to get a job with a place called Today Art Museum and worked there for three years until I was able to open a tea house in Zhongshan Park (中山公园) with an old friend from college. This had been our dream since university and to do it was such a pleasure. It was a very good traditional tea house but it was a struggle to operate it so we sold it after a few years in 2008."

The arts drew Wang Minjie back like a magnet and he devoted himself to study and artwork. He became a *Guqin* teacher and focused on his learning of Buddhism and traditional Chinese culture. His skill of the 5,000 year old instrument brings him a steady string of students, as does his teaching of traditional Chinese culture.

The sage in him speaks again.

"*Guqin*, chess, calligraphy and drawings are the four crucial elements for people who love Chinese culture. I express my love for traditional Chinese culture and our history through the drinking of tea, the wearing of traditional costume and also through my thoughts and spirituality. Most importantly I am a follower of the Confucius way of thinking, dealing with people and the matters of life. Confucianism is difficult to express in a few words but it is an order of things and the social ethics of the family and social relations. There are five elements of social morality. They are: kindness; personal loyalty; respect, politeness and courtesy; wisdom; and trust and keeping your promises.

All of these apply to every aspect of life. The five elements are the basis of society. I practise these in daily life. The application of these is also important for government and the management of a country. Like the influence of *The Bible* to Christians, Confucianism is the basis of civilization."

He fixes me with his calm soft eyes once again. No smile. These are the truths he wishes to impart.

"I believe that Confucianism is the belief that is best suited to most Chinese people. In this world there is no one belief that is suitable for all people. It needs time for us all to see which belief works for us. For example, in order to align with the needs of all the Christian people, the religion itself has experienced many changes. We Chinese are very flexible to changes and we are even used to adapting to big changes."

He leans forward and adopts an almost reverential tone, earnest and deep.

"There are many reasons for our adaptability, but the Chinese people believe that core of change is explained and expressed most practically in *The Book of Changes*."

The Book of Changes or *I-Jing* is one of the oldest 'books' of Chinese culture ...

"I have a study room in my house. I have given this room a special name. Ming Yi (明夷). Ming Yi is one of the 64 trigrams of *The Book of Changes*. This trigram means earth is up while fire is down. It stands for 'the light is hidden'. Corresponding to the situation in society, it references that the power of social morality is currently weak.

"Those who are good and kind are not encouraged to shine and find it difficult to survive. In this situation, *The Book of Changes* advises that you should withdraw from society and hide one's capabilities until the time is right for them to be appreciated again. In China so many people have such a desire for wealth and power it is not easy for a good man to live in this society. I have reflected on this and decided to withdraw."

"Do you not feel you can do anything? Can you not show others, by example, the way of good and social order?" I ask.

"I have not withdrawn totally. I wish to be an influence for good through the example of the application of traditional Chinese culture. This is why I play and teach the *Guqin* and Chinese culture."

I nod, trying to understand this gentle and highly intelligent teacher.

There, is, however, one more thing he wishes me to understand and appreciate.

"Since the Qing dynasty and the Opium Wars, China has lacked cultural influence for 200 years. I want to positively influence society and people to regain their cultural confidence. The British Empire had cultural confidence. Yes, you did some bad things, you destroyed things, and you did some terrible things to China and other places but you moved the world forward. Art, technology, industry and many other things made great contributions to the world."

Right, thanks, I think?

"Now, so long as the US does not start a war with China, then I think China will be stronger and stronger. Along the way of human history, the US started all the world wars. When Empires declined then the US came. The Qing dynasty declined then came the war and, especially the US, became rich by war. The US is war-like and the world is becoming a total confusion."

Right, really?

The sage has one final point.

"Most Chinese people think that democracy is good but they can't accept the whole of democracy. This is a big debate, but China is not ready for democracy just as the world is not ready for the Chinese way."

On that we both agree.

DONG THE DESTROYER

Outside is all bustle and leeks. It is the autumn season of vegetables and the streets are alive with all manner of modes of transport full of the things. There are vans, trikes and bikes everywhere; laden with cabbages and the biggest leeks I have seen in my life. Beijing is settling into late autumn and the people are stocking up like squirrels.

I had visited the tea house in Lumicang Hutong (禄米仓胡同) just behind Jingbaojie (金宝街) in central Beijing before. Then I had been interviewing Wang Minjie (see his views on withdrawing from society in Chapter 40). Today the place is almost finished with a few electrical items being completed and Mr Ji and his wife Ms Zhang, the owners, are justifiably happy with the result. It is a perfect balance between the traditional and the modern and I really hope it becomes the success they hope for.

"I don't want this place to become an empty shell. We want to fill it with young and old, but we also don't want to advertise it heavily. This is a place for the more sophisticated and discerning, not the general public. I'm hoping word-of-mouth will be its most successful marketing."

Ji Dong has spent a good deal of time, and not an inconsiderable amount of money, creating this place of calm and serene homage to tea and it's time to start recouping the investment.

"This place is owned by the state-owned enterprise I worked for. I used to be responsible for demolishing many of the *hutongs* in Beijing. We wanted to put a bit back into the community."

Many have bemoaned the demolishing of the old style, low rise, residential dwellings of Beijing, in what some have described as wanton destruction. Here, sitting in front of me, is the man that signed the death warrant of thousands of properties.

"I really felt I should do something good with my life. I am very interested in Chinese traditional culture and the history of Beijing. I regret that we knocked down so much."

Mr Ji is an unassuming man, bald, with a genial round face, which is the hallmark of the majority ethnic group in China. He is dressed in a traditional collarless shirt and jacket, held together with the old-style toggle fixing. His wife, Ms Zhang, also dressed in typical traditional style, sits quietly and demurely beside him preparing tea. Mr Ji is understandably proud of his tea shop and his knowledge of tea is, at least in my mind, significant. We wait as Ms Zhang prepares some speciality tea sourced personally by Mr Ji from a small village in the mountains of south east China.

"My father worked at the same state-owned business as I did. It was set up in 1986 to improve the living standards of the people of Beijing and they developed a lot of Beijing's residential areas. It was and is a very big company, it's a flagship company called the Beijing Capital Development Group now. When it first started it was called something else then, but after a big merger it became the company it is now, the biggest development corporation in Beijing. It was and is responsible for government backed developments, as well as demolishing the old, poor, dangerous and decrepit residential areas that so many people were forced to live in for so long in Beijing."

Mr Ji started working at the company in 1992 when he was 22 years old. His father being there obviously helped in his application and he had spent the previous two years working in a local leather factory.

"I have good memories of my childhood. I lived with my mother, father and grandmother near the second ring road of Beijing in the north east corner of the road. One big thing I remember was the earthquake of 1976. Even though I was only 6 years old I remember it. There was a fair amount of damage and I remember that we had to live in tents as we were afraid of the aftershocks."

The Tangshan earthquake (唐山大地震) occurred on 28 July 1976. With the epicentre just to the north east of Beijing, it is believed to have been the largest earthquake of the 20th century by death toll. Unofficial figures put the number killed at over 660,000 and 164,000 injured. The region was home to at least one million people and the high population density, coupled with relatively poor quality of dwellings, contributed significantly to the huge death toll.

The Chinese associate significant natural disasters to a major portent of change in society, and this turned out to be no exception with the death of Chairman Mao Zedong on 9 September that year at the age of 82 just 43 days later.

"I have a younger sister too, but when we were young she lived with my mothers' mother as my parents were allocated to work in factories in very different locations. They were a long way apart so we ended up being in very different places. That was how it was back then. They were also allocated houses which were also far apart. They had no choice but to be apart. You went where the government said you went. The houses were allocated when you were married too but owned by the government."

I ask him if he remembers the death of Chairman Mao.

"Of course. I was in kindergarten and on my way home when I saw people with black armbands in the street. I didn't know what it meant or what had happened. I was walking with my mother and saw a lot of adults crying. I thought it was so odd. I remember laughing about it, I guess I was nervous. My mother scolded me but I kept laughing. When she got me home she beat me for being disrespectful to the leader."

Mr Ji enjoyed Beijing as a child and, like so many of that era, remembers odd details which made up the mosaic of life.

"I went to primary school at the age of eight. It was just behind where we lived, on the next street almost. I remember the name of the street well. It was called Anti Revisionism Road and our school was called Anti Revisionism Primary School. It was next to where the Russian Embassy is now in the Dongzhimen (东直门) area. We lived in a flat house compound where there were about seven or eight people living together. Of course, the road names have all changed now. There was a lot of change at that time.

"I recall something odd about primary school. There were the soldiers who came to give us patriotism lessons."

The Sino-Vietnamese War of 1979 was an attempt by Deng XiaoPeng to neutralize what he saw as the Russian influence to the south of China. The Chinese invaded North Vietnam in response to the Vietnam occupation of Cambodia. After a few months of conflict, the Chinese withdrew claiming victory as they did so. Vietnam exited Cambodia but claimed victory over the Chinese invasion too. Known in China as the 'War of Defensive Counterattack Against the Vietnamese' the government of Deng XiaoPeng ordered returning soldiers to visit schools with their stories of victory and experiences.

"There were lots of newspaper and television reports about our victories and I remember soldiers singing famous songs about the war."

Mr Ji spent three years in the junior middle school before being sent to learn about chemicals and leather processing at Technical Secondary School for a further three years until he was almost 20 years old.

"I lived at home the whole time I was at school. We were not a wealthy family so, as soon as I could, I went out to work even though I was in the technical school. I did anything I could. I got a job as a construction worker, moving big steel bars around. I was young and strong then. I also had a job as a salesman, selling workbooks to students and also calendars. It was good money. For a student I was wealthy and I recall going out and buying a top quality suit for ¥800 (£80). My friends were really jealous.

"I do remember 4 June 1989 but I was at home then. We had moved to a place close to Tiananmen Square so I remember looking out of the window that day and the streets being empty. Then I saw four or five people running down the street pushing a hospital trolley. There was no one on the trolley but I thought there was something wrong and someone must have died or been badly hurt for them to be doing that. It's all I remember. It is a sensitive day in Chinese history."

We move on. It was almost 30 years ago and every country has times it needs to leave behind. Mr Ji left technical school and worked in a local leather factory for two years then moved to the Beijing Real Estate Company. However, in his last year at the school, something happened that was to change his life forever.

"One of the jobs I had was working in the school student union where the students would put on entertainment shows from time to time. I was in charge of lighting as the lighting engineer. We had a show that last year and Ms Zhang was in my class and going to be on the stage dancing. It was a great honour for her to be chosen to dance so I had to make her look good for the sake of our whole class."

Ms Zhang smiles shyly.

"What was the dance you did?" I ask.

Ms Zhang lowers her eyes. "I was a break dancer."

In those days, when jeans were banned and Western music was not only frowned upon but actively shut down by both authorities and citizens alike, it was an act of almost outright rebellion to have this type of music and dancing.

"She was great and very beautiful." Mr Ji smiles at his wife and she blushes visibly.

"We started dating and after school each day I would walk her home. We both lived quite close to each other and the school. One day we went to Tianjin on the train together and on the way back we went to have a meal together. Ms Zhang's parents were very strict and they never would have allowed her just to go out to have a meal with me, so our meal was the first one either of us had ever had out away from home. It was a very special occasion and meant a lot to us both."

Mr Ji and Ms Zhang were married in 1995 in a low key affair with very few friends and a few tables of guests. It was, and remains, the tradition for Chinese marriage ceremonies to be grand and lavish affairs, often with as many as 30 or even 50 round tables of up to 12 people at each.

"Our wedding was low key, we didn't even have a wedding car. Interestingly, many of our friends got married around that time and they all had huge wedding events. Many of them are divorced now but we have had a very stable and happy marriage. We could not get married for a long time as all staff had to sign a contract with the companies we worked for to say we would not marry until the men were over 26 and the women over 25. We also had to sign a contract to say we would only have one child. Then when you wanted to get married, you had to get permission from the business to do so. You had to get the permission of the enterprise and the certificate of permission with the correct company stamp. No stamp, no marriage. Then when you wanted a child, you had to get permission again and the right certificate and stamp. No stamp and your baby would not be granted the residence permit or *hukou*. We had our child, a boy, in 2000. He is in high school now in the second year.

"The last 20 years have seen enormous growth in China's economy and living standards have also gone up a lot too. As a couple we have been a mirror of China's development. I joined the company in 1992. I started in the land purchase and demolition department from the day I joined until 2005 when I left that department. I must have been involved in the destruction of thousands and thousands of homes. The last job I did in that department was to authorize the demolition of the housing in the area which is now the new CCTV building in Guomao (国贸). From 2005 to 2016 I have been working in a new department responsible for real estate development."

"Why did you move departments?"

"I was ready for a change. We knocked down so much. I helped to destroy the city I love. We did too much. I didn't want to do it any more. I had a real sense of guilt. China has special circumstances. The population has expanded significantly, specifically here in Beijing. There are so many people and just not enough space. The government had to make some difficult decisions to improve ordinary citizens' living conditions. I remember a day I was working in Xizhimen (西直门 (a suburb in the north west of Beijing just outside the second ring road)). There was a family of nine people living in a 9-square metre house. It was crowded, shabby and of poor quality. There was little we could do to improve things except pull it down. They were quite happy to move to the new housing we were providing for them. These were slums by any Western standards. I'm not saying we didn't pull down some places which we regretted doing later, but there was collateral damage in the planning. Broadly speaking, we were trying to make decisions to benefit the many even though the few had to suffer sometimes. When the Beijing government made a policy to improve public health and standards they were making big decisions. Everyone knew what we were doing and everyone agreed to the demolition. It was the only way to improve the standards of living. I admit it was hard to keep the right balance. It is still hard to do so. I try to regain some balance through photography."

Mr Ji is an accomplished photographer and has taken it upon himself to record many of the remaining *hutongs* and the life within them for posterity.

"I know the policy and it's the right one. I thought what could I do, even in a small way. That's why I do the photography. It's not much I know. But it is something."

As I speak with Mr Ji and his wife, I have a real sense of genuine concern for some aspects of the execution of the current planning policy. He has no regrets for the past, despite acknowledging that they had sometimes been over zealous in the scope of demolition. But he believes that many have benefitted from the destruction of what were badly built, poor quality, cramped places with limited access to sanitation and basic, usually shared, cooking facilities. I have to admit that the UK and many Western cities went through a similar regeneration, just a good while ago. Back to back housing in the major industrialized cities and towns of the West was knocked down and regenerated in the late 1800s and early 1900s, even before the bombing campaigns across Western Europe flattened many residential areas which have since been rebuilt. Has too much gone in Beijing? Perhaps. But it is worth reflecting that few people objected to the offer of new accommodation, sanitation and other facilities. Whether they were compensated sufficiently is another debate, but it is worthy of being aware of the history before we jump to decry the present too much.

"My wife and I have a dream for our son, for ourselves and for China. I want to do everything I do as well as I can, through whatever obstacles I may face. I want China to be stronger and stronger, but not at the expense of other countries. We are peaceful people, we always have been throughout history. I believe that we can all live in this world in harmony and, the better we understand each other, then the more likely that is to be a reality. I really hope the whole world can respect China too and the Chinese people. Of course, some Chinese people need to improve and there are a few who go overseas and are a bad example for us."

"And for your son? What do you wish for him?"

"The same as any parent. We hope he will go to university and be well educated about the world. Ultimately we want him to do something he loves and to be happy."

It's what any parent wants for any child.

PORRIDGE AND MARRIAGE

Miss Zhang Ying was full of small smiles and nods. She had not known what to expect, but now the pleasantries are over and tea ordered she is feeling more comfortable with this foreigner.

"My father was sent to prison and my parents divorced. He was an angry young man. I had been born only a year earlier in December 1956. He was very strong in his criticism of the new socialism and was locked up for his outbursts. He ended up being in prison for over 20 years."

She has clearly decided she can be open with me and the conversation loops backwards and forwards through her life. She describes herself as an ordinary person but there is no such thing in China.

Zhang Ying's mother was from Shandong originally but moved to Beijing with her parents at the age of five. Her grandmother was a business woman, buying and selling real estate as investments, mainly in Qingdao (青岛) Shandong Province (山东省) and Harbin (哈尔滨) Heilongjiang Province (黑龙江省). Her father was in the diplomatic affairs department of the government of the Kuomintang (国民党) but left after the war with Japan, and then the Chinese civil war, started. The Kuomintang was the Nationalist party which emerged after the fall of the final (Qing) Chinese dynasty. Famously founded by Song Jiaoren and Sun Yat-sen, eventually, under the leadership of Chiang Kai-shek, it gave way to the Communist Party led by Mao Zedong which defeated it in the Chinese Civil War.

Zhang Ying's grandfather was on the wrong side of history.

"My mother agreed to the divorce as my father had always loved dancing and going out with other women to dance halls. My mother was fed up with it so when he went to prison she got the divorce. A friend my father had in prison introduced him to his sister and my father married that lady when he eventually got out of prison."

She grins. Zhang Ying turns out to have a well-developed sense of humour.

"My maternal grandmother was very rich from all the properties she owned but with the Cultural Revolution we managed to lose our wealth in Harbin. When my father went to prison, my elder brother went to live with my aunt. Under the law of the time the son of any divorcee could not stay with the mother. Only the daughter could be with the mother, so I stayed with her. When my grandmother died she left all her properties that were in Qingdao and Harbin to my uncle, as he was the first born son. Then when he died the local government in Harbin put a notice in the newspaper about the property, asking for the owner to come forward and claim it, but we all lived in Beijing and never went to Harbin. We never saw the advertisement so the government took it. We never ever got it back."

She grins again.

"My family is a bit of a mess. A sort of bowl of porridge, lots of lumps!"

She laughs. Her humour is irrepressible and infectious. For someone who has had to endure a good deal in her life, she is an incredibly positive and upbeat individual.

"My mother found me a stepfather. He was a revolutionary soldier and had joined the Red Army in 1937. My mother wanted such a husband for political reasons, as he would look after us and protect us from everything that was going on at the time. He became a division leader in a factory. He was a good soldier, straightforward and well educated by Chairman Mao. My mother married him when I was in the third grade at primary school. My grandmother didn't agree to the marriage, she said that the marriage wouldn't work since my mother was a well-educated capitalist from a wealthy and high ranking family, and he was a communist from a poor farming village. She was quite sure it wouldn't work."

But my mother thought if she married this soldier, then it would be good for my future.

She grins again.

"I remember when my mother and my step father were dating, I was there of course. Once day my mother wanted to talk to her new boyfriend alone so she bought me an ice cream and ordered me to sit on a different table while they ordered coffee and chatted. I remember it quite vividly. It was a fair trade! I also remember that my stepfather was already married. He had five sons from his other marriage. He always quarrelled with his wife so he decided to get divorced and marry my mother. Because he was in the army then, his superior had to agree to his divorce and give permission for it all. Those were the days when superiors had total power over their staff and their lives. The ex-wife took the five boys away to Nanjing (南京) and he had to pay for them all. It was a big decision for him to marry my mother. He was ordered to pay ¥20 (£2.0) a month for each boy until they were all over 18 years old. That was ¥100 (£10.00) a month and his salary was only ¥137 (£13.70) a month. My mother was earning ¥50 (£5.00) a month which was relatively high in those days when ¥6 (60p) was enough for the family to survive for a month.

"So how did the marriage work? Was your grandmother right?" I ask.

"Actually, she was wrong. He was from the right political group at a time when it wasn't certain what was going to happen. My mother made the right judgment. She was only 30 years old at that time and very beautiful. Even though there were many more women in China than there were men, because of her beauty and background, she could have had any man she wanted but she wanted this one."

"Where did you live?" This was a loaded question as the stigma of divorce and remarriage at that time was likely to have weighed heavily on the couple.

"My grandmother didn't agree with the marriage so she threw my mother and I out of her house. But the factory where my step father worked, at the Beijing Gas Analysis Plant, was able to give us a small house. It was a start. When I was 12 years old they gave us a bigger apartment which was 49 square metres and we were very happy then! It had two bedrooms, a bathroom and a kitchen."

Then came the Cultural Revolution. Everything changed. Her step father, ironically as an ex Red Army, was denounced for being an 'Alien Class Element', possibly for marrying a wealthy bourgeoisie. Luckily, her mother for some reason was not denounced, but those were strange and turbulent times. They managed to avoid trouble.

"My mother was sent away to a factory to be a cashier. The factory was a long way from the house and from my father's work. She had plenty of time on her hands so she decided to learn English. My stepfather wanted his wife back but it was very difficult, so eventually he bribed the leader in his factory with a watch and somehow she was allocated back to his factory and we were together again. It took him five years to get her back."

Despite the forced separation, her mother had used her time well and the skill in English got her a job as a translator, which meant she was able to work until she was 55, when others were forced to retire at 50 years old. When her mother retired, she had managed to rise to the rank of cadre in the factory, no mean feat for a capitalist, educated and rich woman in the wake of the Cultural Revolution.

"I was 15 years old when my mother went away to work and nearly 20 when she returned. She came back when she was 50 years old. I never went to college. I liked to study but during the Cultural Revolution there was no school. The Party said we had to learn from the workers, soldiers and farmers so there were no classes. I was seen as the only child of my parents. The boys were in Nanjing so didn't count as far as the Beijing authorities were concerned, because of that I didn't get sent away to the fields. I stayed at home as the only child to look after my father. In 1976 I started work in the Beijing Grain Administration as a clerk in the department which checked all the food coupons. I was there from 1976 until 1981. By that time I was tired of working there. My step father didn't want to use his contacts to help me get a new job so I did it myself at 25 years old. I searched for opportunities. I managed to find an industrial company, Haidjan District Industrial Company (海淀区工业公司), which was recruiting staff. It was through some friends. I ended up working in lots of different departments but then settled in supply and sales as a cashier. There were 20 of us in the department and it was quite a good atmosphere."

"Did you get married around then?" As a young woman around 25 she was expected, by everyone, to be married and I understood the pressures must have been pretty intense from home and from her grandmother too.

"I started looking, of course. The first boyfriend I had was introduced by a friend of my mother. He was very handsome, a print worker. His father worked in the foreign ministry. He wrote me beautiful love letters."

She pauses and looks away. There is a long and thoughtful silence. Then a wistful smile and a little laugh.

"My mother and father didn't agree with him. They thought the family was rich and he was too handsome. There would be trouble they said, if we married. So we parted."

It is worth remarking here that this review by parents of their child's marriage prospects was an essential part of Chinese tradition in those days. In many parts of China, parental approval is still regarded as an important requirement. The view of 'too rich and too handsome' for the daughter is not uncommon. The consideration here is that too much family money allows the boy to be lazy and the looks might make him attractive to others as alternatives from the wife. Both spell trouble for retaining the wealth and future of pure lineage for the later lives of in laws and offspring. Infidelity is common among the wealthy of China, Some wear mistresses as a badge of honour and power.

"My second boyfriend worked as a mechanic. A mutual friend introduced us. He was a good worker with five brothers and sisters. This time my mother didn't agree with the marriage so we had to part."

"Wasn't this just a little frustrating?" I ask. A wealthy good looking boy, then a nice stable one, both not good enough?

"I had a third and a fourth boyfriend and my friends kept introducing other boys to me, but we were only together for a very short time and then parted. It got to a point when I decided to be on my own. My parents agreed. Marriage is also destiny. It wasn't for me."

Marriage wasn't her destiny but fate had something else in store for Miss Zhang. In 1989 she was allocated a small 'flat' house, or bungalow. However, in 1996 it was demolished by local developers and she received a 65 square metre two-bedroom apartment on the fifth floor of a six floor building, from her factory. Her company was based inside what are now the extensive gardens attached to the famous yet ill-fated original Summer Palace (圓明园 Yuanmingyuan) of the Qing dynasty. The area had been famously, at least in all Chinese history lessons, burnt to the ground by the Eight Power Allied Force, which essentially ended China's dynastic history. I'm regularly reminded that the British led the destruction. In 1999 the government decided to renovate the gardens and the entire factory was closed as a result. The office was given a substantial amount of money to compensate the retired workers and each received around ¥50,000 (£5,000).

"I had been given that small house the year before the factory closed. As I was single it was very difficult to get a house, but I talked to the committee and they decided that I should receive one. I then managed to buy the house from the company and so I became a home owner. When the factory closed I was ok. I had no husband and no children. I was quite well off."

Miss Zhang had, as so many workers in state-owned enterprises in those days, managed to hold down a few jobs outside while the Haidian District Industrial Company struggled on. It was common for state-owned businesses to encourage their employees to try to develop careers elsewhere. Miss Zhang tried but, after a few failed attempts, returned to her cashier role at the company until it was forced to close.

"I looked for other jobs, and for a while worked at a company producing pens and owned by an American Chinese guy. I was there for less than a year. It was down in Hainan (海南) itself in the far south of China. However, it was just too hot there for me so I quit and came back to the Beijing office, but quit that after two months. Then I went to the Beijing Agricultural Research Institute as a cashier for six months but then that closed."

Miss Zhang's story is a common one for those who were working for state-owned enterprises in China in the early 1990s. This was the time of great change in China and the government of the day was trying everything to kick start the economy. There was a wide policy of encouragement for people to go and try the private sector with low or no risk. Jobs were held open for those who tried and failed, for whatever reason. One could say this was an enlightened time. State-owned enterprises were safe and stable 'iron rice bowls' but they were also slow, inefficient, poorly managed and unproductive. The government hit on the idea of encouraging risk taking with limited consequences. It was an inspired policy and resulted in the establishment of hundreds of thousands of new businesses, many of which failed but some of which have become the largest and most successful private enterprises in China.

Miss Zhang recounts how, on a limited but reasonable pension, she has started gambling.

"When I retired, suddenly I had a lot of time on my hands. At first I was given a pension of ¥1,200 (£120.00) a month and each year it went up so after ten years it was ¥3,500 (£350.00) a month. I'm very satisfied with my life. Happiness is the most important thing to have. But I did have a problem. I liked to play Majiang and I was losing ¥500 (£50.00) to ¥600 (£60.00) a day! I needed to get a job just to allow me to keep playing so a friend introduced me to a job at a local shopping mall where I worked for 20 months to sort things out then I decided to quit. I didn't want to work as I really needed to look after my mother, and not play Majiang so much."

She managed to find a new apartment for her ageing mother.

"Now I cook for my mother every day and look after her. Next year she will move to a special place for the elderly where she will have good care and people to look after her as she gets much older. I have arranged it all. We sold my mother's old apartment and got around ¥1.0 million (£100,000). She wanted to give some money to her second husband's boys so we arranged for them to have ¥30,000 (£3,000) each. My mother can still afford to live and I can pay the rental for her apartment with no problem. The new place will cost ¥5,300 (£530) a month for a one-bedroom apartment with good facilities. It's going to be perfect for her. She gets about ¥4,000 (£400) a month from her pension so with a bit of investments and my pension we are very comfortable. It's all worked out well. And I don't lose so much at Majiang either."

She has it all planned out. Her mother is happy, secure and cared for and she herself will take a trip to Europe during 2017 with her old workmates as a special once in a lifetime experience.

"In the Cultural Revolution, Chairman Mao said that we should use all channels of our own efforts to work hard and have a good life. In 1978 Deng Xiaoping gave us the open-door policy. This was carried through by the Party and China went out into the world. Now China is stronger as a result of all we have done. When I was young, even if you had money, there was nothing to buy. Now you can have what you like if you have money. The standards have been raised and there is a good material life for so many people. I am satisfied and happy with life."

I am left with a real feeling from Miss Zhang that, although she was dealt a card of fate not to be married, she feels she owes a lot to the leadership of China and the Party who have increased material wealth, allowed entrepreneurship to flourish, are lifting the people out of poverty and placing China squarely on the world stage.

Not a bad track record for a country barely as old as she is from her perspective. To her the cost of the Cultural Revolution has been worth it for the China of today to have risen so high from a place so low.

A PROUD MEMBER OF THE PARTY

Mdme Li Shuling opens her voluminous handbag and produces a small digital radio and music player. The song suddenly blares out across the otherwise quiet coffee shop and she begins to sing. After a few bars, she becomes aware of the look of surprised bemusement on my face and stops. No one else in the place even looks up.

"That is one of my favourite folk songs performed by President Xi's wife."

"Oh sorry. Please continue." I couldn't believe what I was saying but this is Beijing and China where people still spontaneously combust into patriotic songs at the drop of a hat. This is a common phenomenon in all sorts of places, from the lift in my apartment block and the local bus, to the parks and other open areas at weekends and early mornings. I have gotten used to it.

Well almost.

She produces a swathe of music manuscripts and waves them in front of me.

"These are all famous and patriotic songs but I do have some others including some English ones. I can sing some more. I have an excellent and strong voice. I sing in Ritan Park (日坛公园) often at weekends and many people stop and listen to me. Many will join in to sing the famous songs with me."

"It's ok, maybe another time." I do remember hearing an older woman singing in my local park, which is, by odd coincidence, Ritan. Maybe it was her, but who knows. There are often people dancing to music, playing instruments or singing in the park and it's difficult to pick out anyone specific.

"I am very proud of myself as I am an excellent woman and the experience of being a Chinese teacher is very enjoyable, even though I don't get paid very much. My pronunciation is excellent and I help many people who want to improve their Chinese."

Mdme Li Shuling was born in 1951 and she has lived in Beijing all her life. Her husband, who she was introduced to by friends when she was 24 and who she married at 26, is now 73 years old. Her only daughter, who she is clearly very proud of, is now 38 and a lawyer in the Bank of China legal department.

"I don't cook. I never have. My husband cooks for me. I have never had time for cooking. I am an excellent woman. I do not do any cleaning. I have never done any cleaning. I have an *ayi* for that. I am an excellent woman. I am a communist party member. I have been since I was at my work. I have worked tirelessly for the Party."

I see.

"Although I was just a worker when I was young I was responsible for 70 people. I started work in March 1969 at the age of 17. 'The Plan' was being implemented when I was young, when I worked for a state-owned enterprise and I lived in the same area in a dormitory with my comrades. When I got married the enterprise rewarded me by providing a house for us. Only five people were awarded an apartment. At that time you had to attain certain conditions and requirements to be allocated an enterprise house. The committee allocated the apartments to those they believed were qualified. There was enormous competition for the houses. I had very good relationships with everyone and I played basketball at the enterprise, so everyone knew me. I had good relationships with five or six committee members, so they were favourable to me and I got the apartment. Other people didn't fight for the apartments as hard as I did. Also you had to pay the enterprise ¥5,000 (£500) which was a lot of money in those times, but I decided I would try, so I managed to borrow the money and I got the house. When I told my husband he just couldn't believe it!"

They lived in a 9 square metres room at the start, but when their daughter was 13 years old, Mdme Li managed to get them moved to a 69 square metre apartment, much to the obvious envy of her colleagues and her delight. They have lived there ever since.

"I want to tell Chinese women that they should not rely on men. Do things yourselves. Chairman Mao said, 'Women hold up half the sky' and he was right. Men can't help you. You have to try for yourself."

She is sitting bolt upright with her finger wagging at me. Stern faced, she lectures me.

"China was born in 1949 and I was born in 1951. So I am China. My life is like China's experience. When I was young I lived in the Gulou (鼓楼) area."

Gulou is the Drum and Bell Tower area directly north of the Forbidden City area. In those days, like much of Beijing just around what is now the second ring road, it was a maze of *hutongs* and factory buildings.

"My father didn't live in Beijing, he worked a long way away as a construction worker and only came home twice a year at holiday festival times. I lived with my mother and two younger brothers. When I was in the second grade of primary school we moved to a small village in a different area of Beijing, to the east part of Chaoyang District (朝阳区). It was all fields around there then and I could easily see the hills. I remember being very happy as I walked to school through the corn and along the country roads."

This is no longer the case. You can now only see the hills when the smog clears and if you live high up on the expensive side of an apartment block in what is now a concrete jungle of high class hotels, high rise offices, shopping malls and expensive accommodation.

"As the first-born child I had to look after my younger brothers. My mother was not healthy and could not work. She had a problem with her spine so I had to do most of the work. Actually, I only went to middle school for two years before the Cultural Revolution started in 1966. Then there were no classes. I joined the Red Guard."

The Red Guard was an often-armed paramilitary group of predominantly fanatical students mobilized by Mao Zedong in the late 1960s to support his political and revolutionary movement.

"We made leaflets and booklets all the time and often worked through the night to produce them. Then we would distribute them to the people the following day."

She sits bolt upright again. Her fists are tightly clenched as she recites the slogans and words of 'The Chairman' from her youth.

There is a somewhat unnerving shuffling around us as other coffee drinkers vacate the immediate vicinity. Mdme Li has declined a coffee, preferring to bring her own water. She has, however, insisted I buy something, as otherwise we will be taking up the space for free and that, she deems, isn't fair.

"I was there on 18.8 you know. When he addressed us all. I was there in Tiananmen Square. There were over one million of us in the square and the surrounding wide streets. I remember we all gathered at our school the previous day at around midnight and went to Tiananmen to wait. He came out at 10.00 and said that the Red Guard were good. We were very excited."

The 18 August 1966, or '18.8' as it is widely known and referred to, was the first of eight rallies held by Mao for the Red Guard in 1966. Mao was mobilizing millions of teenagers to 'turn the world Red'; on that day he wore the same uniform as them, the drab olive green they favoured and became feared by millions. He stood in stoic solidarity with them for over six hours as their leaders made speeches in support of the Revolution.

"We had no teachers. We had denounced them and beaten them in the streets. We were the fire of the Revolution against the Bourgeoisie and elite. I learned so much from my leaders. That my children should be part of the majority, not to stand out or be different, and that for us all to be the same was best and the safest way for all. We often went to the ministry buildings to listen to our leaders criticize and denounce those people who sat in tea houses, the professionals, the intelligentsia, the capitalists who did not follow the true communist way. We really believed that Chairman Mao supported us and wanted us to be the fire in the streets of every village, town and city."

She sits back and closes her eyes, reliving those glorious times which had, in her mind, created the China she loved.

"We had to create national alignment. We all went to different cities to criticize the elite and spread the fire. I remember we decided, my cadre, to go to Guangzhou (广州) by train but somehow we got on the wrong train and ended up in Shenyang in the north. Our leaders said never mind, let's go and spread the revolution in Shanghai, where it was warmer. I was only 15 years old. It was chaos. We got to Shanghai and went to a middle school where we slept on the floor and ate for free because we had our student cards. Then our leaders said we would go to Sichuan Province (四川省), to Chengdu city (成都市), so we did and again, stayed in a school and ate for free. We went to the concentration camp at Xifeng (西峰) outside Chongqing (重庆) where the leaders of the Party had been persecuted by the KTM nationalists."

You can read of these places elsewhere but suffice to say they are ingrained in the history of China as much as the Ming Tombs (明十三陵), the Forbidden City (紫禁城) and the Terracotta Army of Xi'An (西安兵马俑). This part of Chinese history is overlooked at your peril if you wish to even scratch the surface of the real China, grounded, as it inevitably is, in as much of the recent as well as its ancient history.

"We were only 15 or 16 years old. Even our leaders, who we adored, were only maybe 17 or 18 years old. We saw them as our big brothers and sisters. But we had power. We criticized many people, we denounced them. We rooted them out and destroyed them. We were totally out of control. Later the government arrested some of the Red Guard leaders. It had all become very extreme very quickly. Some went to prison and some escaped overseas to be spies. Many of the leaders were being used by people, by someone, I can't say who, I don't want to say, we should not talk about the end of the Revolution."

She descends into a deep and dark silence.

Ok.

"My view of the world was changed by the book *Red Rock* (红岩)(which recounts the experiences of the inmates at the 1948 Chongqing concentration camp). I realized how Party leaders were persecuted by the Nationalists, but also how the Revolution actually succeeded. After the Revolution, Chairman Mao said the Red Guard should all go to the fields and learn from the peasants and workers, to experience labour and hard work. This was the 'Movement of Educated Youth to Go and Work Among the Countryside and Mountainous Areas'. It was a major part of the next stage for Chairman Mao."

She decided she didn't want to go. Most had no choice but she seemed to believe she did.

"I had to stay and look after my mother and my young brothers. I was allowed to stay in Beijing. I started work at the Beijing Pharmaceutical Factory on 8 March 1969 at the age of 17 and worked there until I retired. The Party taught me to work hard for others, for the country. I joined the Youth League at the factory. In 1995 I bought the house we had lived in since our marriage. They wanted ¥30,000 (£3,000) for it and I got ownership."

It is probably now worth in excess of ¥5m (£500,000).

"I have grown up with China. China is 67 years old and I have experienced all that China has experienced. The most ingrained memory I have is of the Cultural Revolution. Since then people have changed, the environment has changed and politics have changed. China can't be China without the Party. Without the Party there is no China. In 1949 China was poor, people were hungry as there were no crops. Now, through the efforts of the Party, we are a great nation of 1.3 billion people. Our lives have changed. Especially since the open-door policy, all good things have come to our country. We have gone out into the world and the world has come into China."

She recounts the many changes in her life she sees as positive, and only because of the stability and guiding hand of the Party. She recalls the first time she owned a television, in 1982.

"I bought it using ration tickets I had saved up. It was unbelievable. Without the Party I could never have done this."

She explains how she has paid so much attention to her daughter's education, something she had never had. She saved up and was able to send her daughter to the best kindergarten, then the best primary school and the best middle school in Beijing.

"They were not too expensive but they were the best. I paid ¥15 (£1.5) a month for her kindergarten and if I provided her with food each day, then I could save ¥2 (20p) a month. It was worth it! Now I have heard that the kindergarten over the road from where I live is charging ¥10,000 (£1,000) a month. It's ridiculous!"

Mdme Li knows the value of money. She would rather buy her water in the big containers and decant it into the same old carrying bottle she sips from during our conversation. She has seen people starve for the want of a simple amount each day.

I ask what her dreams for the future of China are. She turns back on the Party rhetoric. So within her it is etched into her DNA.

"I dream for personal health, to have a harmonious family and no bad things. For China I want us to be stronger, richer and excellent in technology, satellites and space, in our defence and armed forces. I want the world to be peaceful."

She smiles in comfort to me as a foreigner across the table.

"I hope for a peaceful world. Iraq, Russia, Syria all only have problems because of the Americans you know. When I saw the news of a poor baby refugee drowned on the beach of Europe, I was angry that the Americans are so warlike. Even though there are a lot of bad men in the world, even in China, cheating the people, I still am hopeful."

We wind the conversation to a close. She reminds me that she is a poor woman who has given up her time to tell the story of her life correctly, and that she swims every morning and is now learning English, though no trace had been visible for the last two hours or so.

"I am a very excellent woman and I am very happy."

As we leave, I slide a small box of sweets from the UK across the table to her by way of thanks. She picks it up, turns it over, and examines it carefully.

"These sweets are from my home town in Yorkshire in the UK. You can only buy them there. I wanted to give you something personal."

"You are a good man. You understand the Chinese way."

Gifts, and personal ones at that, go a long way in China.

"Thanks."

TEA AND HISTORY

We sit in the old style One Tree tea house in the Haidian District of Beijing. Mdme Lin Yaling greets us with flowing shawl, purple polo neck jumper and elegant gestures. She is immaculately groomed and dressed. We are served in the small private room reserved by Mdme Lin of the upmarket establishment, as tea is prepared and served delicately and correctly. Mdme Lin places her new(ish) Burberry handbag and iPhone 6 conspicuously in pride of place.

"I was born in December 1959 in Beijing. My family have lived in Beijing for three generations, with my grandfather coming here from Fujian Province (福建省). I remember when I was very young, maybe only 6 years old, my friends, my two younger sisters, my younger brother and I would play on Lugou Bridge (卢沟桥). We lived near the bridge at that time and we were very happy to play around there."

Lugou (or Marco Polo) Bridge is ingrained in the minds of many Beijingers, if not the Chinese as a nation, as an icon of the War of The Chinese People's Resistance Against the Japanese Aggression. Its elegant stone arches bridge the Yongding River (永定河) some 15 km south west of the centre of the city. Now preserved for posterity with the building of another bridge close by, it was the site of what historians have identified as the start of the second Sino-Japanese war (1937–1945) with the battle of the Marco Polo Bridge on 7 July 1937.

"During the mid-Autumn Festival every year, we all used to go down to the bridge to see the moon. You have to pay to go on it now! After several years, all the trucks crossing it damaged it so they built another bridge and it became a beautiful place and park."

Mdme Lin pauses to inspect her phone and pick delicately through her bag for something which doesn't emerge. We drink tea from the traditional small delicate china bowls, so prevalent in such establishments. We have our own dedicated waitress to serve us.

It's not cheap tea.

"I once wanted to travel abroad very much. However, a holiday I had in China in 2003 changed my mind totally and I have subsequently never felt the need to travel abroad."

Really?

"We have so much in China. I went on a self-driving tour of Yunan and what I saw was so very beautiful it confirmed to me just how much we have here."

China has many beautiful places.

"I had been very lucky due to my hard work. I was able to afford the self-driving tour. It cost ¥10,000 (£1,000) at that time but I had made a lot of money from having worked in design and landscape garden design for the government."

I see.

"In the days of my youth, Beijing was very different to today. When I was a little girl, even if you had money there was nothing to spend it on! Now you can buy pretty much anything."

She sips tea elegantly. I'm reminded of the quintessentially British afternoon teas of the early 1900s, when elegant women poised delicately in hushed tones with their regulation extended little fingers balancing the Royal Doulton, Derby or Wedgwood 'fine bone china'. Mdme Lin would have fitted in perfectly around the linen clothed tables of Edwardian London or Paris.

"You are English, aren't you?"

I tell her, "Yes." She had asked me this question shortly after I had arrived. Now I understand why. The historical grenade rolls gently across the wooden table then goes off without collateral damage.

"My father went to fight the Americans in Korea in 1952 with the People's Liberation Army."

You can search elsewhere for information on this conflict, known in China as the 'War to Resist US Aggression and Aid Korea'. History records that the combined Soviet, Chinese and

North Korean troops pushed the American army back below the 38th Parallel, around which the current demilitarized zone still lies in suspended standoff.

"My father was a secretary to the leaders at that time. He was only 19 years old. One day a bomb fell very close to the leaders and my father threw himself in front of them as protection. He was seriously wounded in the waist, though he saved the leaders. He was seen as a hero. However, he was badly hurt so the leaders sent him back to Beijing in a truck to hospital and then to a nursing home. Although he was very young, he was unlikely to be able to work ever again as he could not walk, so the government gave him a war hero's pension. He was in hospital, which was all paid for, but every year at the Spring and Autumn Festival, the government would send him back to spend time with his mother at home. They sent him in a wheelchair."

This man was your father?

"Yes. My mother was his mother's neighbour and saw that he had no one to cook for him, or care for him, or look after him. She took pity on him and decided to marry him to look after him. They were both very young. My mother still gets two pensions, one from her work and one from the government, for being the widow of a war hero. My father was so grateful to my mother because she had looked after him, given him children and a good life. He used to do all he physically could for her. He would make tea and washed things as best he could. When she was very bad tempered through her life change later, he tolerated and supported her. He just couldn't believe what this woman had done for him."

Mdme Lin smiles at me somewhat awkwardly. I smile back as reassuringly as I can.

"I was the first born. I didn't have a very happy childhood really. We were quite poor, though my father got a small government pension. I had a heavy burden from a very young age.

My father died in 1998 and then we, the children, had to do everything we could to support our mother, who was then 79 years old. We have a filial duty to give her back some of the life she gave up for our father."

She pauses for another sip of tea and a long cooling silence descends on us.

"What was it like in those early days of your childhood?"

"Growing up in Beijing in the 1960s was a difficult time. The streets were quite narrow in the *hutongs* and there were very few buses then, and no subways of course. It took over an hour to get from our area near the Lugou Bridge to the centre of the city. At that time the bridge was a long way out in the suburbs. Every winter it got very cold and there was no heating, so we all wore very heavy cotton clothing. Also, there was almost no meat. In the winter, we ate a lot of cabbage. It was all you could really get and we would buy it from the farmers. We would bury it in our compound courtyard and keep it throughout the winter. We could only get meat, pork, once a week and it was rationed with coupons, each family only being allowed 1kg a week. Our family included my mother and father and my mother's mother, as well as four children. That meat didn't go very far. We sometimes could get turnip too. That one day a week we looked forward to it. We could have fried meat with a slice of turnip and some cabbage. It was always so delicious!"

In those days, Western Europe, and especially Britain, was experiencing the flower-power hedonistic times of the swinging 60s. Rock and Roll was everywhere, Leyland Cars launched the iconic mini, miniskirts stopped traffic, The Beatles, drugs and rebellion against social norms were the order of the day.

"During the Cultural Revolution in China no one was allowed to wear flowers of any description. You could wear blue, grey and military green, that was it. Male and female, old and young, so-called rich and all the poor. We all looked the same. In the streets you couldn't tell the difference between a man and a woman. So being a young girl was hard. You yearned to wear beautiful clothes, dresses with patterns and especially flowers, but of course these things were forbidden."

There was an upside to it all though.

"The government provided us with a small brick house with a central yard. All of us were there together.

"There were almost no classes at school at that time and no real teachers as they had all been sent to the villages. We were told that we should learn our lessons from the workers, learn from the peasants. I tried to be the best student I could, whether it was climbing mountains or doing physical education. I got lots of awards for being the best in the class. Most of the time, though, we were on holiday. However, my father believed that education was very important so he taught us at home as best he could. He also taught us to be good and positive people, always to be honest, to obey our parents at home, our teachers at school and the government."

As the eldest child of the family, her father instilled in her the requirement to look after the family, work hard and take responsibility. Her mother was designated to be a street cleaner and they lived about 15 minutes from where her mother worked.

"My mother's job was to go to the local workers factory and then sweep the street clean all the way back to our house. That was the job. Every day, from early in the morning until the evening, one end of the street to the other. To start helping her, I was woken early every day, and she took me on her bicycle to work. It was my job to wheel the big bike back to our house before I went to school. As I got older and the bike got smaller, I learned to ride it myself so I could ride it back home. Older still and I rode my mother to work and then rode home.

"Another job I had was to go to my grandmother's house with the bike and collect wheat from her, then take it to the local street mill to be ground into flour. I waited for it to be done and then took the flour back to my grandmother. I also had a big job every so often when I was at high school. In those days, when heating started to be more widely available, it was gas fired using big gas canisters. I had the job of taking the empty canister to be filled up and then taking it back home. Going was ok, but coming home, it was so heavy! It was hard work. I really thought I was being brought up as a boy! In a way it was much better than before though. Everyone was very happy when the gas canisters came out, as until then we had to heat the homes and cook using charcoal. This was a good sign of how China was progressing."

Mdme Lin is a strong character, refined, as she was elegantly but firmly articulating, through the fire of the Cultural Revolution. As a result she prefers to do everything herself. She learned through bitter experience that if you wanted anything done properly, then the best thing was to do it yourself. Time passed and with the arrival of the 1980s came the open-door policy.

"People were suddenly allowed to go to university and there was an entrance exam, the *Gaokao* (高考). I took the *Gaokao* but failed. I had never really studied like a proper student, there had been no real classes anyway. Proper study would have required extra lessons, which required money which we simply didn't have. So I waited to be allocated a job."

Mdme Lin had not been sent to the villages along with her peers, partly on account of her father's position as a war hero and his disability. Through her father's contacts in the local army, he managed to get the local officials to recognize his daughter as his carer and the main person responsible in the household for looking after the younger children while her mother worked. It seemed her father and mother had had immense foresight when they sent her to work. The result was she remained at home when so many others were separated from their families.

"I didn't go away, but, at the age of 19, was allocated to the weather bureau as a weather woman. I thought I should start looking for a husband but I was still very young and my expectations of a boyfriend were very high. Quite frankly, no one came close to my aspirations!"

She worked there for nearly 20 years.

"Then I thought about my life. I realized that if I did nothing, I would be there in that bureau until I retired. I might be promoted though, from assistant engineer to engineer. One day I saw an old engineer lying on the cold ground taking a soil temperature reading with an old thermometer. I couldn't bear the prospect of ending up like him so I decided to leave.

"That was the time the opening up was happening and the government was encouraging people to go and start businesses. They were telling work places to let their staff go out and try to start businesses. Even just selling one bag of peanuts for ¥2 (£0.20) would mean you were going to earn ¥20 (£2.00) from 10 bags, and that was a lot more than my day's salary. I was lucky as the leader at the bureau said I could leave but could go back at any time. I was strong minded and stubborn and believed I could make it without a safety net, so just left and lost that opportunity. It was a risk, as I eventually got married and had my son. But I wanted the chance to do something myself."

She opened a small restaurant near the weather bureau. There were a lot of small 'township' shops and small businesses around the area so she felt there would be a lot of customers for a restaurant. She struggled to make it work.

"I called it 'Big Harmony' and I thought it was going to be easy. It wasn't. Not many people came. I needed to do something different so I hired a really good cook. He was a Muslim and excellent at his job. He prepared a Beijing delicacy made with sesame called *shaobing* (烧饼). These pies became more and more well-known and more and more people would come for breakfast. Suddenly, I had a success. Although each pie was only ¥0.35 (3.5p), I sold a lot and we made good money."

Three years later the factories and small businesses

associated with them started to go out of business, so she closed down and took a break. It was the end of the 1990s. She decided to do something different. Through her relationships at the Bureau of Urban Landscapes, she managed to get some work looking at the design of some government land. She became wealthy from the projects and went to study English at Wall Street English.

Wall Street English was and remains one of the foremost English language school services in China. Its consultants and teachers cater for the growing number of ambitious Chinese wishing to learn the global language of business. Mdme Lin believed that she could learn English as she was talented and successful already so she could then develop a business abroad and emigrate. The 2003 self-driving tour seemed to be the catalyst to end her overseas ambitions and she decided to stay, so she told me.

Interestingly, our entire interview has been and is conducted in Chinese.

"I had been working very hard for so many years. I took a rest and time off to learn calligraphy. Then, as I had become more knowledgeable about old manuscripts and historical relics, I started a job in a collector's association. These people were academics and experts in verifying antiques. At that time, there was a huge interest among the wealthy for old art and it was important to know if what you had was genuine. The association verified and issued certificate of authenticity. I stayed for five years until the increase in fakes started to compromise the process. Each certificate attracted a fee from the experts. Of course, the experts were of high integrity, but many customers wanted a certificate even if the item was a fake so they could then sell it for a big profit. They offered big money for the experts to issue certificates for the fakes."

"So, there was corruption?"

"Of course, but we all discussed the situation. Many of the

experts were academics. They had their personal reputation to think about. We decided to follow our hearts and close the certification office. It was an easy decision."

"So, what next?"

"I decided to become skilled in beauty and healthcare. I wanted to study it and then help women to stay beautiful and healthy."

"You are a good personal example," I fawn a bit.

"Yes, I am."

Oh.

"I look very beautiful, youthful and healthy, as I personally practise all I teach."

She does look well.

She started in 2010 and has grown her modest but successful Chinese medicine business over the last six years or so. First, she studied the art of 'cupping', later she moved on to moxibustion. This is an ancient form of Chinese traditional medicine where dried mugwort (moxa) is ground to a fluff and then burnt as a small smouldering ball, either in direct contact with certain parts of the patient's body or through the use of acupuncture.

"I wanted to stay young for my family and to help them and my friends to defy the ageing process. That's what I've done. I also use jewellery made from meteorite fragments to help cure illnesses. I have learned all the theories from a teacher over the years, and now apply them to my clients. They are simple and particularly moxibustion is a very cheap but very effective form of therapy. It can be used to treat many different illnesses ..."

She embarks briskly on a more detailed explanation of the merits of Chinese traditional medicine, which is seeing a resurgence in China and being more accepted in the West.

But that's for another day.

CHAPTER

45

THE POWER OF BELIEVING

We meet in the lobby. The marble columns and waterfall feature at the back dominate. The Beijing Henan Plaza Hotel (北京河南大厦) is as opulent as the upper elite of China like it. We are early so attempt to obtain a coffee. We are directed to the rear of the hotel through a narrow marbled corridor and through a crushingly expensive jade shop to a few leather seats next to a small unoccupied bar. The coffee is a small cup of powdered instant slurry and long life milk. It is also ¥72 (£7.20) a cup.

I have stayed in many quintessentially Chinese hotels and this is an example of a specific type. It is very 'rich Chinese' and certainly not Western. There are none of the niceties found in Hiltons, Holiday Inns and the like in places of such marbled extravagance and show. Many such hotels are state-owned and, until a few years ago, the service was at best perfunctory, with customers being an irritating interference in an otherwise languid existence where you got paid anyway.

Wen Bojun (see Chapter 37) bounces in on both phones. Without his introduction, I would have never met 'The Professor' as everyone calls Mr Chen Linsen. We ascend to the seventh floor and trot along the narrow corridor behind Bojun, who is a man in a hurry. At the end of the corridor he plunges right and enters the open door of the dimly lit, small windowed room without knocking, in a flurry of goodwill.

The Professor rises to meet us. He is enormous. Over two metres tall, he dominates the room and his huge frame blocks an ample framed middle-aged woman of substance in a very expensive coat and slicked back hair. I never learn who she is – wife? patient? friend? business partner? It isn't clear and I'm not going to ask.

The introductions are made and explanations of my intent accepted. Wen Bojun's immediate job is done and he throws himself into a chair and slumps into WeChat. The elegant woman sits to one side, silently examining me in unobtrusive but slightly unnerving detail. The door of the room is never shut and it looks like the bed has never been slept in or any aspect of the room disturbed. A coat is slung over another chair and there is no heating to speak of. It is as if this audience has been specially arranged, booked and orchestrated. There is a slightly eerie aura.

"I have cured many incurable people."

The Professor has a reputation to uphold, as I am about to learn.

"I was born in 1963 in Xi'an in Shaanxi Province, I am a rabbit."

Rather than head for the door, I accept the comment with a knowing nod. This simple statement defines him more than any flurry of opening Western questions. It would be rude to ask any more.

He is a product of the New China, and has experienced all the turmoil of its revolution and change. Xi'an has been the capital of 13 of China's dynasties and was originally known as Chang'an (长安), the start of the famous Silk Road (丝绸之路) and the place of emperors and intrigue.

The Chinese zodiac is split into a cycle of 12 years, each denoted by an animal, each meaning something. The rabbit is the fourth in the cycle and it is a tame creature denoting hope, calmness, tenderness and self-sacrificial love. The year 1963 was the year of the water rabbit and one of its lucky numbers is 7; hence floor seven in the hotel, I guess.

"My parents came from Shandong Province. Xi'an was not a fashionable place to live but they were moved there. They lived outside the city walls. Inside the walls were the rich and outside were the poor in those days. The following 30 years saw a total transformation of the city to become what it is today. A good thing for the development is that the city has thrived, but the downside is that it has broken the quiet and reflective sense of the place that I grew up in. When I was a boy in the 1970s and 1980s, there were almost no cars to be seen – only bicycles – but now it is a busy and noisy place."

Xi'an is now best known to the Western world as the location of the famous army of Terracotta Warriors. Initially discovered by accident in 1974, the huge pits subsequently excavated contain over 8,000 life-size warriors, each one different and individual. It is an amazing place and on the major 'must visit' tourist trail, alongside The Forbidden City in Beijing and the Great Wall of China.

"I went to primary school in Xi'an and continued my whole education there. I started playing volleyball at the age of 13 at junior middle school in 1976 and just kept going from there. I ended up playing through to university. There were many world and national championship players who started in our university team. We all really loved volleyball and, as a result of our time playing sport, we were going to miss the cultural classes so the leaders organized for us to have them separately, for three years! At the end of it all, a lot of students went on to be coaches all over the country and I ended up in the police bureau. As a result I became a government officer."

Despite polite probing, I fail to get much more on what he did in the years between the early 1980s and today. However, what he does now is worthy of a good deal more attention.

"I discovered a way of making metallothionein (MT) relatively cheaply. There is a story that I will tell you."

Metallothionein is a range of low molecular weight proteins which are very difficult to extract, but have the ability to bind heavy metals in the body to support their metabolism, specifically of zinc. Scientific understanding is limited but there appears to be increasing evidence that its balance in the body may affect such diseases as cancer and autism. It is little understood and expensive to create.

"With the economic development of China, pollution became an increasingly difficult problem. By chance I found a new technology to treat polluted water. The new technology was very advanced and remains so even now. It is a revolutionary way of treating polluted water to purify it. As a result of discovering this, I quit my government job to concentrate full time on water pollution treatment."

The details are hazy in Chinese, let alone in English, but it seems that as a result of his discovery, Cheng Linsen worked on water purification projects all over the world, including South Africa, Indonesia, Hungary and Singapore.

"When I was working on these projects I found a royal doctor who was very old indeed. He was promoting healing through the use of herbs and had managed to learn how to create MT through the use of herbs. It had been discovered in 1957 from the renal cortex of horses, but had never been commercially produced. The old doctor understood the way herbs could be blended together so when eaten by animals, they would produce MT naturally. In the beginning, it was still uneconomic and unethical, as well as cruel, as it would have taken 100,000 rabbits' livers to be needed for the extraction of only 1 kg of the crude and 0.6 kg of the pure protein. It was also a horribly cruel production method, as the only way to extract the protein was to inject the rabbits with a chemical base of the active ingredient. This made the animals' flesh and skin start to rot. Only when the animal had rotted alive could the liver be taken out and the protein extracted. It was never going to be practical. However, in 2003, having worked on this for many years, I found a way of creating the right animal feed that allows chickens and cows to eat it and the protein is created naturally in their eggs and milk. This is a breakthrough and we can now create commercial quantities, though it is still for only a short period of time in the year when the animals actually produce the pure form of the protein."

Chen Linsen studies me carefully. I haven't reacted at all. I have learned a little of the inscrutability attributed to the Chinese and am broadly impervious to most shock tactics or outrage.

"Actually the ancients in China understood the use of proteins extracted from herbs and some animal tissue for the promotion of health, but they didn't know the actual reason it worked or the content from a scientific perspective. We do now. I'm sure you know about the sword of Emperor Qin Shi Huang?"

I do. Emperor Qin Shi Huang is best known for being the founder of the Qin dynasty and the first emperor of a unified China. Amongst his more notable legacies are his vast tomb, in what is now Xi'an (same city the Terracotta Warriors were found in). His body has yet to be discovered. He also spent many years searching for the elixir of eternal life, while destroying what he regarded as subversive books and texts and intellectuals, including the alleged live burial of 460 Confucian scholars in 210 BC. The swords found in the Warrior pit are immaculately preserved. It appears that the ancients had perfected a method of welding and chrome plating not invented in the West for a further 2,200 years.

"The ancients knew many things and if you look on the chariots of the tomb, you will see another example of high technology developed by the Chinese. They perfected the welding of gold and silver chains together. This is still deemed impossible as the melting point of gold and silver are quite different, so theoretically you can't weld the two together. But the ancient metal workers did."

We pause to consider the skill of the ancient Chinese in so many areas, until our discussion returns to medicine. I have a question for Cheng Linsen.

"So what do you think about Western medicine?"

"There is no such thing as Western medicine. It is all data and chemicals. It just treats symptoms. Western medicine does not cure people. At best, it puts them in a state of permanent remission. A Western doctor will give someone medicine they may have to take for the rest of their lives. A Chinese doctor will nurse the whole body, so if someone has a cough, a Chinese doctor will let them cough until all the symptoms are shown and only then give them the food or medicine to cure them. The process is to clean, amend, repair, supplement and finally cure. Sometimes we believe that first you must get fully, or even more, ill and only then can you be cured."

To the Western ear, this is a controversial perspective and calls to question the hundreds of years of developed medical thinking. However, sitting listening to The Professor as he has become known to the many people who listen and follow his teachings, what he says has a logicality and simplicity which is beguiling.

"People call me Professor as a mark of respect for my skill and the results I have been able to deliver. I was even asked to go to Cyprus by the President of Cyprus a few years ago, as I treated a couple of people there who had terminal lung cancer. Those who had the Western medicine treatment all died, but the ones I had treated recovered fully. They thought it was a miracle. They had taken the MT I prepared for them in the special doses I required, and they were cured. Totally. When President Anastasiades of Cyprus came to Beijing in 2015, he came to see me to discuss how I can help people in Cyprus. I will go there again soon to see if I can enter the European market through Cyprus."

The Professor is a regular lecturer at the prestigious Chinese Academy of Sciences and is an acknowledged expert in traditional Chinese medicine. As we talk, Wen Bojun has been filming and recording, seemingly half asleep, in the chair. The phone in the room rings and before The Professor can move, Bojun is up and answering it in hushed tones, so as not to disturb our discussion or the sleeping woman who had transferred to lying on the bed fully clothed, complete with coat, earlier 'to rest'. The Professor barely notes or acknowledges the interruption.

"MT has now become well known all over the world and is exported to the US and to Germany. MT is a biologically active product with a number of special functions. First, it eliminates the free radicals in the body to increase immunity and prevent ageing. Second, it removes the poisonous heavy metals in the body. Third, it supports the metabolism of trace elements essential to the human condition. Fourth, it increases the adaptability of the body when it is in a state of negativity. Fifth, it is the 'zinc tank' for the body. Sixth, it prevents radiation and stops transformation of normal cells into cancerous tumour cells. Seventh, it adjusts and lowers blood fat. Eighth, it cures diabetes and kidney ailments. Ninth, it cures stomach and intestinal ulcers; and tenth, it improves skin nutrition and the metabolism to make the skin beautiful."

"A miracle cure," I say without emotion.

"Not entirely. It also requires the patient to believe."

"Believe what?"

"Effective traditional Chinese medicine relies not only on the physical ingredients, but also on the spirit. The patient must believe that it will heal them too."

"So, it's just a placebo?"

The Professor eyes me with a look which makes me squirm uncomfortably a little, but I can't let the claims go totally unchallenged.

"Herbs are very important, as is the way they are cooked and mixed, but the patient also needs to want to be healed. The diagnosis in traditional Chinese medicine is a four-stage process; observation, listening, interrogation and pulse-taking, like anywhere in the world. Then the patient needs to awaken their *chi*. This is the essential element of success to support the medicine which is prescribed. When the vital *chi* awakens, then the diseases will disappear, led by the medicine."

The Professor claims to have healed many people and illnesses including breast cancer, uterine cancer, prostate cancer and a number of serious diseases in people who were rejected by the hospitals. Our discussion ranges from herbal preparation to the potential loss of the ancient art of traditional medicine in China itself. He feels that some herbal medicines are wrongly prepared even now as many are not the original herbs from the proper regions of China where they grow best. Supplements and frauds are creeping into the system and there is a need to return to the use of true regional drugs, as well as improving the technology for their production.

"Let me tell you a story about how important the spirit and belief is to healing and to illness. I once met two young women on a boat. They were both sea sick. I gave them a tablet, it was nothing. But I told them that it was the best medicine for sea sickness in the United States. They believed me and both were well very quickly. In another instance, two men went to a doctor. One had terminal liver cancer. The other was healthy. Interestingly, the doctor found out later that he had given the wrong man the wrong diagnosis papers. The healthy one died of liver cancer three days later, and the man with terminal liver cancer lived another six months very happily. Just because they believed the results, of the wrong man!"

The Professor is clear that his is only one way of developing the ancient art of Chinese medicine and he admits to the MT he produces being very expensive.

"The price of MT is 300 times more expensive than gold. This is because it is difficult to produce in reasonable quantities and very seasonal for the animals to produce. It's only between April and October that the animals produce the protein so it's a finite quantity."

One of the ingredients of the MT produced by The Professor is derived from a bitter courgette-like vegetable called *ku gua* (苦瓜). The Professor gets up and crosses the room. From a small sachet in the pocket of a voluminous bag, he extracts three small withered and dried light brown shards of the vegetable.

"Put it in your mouth next to your cheek. Chew it slowly until it loses its bitter taste."

"Why?"

"It will give you an idea of the healing properties of MT."

"But there is nothing wrong with me to be healed," I suggest gently.

"Nothing?"

"Well I get a bit bloated after eating," I admit, rather ruefully and not sure if I am ready for what might happen.

"Hmmm, that's a different problem I can solve with a meal together if you have time? We can go for Hot Pot and I'll put some MT in and that will solve your bloating forever."

I'm sorely tempted but have another dinner engagement. "Next time," I suggest.

"Ok. Anyway, try this."

It seems rude not to, so I slowly press the gnarled dried gourd sliver into my mouth. It is genuinely bitter but not as unpleasant as some things I've tasted in China. To be honest, I never experienced any ill effects.

"With the use of MT, some people recover from their illness after taking a course of only one or two bottles. Normal treatment is two tablets a day and that's enough. You should try it. Come back and we can talk more."

If this is a sales pitch, then it is a very soft one.

We leave soon afterwards, Wen Bojun bounding down the corridor and then rushing to his car to retrieve a special gift for myself and my translator. A bag each of multicoloured granular pills. He will send me instructions later.

There is much written on the subject of traditional Chinese medicine and I am no expert, not even an informed amateur. Sitting there in the lucky room (708) of the lucky (7) of the traditional Chinese hotel listening to story after story, with the offer to verify every one with the person concerned, I was fumbling somewhat schizophrenically with the fuzzy line between belief and scepticism. Maybe I am both right?

THE DAOIST ABBOT

The car winds its way through the mountains to the south west of Beijing. As we gain height, the flat plain which the capital of China sits on recedes behind us and gives way to rugged hills and narrow gorges. The new highway we had sped along to start with suddenly ends in a terminus of concrete lorries and dust. The driver studies the satellite navigation system intently. Then we are twisting and turning around an ever-rising landscape, heading for a somewhat unusual location and an unusual man.

Abbot Li Zhijie welcomes us in the small rectilinear refectory already busy with young women eating noodles, soup and vegetables. At a long set of linked tables with wooden stools we sit with our coats half open against the bitter wind that blows in with visitors.

"You will eat," Abbot Li gestures to the laden table.

Not so much a question, more so a hospitable instruction. My interpreter and I duly tuck into vegetables, noodles and soup. Time slows down. Outside happy music blares across the courtyard and the dogs we had seen earlier, growling their warning of unwelcome, bark at arriving monks. The pair of peacocks in the cage behind complain at the attention the dogs get. We had arrived at the ancient, 600-year-old, Daoist temple the day before a big conference and delegates are arriving all day in readiness for the celebrations and teaching. Abbot Li Zhijie instructs food, tea and a tour with waves of his one good arm. His right arm was badly mutilated in a car crash which almost killed him a few years ago and he manages his injury with fortitude and a bevy of helpers. The food is delicious and the tour insightful, conducted as it is by a young monk with a slow walk and an encyclopaedic knowledge.

We are told to sit and wait on the wooden raised seating in the upper teaching room.

Abbot Li will be here soon.

Time slows further.

Green-backed beetles wander over the floor randomly.

Green tea provides sustenance.

The village far below us is deserted, a warren of disappearing lives and empty yards. All around are the persimmon trees that are the main source of income to the remaining older community, the fruits holding tenaciously on to the otherwise totally bare branches like small bright orange lanterns. Beside the road the old and infirm patiently sit, selling 5 kilo baskets for ¥20 (2p) or next to nothing.

Abbot Li will be here soon. He is attending to business and is very sorry. We wait.

We wait a little longer.

Time almost stops altogether.

Abbot Li is genial and apologetic. He is a busy man. We start to chat but are almost immediately interrupted by an old monk dressed in traditional Daoist robes, gaiters, felt shoes, a straggling white goatee beard and grey hair tied back into a rough pigtail with a ribbon.

"The female dog is pregnant. We need to build her a separate place to rest. Is this ok?"

Abbot Li dispenses instructions and ¥100 notes (£10.00).

We recommence our discussions for two minutes and another interruption from another monk, then another, then another muttered side meeting, a greeting of new visitors and a phone call on the smart phone which emerges deftly from an inner pocket.

Abbot Li smiles apologetically, then wanders around the room, crushing beetles and requests for further audiences.

We are left alone.

"I was born in Qingdao (青岛) in the early 1960s and grew up in Henan Province (河南省). My family moved from Qingdao to Zhengzhou, the capital of Henan Province when I was around four or five years old. My parents were sent to Manchester in the UK by the government to learn about textile technology before I was born. At that time Zhengzhou was an emerging textile city in China. My primary and secondary schooling was in Zhengzhou and then from 1981 to 1984 I studied at Zhengzhou University of Textile Technology where I also learned English. After graduation, I was allocated to work in the local government office responsible for planning, statistics and other aspects of central planning for the provincial government."

Clearly a very able student, Li Zhijie progressed quickly and after a short time moved to the Overseas Chinese Federation, which was set up to manage government investment and international trade in 1990. At that time, many Chinese people who had been abroad chose to return and Li Zhijie worked in the department which supported them to do so. He was there for five years and travelled extensively. He would have been one of very few to travel and would have needed government papers and travel documents sanctioned at the highest level.

"I went to many countries, including Eastern Europe, Africa, South East Asia and the Middle East."

At that time these locations were not on most Western governments' wish list for liaison, and China was investing in some countries where the scope for building strong economic ties was heavily tinged with political overtones. It was unclear if Li Zhijie had been a visitor to places such as Lybia, Syria, Iran, Iraq, Zimbabwe or the likes of what became the slowly break-away Confederation of Independent Russian States, but my suspicion was that some of these at least had been on his itinerary at some time.

We gloss over the details.

"Then I was appointed to the Shaolin Charity Foundation. In 1999 we went on a tour to the UK and performed in front of Queen Elizabeth and Prince Philip in London. I met them both as I was the tour manager. We performed as part of the millennium celebrations in the Wheel of Life show at that time. It was a memorable occasion to meet the Queen of England."

The Shaolin Kung Fu Monks team are of international fame and perform astonishing feats of Kung Fu mastery as part of the government-sponsored Chinese cultural outreach to take Chinese culture to the world.

"We also toured in Edinburgh and Manchester that year, as well as London and were filmed on a regular basis. I spent three years as the team manager and we went all over the world including France, Italy, Germany and Sweden. Then I became the chairman of the Shaolin Foundation for the following ten years. I was the chairman as I was not a monk but the government official responsible for the place. During that time I also was able to go to the US and get a PhD in economics and management from the University of Southern California. Because I was not a monk I was able to go out and meet people, talk with them and do these other things. I returned to Beijing for a year and then went back to the US to Harvard for a year from 2006–7."

In 2008 Li Zhijie moved to become the general manager of the Beijing Jinshide International Auctioning House (北京金仕德国际拍卖有限公司). This was an officially sanctioned organization for the sale and export of Chinese art and artefacts all over the world.

"Because I had a deep understanding of Daoism, Buddhism and Chinese culture, I was asked to stay for nearly five years and dealt in a lot of sculpture, paintings, calligraphy and other Chinese art. I was the general manager, sort of president of the business."

We talk and talk, and time passes in a respectfully slow and paced manner. Abbot Li exudes a complex blend of capitalistic entrepreneurialism and devout, deep religious karma. It is clear that he is held in awe by those around him and, after an hour or so, I start to understand why. We get on well and he has long since slipped from the formality of Chinese into a delightful mix of Chinglish, which allows us to converse without the need for much, if any, translation.

"So how do you come to be here, half way up a mountain in a 600-year-old monastery in the middle of nowhere?" I ask with a half-smile.

He gently sidesteps the question and I have to read between the lines.

"I have studied religions for many years. I have always believed deeply in the basic principles of Daoism. Confucianism, Buddhism and Daoism all have the same origin. Indeed, all religions have the same basic belief behind them. All have but one origin. There are a hundred theories, but all talk of the same reality and there are thousands of ways to pursue that reality. All doors to enlightenment have common doctrines and wisdom. Because there are many ways, and because Daoism is in the roots of Chinese culture, that is why I chose Daoism."

He pauses to ensure he has my full attention.

"This is a very old and famous monastery. Tomorrow we have a big Daoist conference here and people are arriving from all over China. Daoism is an important part of Chinese culture and is under the leadership of the Communist Party. This monastery is open to the public and I am responsible for managing its affairs in accordance with the rule of law and the direction of the Party. They needed someone to have responsibility for the proper management of this place. I was chosen."

"So you are the CEO here?" I enquire, playfully. It certainly seems that nothing happens in the monastery or the surrounding area without his express knowledge and approval.

"More of a general manager really," Abbot Li smiles knowingly at me. "I'm the one responsible for General Temple Management, or Temple General Management."

He chuckles, as he rolls the English around his tongue.

"I have been here for the last six years. I'm not really a government official."

Abbot Li smiles knowingly at me again.

"Anyone who has a position as I have has to be checked by the government for approval of the appointment. Only qualified monks can be an abbot. The temples are a kind of religious corporation based on the rule of law. The qualities of an abbot are that we must ..."

Abbot Li ticks off the qualifications on the fingers of his only hand.

"First, you must love your country. Second, you must love Daoism. Third, you must obey the law. Fourth, you must cultivate morality according to the Daoist doctrine. Fifth, you must have a kind heart. Sixth, you must bring unity to the believers and practitioners of Daoism. And seventh, you must make a clear contribution to a harmonious society."

"Do you think all Chinese have a good morality?"

"We are on a journey. Some Chinese people give a very bad impression of China when they are abroad. This minority is a problem. Generally, the Chinese are a friendly people. We pay attention to courtesy, culture and harmony. Most religions in China stress the cultivation of an ethical mindset. As a religious leader, I will continue to promote Chinese culture and believe that things will get much better as the Chinese people embrace religious beliefs more and more. The way for the Chinese to improve their morality is for them to truly understand Chinese traditional culture. The more people respect the heaven, the earth, their parents, the ancients and the spirit world of ghosts and gods, then the better our collective morality will become."

"What do you think of the recent generations of the 1990s and 2000s. People tell me these are an unruly and selfish generation. Do you agree?"

Abbot Li thinks for a while, and the silence of contemplation envelops us.

So does the cold which penetrates the upper teaching room we are sitting in. I notice it is so cold now that the ink in my pen has stopped flowing and my notes have to continue with a stubby pencil and tight fingers.

"This is a global issue. Economic development has been very fast in China, but elsewhere too. Everything is perhaps moving a little too fast. The whole world is in a state of flippancy and fickleness. There are natural disasters, regional wars and religious chaos, as well as a lack of water and energy everywhere."

We pause to ensure his Chinese is translated correctly as he wants to make this observation very accurately. I sense a wider power is speaking. There is a long traditionally held view in Chinese culture that dark days and natural disasters precede tumultuous change in the world.

"These are global problems and we cannot blame the generation of the 1990s or 2000s. We have the responsibility to educate them. When they become older they will be reserved and understand and take their responsibilities seriously. All religions are actually loyal to the basis of education which is to teach people the moral code they need to follow. Religious education in China flows from traditional Chinese culture. The core precepts are firstly of proprietary, righteousness, integrity and honour. Secondly, to comply with the rules of the law of nature and thirdly to conquer the devil of the mind.

"I want to promote the spirit of Daoism. I would like more and more people to come here to experience and understand Daoism. Business and religion are the same you know."

I'm not sure I do.

"We have a business morality in Chinese culture and we should conduct business in a moral way, not cheat and dupe others. Without a sound business morality, there will be more troubles, disputes and conflicts."

I am drawn deeper and deeper into the philosophy. We talk of the detail of the *dharma* and the importance of belief, the interdependency of religion, state and business. I am invited to share food again, but the fading light outside means we must return to the bright lights and choking traffic of Beijing. My translator looks visibly worried at the prospect of a late return to her family, so I make polite moves for departure.

Abbot Li is in no hurry. Time is of little importance up here amongst the old stones and the incense.

"I have a dream for China."

We pause on the steps to the wind-seared courtyard.

"Of course, I want my country to be stronger and richer in the world. But I want people's lives to be richer and stronger, for them to be happier and more harmonious. Then China and the other countries of the world will live happily on the Earth in friendship."

I depart suitably enlightened.

In the comfort and soporific warmth of the car, we wind our way through deserted villages in the fading dusk.

After a short distance, I call the car to a halt to buy fresh persimmon fruit from an ancient wrinkled roadside vendor. She is surprised by my refusal of change for the kilos of fruit that the driver, my translator and I purchase. It seems a small price to pay for respecting my elders. Maybe Abbot Li would have frowned on my lack of business acumen.

THE GOVERNMENT TRAVEL AGENT

Wu Yandong is already sitting at the Formica-covered table when I arrive, as instructed by my local fixer, at precisely 09.00. The ubiquitous tea has been ordered, cold tea since the temperatures outside have already soared to the high 30ºC in another baking Beijing summer. We exchange pleasantries and gifts while the waitresses scuttle between tables around us. The barn of a restaurant, with its serried rows of neatly arranged tables and chairs, is almost entirely empty, but a sense of relief pervades the place after the breakfast onslaught. A couple of staff are asleep in a corner, steeling themselves for the inevitable lunchtime mayhem.

"I was not a good student," Wu explains with typical Chinese respect and humility.

I am used to this self-effacing and self-deprecation in China so I respond with the obligatory, "I'm sure your parents are very proud of you."

"No, no, really, I was truly a poor student. My mother was working at this company and I was lucky that she was able to get me a job as a trainee many years ago and I have been here ever since. We are Cantonese, from the south of China. Actually, my family is from Malaysia and they moved to Guangzhou in the 1950s. We still have family in Malaysia."

"So where is your *hukou*?" I was curious to know how a Malaysian Chinese family member was now working in Beijing for a state-owned company, somewhat unusual at best.

"Oh, I've got a Beijing *hukou*. I studied foreign trade and English at Beijing Capital Normal University. My mother is from Xiamen (on the south east coast of China) and she speaks the Cantonese, Taiwanese and Fujianese dialects."

So, not such a poor student after all. And a mother with a Beijing *hukou*, so a son eligible for a mainland university. It is becoming clearer. Wu Yandong now has responsibility for arranging tours for visitors predominantly to Australia and New Zealand as a manager in the rather grandly named

'North America & Oceania Department' of the state-owned travel agency he works for.

"South East Asia is the first choice for travel among Chinese people. Often, they may first go to Hong Kong and then they get more adventurous and travel to Thailand or Malaysia, then Japan and Korea. We are still state-owned. Around 15 years ago, all travel agencies were state-owned. Since then the industry has totally changed. If we go back only 20 years, it was almost impossible to even get a passport, let alone have permission to travel outside China. As recently as the 1980s and 1990s, only government officials were allowed to travel and even then only a few were issued with passports."

It seems so strange that at a time when most of the developed world was flying at will, and there was an explosion of low cost airlines in the West, China was still restricting travel and the issuance of travel documents. However, an appreciation of this helps understand some aspects of Chinese society and the significant lack of understanding, even fear, of the West and Western ways that was all pervading only a few short years ago and is sometimes still evident.

"At that time there was no real experience or expertise in arranging outbound travel. For the bulk of the population, it was an unknown and frightening world beyond China. Even those who could afford it, and there were not many, they were very cautious and wary of travelling. That's why it all started with Hong Kong and Macao and slowly grew from there. It was a very complicated and lengthy process to get the necessary documents to travel. In those days, it cost over US$24,000 for a two week holiday in Australia, for example. Only Air China had flights and they were very expensive. The first flight by China Southern Airways to Sydney was in 2001 and then prices started to drop. Now a flight to Sydney can be as little as US$450!"

As more and more people began to travel and government restrictions were relaxed or lifted altogether, then prices tumbled.

"There were big changes. It started small, then grew and grew. Everything was strange and new. People were curious and interested in everything. You also have to understand that between 1950 and 1980, the main foreign language taught in schools was not English, but Russian."

This aspect of language alone made it less attractive to travel to English-speaking places than to those where Chinese or Russian was, or at least might have been, spoken.

"Now the internet has changed everything and people are no longer worried about overseas destinations. They have much more information about places. However, the reason for travel is not the same as why Westerners travel. Chinese travellers are not so bothered about visiting places to learn about history or culture. It is to have face. It is all about showing their friends and families that they have been to places that others have not. So there is a real increase in travelling to exotic places and unusual locations, but ones that other Chinese people might have heard of and be jealous of their friends going to."

This is borne out every holiday season when my WeChat 'moments' messaging is full of pictures of the beaches of Bali and Bondi, Scottish castles, or South African vineyards. As one friend said to me, "You travel and take pictures of the places you visit, while the Chinese travel and take selfies."

Wu Yandong's experience spans almost a generation of Chinese travel and his observations are a window on the changing social dynamics of China.

"Around 20 years ago the rich travelled and were only able to share their experiences with friends and family. Now the middle classes can show everyone they have ever met how well travelled and sophisticated they are by posting pictures on WeChat in real time. Now there are no rules. You can go where you like. Back then there were rules prohibiting and constraining people so much. It used to be that you could only travel with organized groups led by government sponsored and approved guides. Twenty years ago, when I first started, over 95% of Chinese visiting Australia were in government approved groups. In 2015, over 700,000 Chinese visited and less than 20% were in groups, and those were not organized or overseen by government. In the old days, people felt safer in groups as they didn't know about places or what they were doing. That has all changed now."

The freeing up of travel, and almost total abolition of government intervention or restrictions, has led to an explosion of everything from private online travel agencies to low cost airline tickets and reducing room rates worldwide. Everyone wants a share of the Chinese traveller and their money. UnionPay-based credit cards are now more readily accepted around the globe and the availability of two year repeat entry visas to the UK and up to ten years to the US and Canada, as well as some countries such as Jamaica offering visa-free access to Chinese, is opening up new markets and locations. There is even an increase in Chinese visitors to such exotic places as the Antarctic.

Wu Yandong is concerned about his fellow Chinese creating a bad impression of their mother country.

"We know that some people's attitudes, behaviours and moral standards are not the same as Westerners. Some travellers are not good ambassadors abroad for our country. We need to communicate and try to understand each other's cultures much better. We are making mistakes but we also have to accept that we can't just skip this part of cultural learning. Equally, we need Westerners to try to understand the Chinese and our culture a little better too.

"We see Europe as one homogeneous group while the US is seen as the naughty child of Europe, because of your history. Not all places in the world are in political tension with China and we know that governments are different to the ordinary people. That's why so many Chinese go to Japan or the US. We must accept that there are many different routes to the same goals of understanding. Asian culture and Western culture are like night and day. Taoism teaches us to find the balance in life. We must do this with our cultural understanding.

"Now we are only arranging about 5,000 travellers through my department to Australia and New Zealand. They are predominantly 40- to 45-year-olds and their families for the main two holiday periods (Chinese New Year and around National Day on 1 October). We also arrange study tours for students aged between 12 and 18 years old, where they visit local schools across Australia and New Zealand for maybe only one week at a time."

So how has the internet changed the face of travel agencies in China? Are the old-style agencies disappearing with the advent of online?

"Not really. Of course, we were badly hit and continue to be so with the internet agencies and an increase in people arranging their own travel, flights hotels and itineraries. Many traditional tour operators have lost business. However, we are not too worried as the internet is just one tool or channel for sales. It's ok for short-term accommodation and ticket booking, but for more complex tours to more difficult and specialist places, the internet is no good at all. That's where we win with our personal service. Call centres can only answer travel questions from the list of answers in front of them. They don't know the places like the specialists do. We offer a better service which is based on personalized experience."

There are also strict requirements to physically visit the relevant embassy or consulate of all the countries you wish to visit for an interview. This is invariably accompanied by copious form filling, letters of introduction, proof of *hukou*, bank statements and a number of other confirmations, authorities and stamps to obtain your necessary visa. This is assuming that you have already completed the somewhat long and tortuous process of passport application. Then there is the small matter of the government requirement that all travellers must confirm and register that they have significant assets in China, and different levels apply to different countries. This is presumably to ensure would-be explorers return happily to the motherland. So, in reality, there remain some significant, though not insurmountable, barriers to free travel overseas. However, this also means as the restrictions are lifted, slowly, country by country, then there is significant scope for this already growing market to expand further throughout this enormous country.

As we amble through the complexities of visa applications, customs regulations and airport transfers, I sense a well-travelled and competent advisor.

I ask, "Where have you been in the world yourself?"

"Oh, nowhere. I can't afford it!"

He grins at me.

I later learn that Mr Wu is a very well-travelled individual and, in addition to Australia and New Zealand, has been to such places as the Maldives, Vietnam and much of South East Asia, as well as the US.

I never cease to be surprised by China. It was good to share the joke.

I nod sympathetically, grin back and play fight with him to pay the bill.

AGAINST ALL ODDS

Wang Li Ran, was born in Beijing in the 1950s. She has had a long, extremely distinguished and well recognized career in Chinese government departments. Now retired and, rightly, doting on her newly arrived grandson, she remains one of the most highly respected and acknowledged influencers of the post-Revolution era inside the accounting and finance profession in China.

We do not meet in my coffee shop.

The traffic is even more dreadful than normal in Beijing. It is the week of the National People's Congress (NPC) and Chinese People's Political Consultative Conference (CPPCC), the most important annual conferences of the Chinese Government. Security is horrendous and so is the traffic. Chang An Avenue, the main thoroughfare past Tiananmen Square and the Great Hall of the People, where the meeting is being held, is, at best, moving at walking pace. It is a bright, sunny, uncharacteristically smog-free, day in the city.

Li Ran is accompanied by her demure and solidly respectful 28-year-old daughter-in-law, who acts as an accomplished translator. Li Ran's English is very good, but she wants to ensure her story is accurately conveyed. Her daughter-in-law's English is perfect, and she is good at French too, I learn. In her typical well-prepared style, always attentive to detail, Li Ran navigates our meeting with self-effacing elegance.

"So, what do you want to ask me?"

I sent my broad areas of questioning to her in advance, but this is permission to proceed, and so we do.

"Tell me about your life," I say.

She laughs. She is totally at ease, and over a rather refined coffee in one of the best hotels in Beijing, if not in China, her fascinating story unfolds.

"I was born in Beijing, and right after I graduated from middle school, I was 'dispatched' to a small village nearby Baotou."

Baotou is now one of the biggest industrial centres in the Chinese province of Inner Mongolia but, in the days of her youth, it was only just starting to develop. Li Ran, like so many of her era, was sent to the countryside to use her knowledge to help local villagers by the Communist regime of the time.

"I was lucky, really, as I was very young so didn't really find it such a hardship."

The reasons for this emerge later but Li Ran was different. Many youngsters were sent to much harsher and far flung places, often in the crushingly poor areas of south and western China such as Shanxi and Yunnan Province.

"I left Beijing with 14 of my school mates, and headed for a small village in Inner Mongolia. That was 1968. In those days, the authorities looked at your background, your family and your situation. I knew that I didn't have a good background at the time, with my grandfather being a landowner and my parents having a small business, so I decided to leave as fast as I could so I could get a better 'despatch' to the countryside. It was the right thing to do. I left a few months early and it helped. Everyone had to leave by December 1968 but I went four months early. Many others had a very bad time and were away for much longer than me. I, however, only spent three years in the village."

This was the time of the notorious Red Army; there was significant disruption across China, but no more so in the cities, and at its most bloody and sometimes brutal, in Beijing itself. Different factions of the Red Army and the Youth League were vying, sometimes even fighting, with one another to flush out the bourgeoisie and 'undesirable' elements in society, which included 'intellectuals'. There are countless stories of landowners, big and small, being required to hand over land and give up wealth, often hard-gained, in the name of the Revolution. Li Ran's parents and family fell into the category of wealth which was not deemed appropriate in the new order. Many parents resisted the Great Despatch, hiding their children's *hukou* documents to forestall their being sent away.

This is a generation which was lost to the education system, as schools closed and didn't reopen until 1971. The effect on the China of today is still visible in many ways.

"My parents had hidden my brother's *hukou* when the despatch had been called. In my class of 45 students, only one or two managed to avoid the despatch and stay in Beijing due to their family situation, or special circumstances. Everyone else had to leave. Like I said, I left early to help the situation for my family."

"What was it like?" I ask.

"I was lucky, as the people in Inner Mongolia at that time had a perception of women that meant they did not really expect us to work. So we learned to do the work we did part time and knit some sweaters in our spare time, which we then gave to the locals as gifts to show our respect and gratitude. We received no money. In return they often gave us food. It was a good-natured exchange. Life as a part-time worker in the village was a good deal easier than many of my classmates, and many others of my age group, had to endure across China.

"I then went to the Normal University in Baotou (Batou Shifan Xueyuan 包头师范学院). I was 20 years old. I had four months at school until the end of the Cultural Revolution, training to be a teacher. Then I went to a middle school in Baotou. It was one of the best middle schools in the region. I spent three-and-a-half years there as a teacher. I then went to Tianjin University of Economics and Finance (Tianjin Caijing Daxue 天津财经大学). The reason I wanted to go to college was because, compared to the elder teachers of that middle school, my education level was relatively low. I wouldn't have been selected if it hadn't been for the lack of teachers in the post-Revolution era. So it had always been my goal to attend college."

I am confused. How did she manage to get to Tianjin University, one of the best in China, having been a teacher trained in the middle of nowhere in Inner Mongolia?

"I'll tell you. I was recommended by the Baotou school to go to the university. They had a chance to recommend people. There were 28 teachers in all of the Baotou middle schools who were thought good enough to be recommended to be sent to university. Only five were chosen and I was one of them. The Education Bureau in Baotou held a meeting to discuss the performance of their best teachers and to see who should be selected. I was one of them. I was so delighted. I was highly recommended by the middle school and my fellow students who made representations at the time to encourage the Education Bureau to accept me. There were meetings of the students to support my going forward."

I am genuinely amazed. I am more than well aware from studying both ancient and recent Chinese history that local meetings were convened for most things in China. I had never heard of a meeting convened specifically to support the application of one, no doubt gifted, student to be sent to university. But that was the case with Li Ran. The reason for the strong support needs to be grounded in the history of the time, which requires the reader to spend a good deal of extra time in study. However, the bottom line is that local groups had the power and ability to influence local affairs in ways that some Westerners might find frighteningly democratic.

"When I started working, I thought I was not good enough," she continues. "So I really worked hard. I worked every day until midnight, sometimes later. I was an art teacher and I painted all the slogans and loyal [Communist Party propaganda] pictures in our school. Before me, there had been a painting teacher but he had not had the energy to paint as strongly as me. People saw the difference immediately. I was lucky to have skills and put the effort in to be as good as I could be. I really cherished the opportunity to be a teacher and I had had a bit of a hard life in the village in the countryside so I really wanted to excel."

She did and her diligence and dedication to the cause, the painting and the school, were clearly recognized and appreciated by all around her.

"The headmaster went personally to the Education Bureau to recommend me for the university opportunity. They chose me.

"I graduated from Tianjin University with a major in finance. The teaching staff then recommended that I be sent to the Ministry of Finance."

As you can read elsewhere in this book, students at that time were allocated jobs by the university as an arm of government. Li Ran was no different, so in 1978 her cherished *hukou* was moved back to Beijing (it followed her from the village to Baotou, from Baotou to Tianjin, then to Beijing).

She was back home.

"My *hukou* had been away from Beijing for ten years."

There is a pause from all of us around the low coffee table. I am aware of being totally absorbed in the story. We sit in post-Revolution China and reflect on life, history and change.

"I'm interested in your name," I say, thinking it is time to move on. "Wang Li Ran is an unusual name. I know names reflect the hopes and dreams of parents for their children, what is the origin of your name?" This is a super sensitive question in China, steeped in meaning.

"My father gave it to me," she replies. "As a direct translation it means 'beautiful nature' but it has deeper meaning as well, as a status of beauty and beautiful gestures, the appearance of beauty. My father had great hopes for me. He was a teacher before the liberation of the People's Republic of China. There is a story that when I became a teacher in Baotou Middle School, my sister wrote to my father to tell him of my achievements. He was so proud of me; he went around the streets telling people that his daughter had become a teacher."

Her father's pride is understandable in the context of China at that time, just after the Revolution. To have a daughter achieve so much, step in the shoes of her teacher father and succeed, not only so far from home, but so well, must have seemed to be the pinnacle of an impossible dream. Against the odds of the time, Li Ran had been hugely successful. He was rightly proud.

"Ten of my classmates from university were allocated to the Ministry of Finance with me. We were allocated all over the department, but because I had been a teacher and a painter of slogans, I was allocated to the central administration department. Because of my skills and the good name I had managed to create, the leaders of the ministry allocated me to be an editor. Every conference and big meeting had to have slogans and paintings produced. I was allocated the task of producing these for all the big meetings and conferences. I painted a lot of slogans."

I am judicious in my questions but it does emerge that Li Ran was not only good at painting slogans, but probably the best at doing so.

"I painted the slogan for the very first founding meeting of the Chinese Institute of Certified Public Accountants (CICPA). Actually, I should say that I re-painted the slogan as the person who had done it did not do a good job and the leaders felt my painting was better, so I re-did it. I still have the photograph of all the leaders in front of my slogan. I then became famous in the ministry for this, and for my ability to take photographs too. As an editor, I also helped with the founding of the first ever finance magazine in China. That was in October 1978."

The magazine was a runaway success. Under Li Ran's editorship, the finance and accounting magazine became a must-read publication for all those involved in the finance profession in China. She was very well known as the editor for more than ten years.

"We produced the first trial edition in 1979 and it had a print run of 400,000 copies. We managed to get it to a maximum circulation of 700,000 copies when I left. It doesn't have that now, however. I then transferred to the CICPA in 1993, in charge of the training and examination department. In May 1995, I was promoted to the role of deputy secretary general by the ministry. We launched the CICPA magazine in 1999, with me as chief editor, and I kept that job until I retired in February 2011."

She pauses and beams at me. This is an amazing achievement and she knows it. During her tenure as editor of the two magazines, the finance and accounting profession in China was born and grew up. She witnessed some of the most significant changes in China and was at the heart of one of the most important and influential departments and groups navigating the unchartered waters of an emerging profession in an emerging economic superpower. No wonder she is a tiny bit proud.

"When I retired from CICPA, as all officials have to do at 60, I felt that I still had a lot of energy and wanted to contribute. I saw a need to help bridge the Chinese accounting profession to the Western world. Then, at about the same time, the Institute of Chartered Accountants of England and Wales (ICAEW) was looking to expand their presence in China. They were familiar friends, as when I was working at CICPA I'd also helped ICAEW come to China. So I joined the ICAEW, I helped arrange multiple exchange programmes between the two organizations, which have been widely welcomed by Chinese accounting professionals."

"What differences did you experience between the Chinese way and the British way?" I tiptoe through the question.

"Oh, really, not so different. Chinese people and British people have many similarities. We both have a long and distinguished history. We have a culture of courtesy and generosity. We share a lot in common. Unlike the US."

Again, I am intrigued by the perceived differences the Chinese see between the US and the UK, let alone other counties.

"Our English teacher at CICPA was English (English courses, among many others, were and still are offered to employees at the Ministry of Finance and many other government departments). Our teacher talked a lot about the differences between the US and the UK, not just in terms of language, but culture too.

"I have been very lucky to have travelled a good deal because of my job. I often read about the Chinese abroad behaving very badly. But I think the media exaggerates these stories to stir up bad perceptions of the Chinese. I went to the US in 1994 and Malaysia in 1998. Many of the young people we met thought we were Korean or Japanese. They couldn't tell the difference! Now people can tell the difference. The Chinese are the ones with the money. Everyone knows that the Chinese have wealth and cash to spend and the old historical perceptions are changing."

Li Ran tells me a story to illustrate her point.

"In 2002, my son, my only son under the one-child policy, went to France to college. One day he called me. He was really angry. Some fellow students had been asking him if he slept on a mud bench with a fire underneath it at home to keep him warm. He said to me, 'Mother send me photographs of our apartment so I can show these people what it is really like!' So I did and they were amazed that we had, and have, modern apartments with beds and chairs and sofas, washing machines and so on. Just like them. We laugh now but it was serious. People really didn't know anything about China except the old negative perceptions from years and years ago. His classmates needed to be educated.

"There are two extreme perceptions in the West of China: first that we are poor and they look down on us; second that we are the biggest threat in the world. Since China has grown so fast in the past 10–15 years, the story is one of worry and fear."

My understanding of Li Ran's comments is that the seemingly widely held Western perspective on China is the worry surrounding both its military and economic might.

Li Ran continues with a rather more serious story.

"Another one of my son's classmates was a very diligent student. She got an internship working for a French car manufacturer. She was trying to finish work at the end of a day and decided that she would finish it at home that evening. She took the computer home with her to do the work in her apartment. She was arrested by the French police and put in prison. She was suspected of being a Chinese spy. It was all over the French and Chinese media. It happened that her parents lived in Shiyan, which is a car manufacturing centre in China. They believed that she was stealing intellectual property from the French company. It was total rubbish. My son knew her as a diligent and good student. That was it. She spent six months in a French prison. It was a devastating life experience for her."

One has to hope that the days of misunderstanding and misperception are dying out, though not entirely, I fear. In China, stereotypes of other countries are as deep-seated as they are in other countries about China. However, they certainly want the perceptions to change and all the Chinese people I know are far more educated about the rest of the world than the rest of the world is about China.

"Personally, I have always tried to help people, even if they don't help me back. I've always found I get more out of life that way. Through being an editor and being in charge of the training department at the CICPA, I was so very lucky to meet many different people. I know a lot of people. This has given me very rewarding connections and relationships all over the world, as well as in China. I have tried to use those relationships to help the people I know. At the ICAEW I was happy to use my contacts to help them develop their position here in China. It is a great institution and very prestigious, as I said. I was proud to work with them and help them develop and grow here."

Even now, fully retired from all her paid working life, Li Ran is called upon to provide unpaid advice and is regularly consulted by many, including myself, on matters relating to the accounting profession in China. She does this because she wants to help and does it willingly. Li Ran is unique among many retired Chinese, especially retired from official positions, as it is extremely rare for them to return to any form of work, let alone for an international organization. Li Ran is special. The last of Li Ran's stories is in response to my asking her what she is most proud of in her life.

"My son has turned out to be a good boy. People ask me how I raised such a good son. I just say that he is a reflection of me and my values – not to be selfish and to think of others. I let my only son, my boy, grow up for himself, without too many boundaries. My son went to France in 2002, as you know. He didn't come back to visit until 2004. He didn't come back in 2004 for the Chinese New Year, which is a very important time for Chinese families. I called him and asked him why not. He said he couldn't come home at that time but would come home later in the year. Then he told me the reason. At that time, he was working in a restaurant to earn some money for his studies and his life in France. In 2004, the Chinese New Year fell over 14 February. When he told his boss that he wanted to go home for the Chinese New Year, his boss asked him to stay as there would be a very big increase in trade on Valentine's Day and he needed him to help. My son said he would stay and help, and when my son told me, I supported his decision. He was thinking the same as me. I was very proud of him.

"I am very proud of him now too. Through the one-child policy, many children are turning out to be selfish. People blame the politics. I don't. I believe it is more about parenting skills."

She turns to her daughter-in-law and smiles warmly.

Additional note:

The reader should be aware that I have used Wang Li Ran's personal name throughout this chapter and I hope she is happy that I have. I should really refer to her with more re-spect and she would normally be addressed as Wang laoshi (teacher) or Wang shuji (party secretary) to reflect a role she held for many years in the CICPA. To me, however, she has simply been Madam Wang, or in moments of real friendship, 'Linda'. However, I know she prefers her Chinese name, which is why it is used here throughout as my own personal mark of respect to this extraordinary woman.

THE
CANADIAN

Laurie O'Donnell is odd. A Canadian national, having built a successful business, decides to voluntarily move her entire life to China's polluted, traffic-choked and frenetically busy capital, at the age of 60.

"I like a challenge."

"I guess."

Laurie and I are sitting in a mutually convenient internationally branded coffee shop in the plaza not far from her gym. She is on her way back home from her regular Saturday morning workout with a personal trainer. She downs a double espresso almost before she is seated.

"I have harboured a life-long interest in China but in the days of growing a business and bringing up children, it was just not possible. Then when I retired from the business I got an email from the leader asking me if I'd like to come to China and run the business in Beijing. I thought, why not?! I'd spent 30 years working in Canada, my kids were at university and my husband was open and supportive. So we moved!"

"A big culture shock?"

"Oh totally! We left a beautiful house on the side of a lake in a place on the outskirts of Montreal. It was a huge deal to come here and our friends thought we were mad. It shook us to our foundations and it's very hard but then again it's hard to leave. This is an intoxicating place, and I don't mean the pollution. It's an amazing experience and as we have started to understand the intimate side of China we have come to love and cherish it."

Laurie is the Managing Director of Cornerstone International Group in Beijing. It's a global executive search, coaching and CEO advisory business and Laurie not only has her responsibilities as the MD, but also handles a suite of high profile clients herself.

"We are rooted in China, of course, but with a global reach."

"So what made you come here?"

"I guess I was asked to so that warranted at least a look and, as I took a closer look, it just seemed too good an opportunity to miss. I was always fascinated by China and here was someone willing to pay me to follow my dream. What's not to like?!"

"What keeps you here?" I ask.

"This is such a wonderful place and such wonderful people. There is a history here and it is such a vibrant but fundamentally different culture to anything I've ever known. It really gets under your skin and envelops you. Everything is different and that makes it a truly fascinating place. Even though it is challenging, the relationships you can develop with people are so intimate I just can't believe it. I don't think people outside China can appreciate how warm and genuine the Chinese people are."

"So different to that which you expected?"

"Totally. I came with a bag full of prejudices. I thought it was going to be a big risk, that we may not be safe in the streets, that we would be watched and have to watch everything we did. I thought being an outsider would be a big negative, that I'd stand out as different and our sense of 'otherness' would make us suffer for that. It has been totally not so. Quite the opposite in fact. It's such a safe place to be, as an older couple, as a woman, as a foreigner. There is no violent undertone, such as you can find in some parts of some cities in the West. On the subway I am never fearful of the crush. You will not be attacked or robbed or assaulted. Never."

"Back in Canada, what are your roots and experiences, which led you to be here now?"

"In Montreal in my childhood we lived in a bilingual town. We were bilingual by the age of five, both French and English. I studied art at high school and college and hoped to be a sculptor. Then I got into fabric and clothing and design. When I finished studying I decided to set up a business and it did well. I was fascinated by all types of oriental designs and, specifically, the Chinese style with the soft lines and soft buttons. I loved the feel of the lines of the Chinese clothes. I was successful and the fashion editor of the local papers did a big story on me. I was just a kid. The editor needed an interesting setting for the shoot. I was directed to a Chinese Kung Fu master. I introduced myself and asked for his help. We shot the story in his studio, a third story walk up in the old part of the city. The master posed the models in authentic martial arts poses. The piece was so successful that a national magazine covered me and then I was on television. It was amazing. I was only 22 years old. I started a company but to fund the business I couldn't get a loan. The local branch manager of the bank said, 'I can't give you a loan for the business. Why don't you buy a boat?' At first I didn't understand what he meant. Then he told me I'd never get a business loan but I could get a personal one for a boat or a car. Then I understood what he meant. I used the money and then paid it back as soon as I could. Then I asked him for another loan and he asked me if I needed another boat? I said no. A motorhome!"

Laurie continued to fund her burgeoning start up business through personal loans and built a successful company. Then, with this success under her belt, she first joined a design company and, later, a large Canadian design/retail company, advancing quickly. She was approached to manage and reposition a retail property for a public investment corporation; managing five turn around projects in five years.

"Then one of my parents had an accident. I felt I had to leave work to look after my Mom. I was looking for a job so I could manage things and went to a recruitment company. They didn't think I was suitable for anything on their books but asked me to join them anyway! It was all about business people talking to business people. It was an Executive Recruiting business based upon extensive global research; fascinating! World class clients! I ended up staying and was their Vice President for 12 years."

Laurie came up to retirement at 60 years old and was set to leave the business in Canada, but the owner, a Hong Kong Chinese/Canadian, had other ideas.

"He said I'd be bored sitting at home on the veranda with my feet up and I guess he was right. He said, 'Come out to China.' So here I am! It is a sort of return to my youth and back to building a business again from nothing, with no experience of how to do it here. I'm learning and have had to learn fast these past few years. What I feel like is that I've been given a wonderful gift. The chance to do something over again in a new culture, in a new country, with new horizons is just wonderful!"

Laurie is an irrepressible optimist. Enthusiastic, exuberant and driven, she is a breath of fresh air in a city which certainly needs it. She is not a common ex-pat. I've met a lot and there is an awful predictability about many of the old China hands. Except for a few, these are, by and large, full of negativity and frustration about the changed landscape in China. 'Old money thinking' seems to pervade their attitude and permeate their business approach.

"It's a shame," agrees Laurie. "I spend my life as an executive coach and these people are just playing catch up with the speed of change around them. Many are unable to bridge the gap which is widening between the old Western ways and the new Chinese approach. Life has changed here. The big multinational businesses are no longer the only show in town. There are new indigenous corporates playing on the national and international stage to different rules. Globalization is no longer a one-way street into China."

As an executive coach Laurie is exposed to all the stresses and strains faced by the biggest businesses, both multinational and national, in China.

"At home we live a very reflective and quiet life. At work it is a million miles an hour all the time! I have no historical set of relationships to build on. It's all a question of whether you can build trust. Without trust through relationships you go nowhere in business here. I realized from the moment I arrived here that I was ignorant. I've become a student again, a studier of Chinese and the Chinese way. Without a willingness to embark on that path, there is no future for a Westerner here. I have read a book a week about China for almost the last four years. I was in a bookshop soon after I arrived here looking at books and the owner came up to me and asked if he could 'edit my choice of books'. I was intrigued why he should use the word 'edit' so I said yes. He then proceeded to recommend 28 books, I remember that number. They covered the nine periods of Chinese history, five series of five classical Chinese literature books and books of Chinese poetry, as well as books from more recent Chinese and foreign writers. 'Read these,' he said, 'and your mind will be changed about China.' He was right! It was like landing on a new planet!"

Laurie and I compare notes on the books she has read, many overlapping those on my recent and poor attempts. As we compare notes and titles, we become aware that we know so much about China, but know so little. Every time we find common areas, we find the depth of our understanding thin and incomplete.

"There is so much written in the West about China but so little is really well informed by those authors having spent any amount of time here or tried to understand the place. I know I say too much sometimes but it frustrates me that foreign authors or editors remain labouring under the wrong impression. That reputation of the West, to be mistrustful and to assume the worst, creates a shadow in front of those of us who are trying to build reputations and relationships here. My clients take time to realize that I am not here to judge or apply any Western prejudices. I'm on their side but it's difficult to prove against the backdrop of rhetoric and ill-conceived Tweets we all see."

We discuss the unintended consequences of a Western history that has left the Chinese innately suspicious of the likes of Laurie and I. Our task is not helped by the unconscious bias and often poor treatment meted out to Chinese staff in Western or Westernized business based here. An ignorance of language and culture doesn't help CEOs under pressure to grow and expand quarterly with shareholders expecting stellar results from China as the growth saviour of the balance sheet.

"The Western processes we have used in the past simply do not work here. The approach is much more of start, learn, adapt, change, drop or move forward. The notion of strategic planning and steady step-by-step progress is not how it's done here."

What of the current changes in China which are affecting Western business, changes in rules on investment, tightening controls and the like?

"There is a lot going on here and there seems to be a move towards retrenching and drawing power and control back to the centre, back to Beijing. I'm not sure I like it. No one really knows what will happen as this amount of power and influence is vested in one place. It's clear there are many good things happening with the eradication of corruption. However, at the same time, there are lots of little signs of a country under immense strain and contraction, centralization and maybe even a little panic over what can be done to keep this super tanker of a country from hitting the rocks."

So what does she think she will do next?

"Well it's a fascinating place to be right now and I would rather be on the inside experiencing the reality and working with it, than on the outside trying to figure out what the heck to do about it from a distance. Never a better time to be here, though I will have to go back to Canada sometime, even if it's just to breathe in the fresh air again!"

CHAPTER
50

MADE IN
MODERN
CHINA

Wang Yuli, or Sunday, as she has named herself in English, is surprised by my desire to interview her. She has provided me with translation and logistics support throughout the interview stage of this book and didn't seem to think she had a story to tell.

But she has.

Yuli was born in the small town of Tongliao (通辽) in the eastern area of the Inner Mongolian Autonomous Region of China (内蒙古自治区). The year was 1978, the first year of the Chinese one-child policy after which parents opting for a second child were fined and likely to be demoted at work.

"Tongliao is located in the famous Khorchin grasslands (科尔沁草原), best known as the place where two of the first empresses of the Qing dynasty were born."

The Khorchin Mongols were the first Mongol tribe that submitted to the Manchu-Qing dynasty in the early 1600s and were the tribe responsible for the production of fermented mares' milk for the Manchu emperors. To this day, the grasslands of Inner Mongolia are still known to produce the best and highest quality dairy products in China. Empress Xiaozhuangwen (孝庄文皇后) (1613 - 88) and Empress Xiaohuizhang (孝惠章皇后) (1641 - 1717) were from Khorchin.

"Though I was an only child, I spent a very happy childhood playing around the factory where my mother worked. It was a paper company producing paper cartons and every type of paper and cardboard product. There were flowers, green grass, a basketball court and even a horse's stable there. I recall the old trees with flowers on them, berries, butterflies, grasshoppers, beautiful caterpillars and dung beetles."

Yuli's father worked at a chemical factory which produced soap.

"Every morning my mother would ride her bicycle to her factory and my father would ride his bicycle to his factory. We all met up each evening. My happiest time was in the summer. Running around, laughing and playing in the big factory gardens.

Lunchtime was always at the factory with my mother. At that time, all the workers brought their lunch from home. They all left their lunch boxes in the factory boiler house and there were workers there whose job it was to steam the food. At noon, everyone stopped for lunch and the smell was so delicious and irresistible."

We are sitting in a well-known coffee shop not far from my apartment. Yuli is transported back to her youth. A time when sitting in Beijing, drinking coffee for pleasure and working with a foreigner was an unthinkable future.

"Before Spring Festival each year the city would arrange the Yangko (秧歌舞) dance and stilt walking practice. I would go with a group of young friends just for fun. We were very happy."

Yangko is a traditional dance format sometimes performed on the ground but also on stilts across China.

"During the Spring Festival the dancers would perform in the main street of my home town. Thousands of people would line the streets. Everyone was very happy during the dance times and we also had lion and dragon dancing which attracted many people during the Spring Festival period. I also remember that the rich state-owned factories, such as the textile and electricity plants, would put on huge firework displays at the Lantern Festival on the 15th day of Spring Festival. On the night of the 15th day of Spring Festival, it seemed like the whole of the city of Tongliao was at the firework display. It was the only traffic jam of the year back then as all the ordinary people had bicycles and it was just government officials and rich people who had cars. But everyone was there to watch the fireworks and all the houses were empty on that night."

Yuli pauses. Tears are welling up in her eyes.

"I always cry a little when I remember those times. I know progress has been made but whenever I think of those things I get a bit upset and I think we have lost something in their passing. There is none of that left now, no street dancers, no stilt walking, no factory firework displays. Even my mother's factory has disappeared. It's just a memory but I feel that those were happier, maybe a little naive, days of my childhood."

Yuli explains that in the early 1980s there were no high-rise buildings at all in Tongliao.

"They were all flat houses, not quite so convenient as today as they were cold and sometimes difficult places to live, but everyone helped each other back then. Neighbours knew neighbours and we all went to each other's houses. In 1984 my parents were one of the first in the neighbourhood to have a TV. It was a very small black and white one. All the neighbours came to our house and sat and watched a series on TV with us. I remember it was a Kung Fu TV series and everyone wanted to see it."

We meander through Yuli's childhood. Her kindergarten with the strict teacher who would box the ears of miscreants at a moment's notice, the Liberation Primary School with the huge playground and strict management.

"I wasn't a very good student but I did join lots of extracurricular classes. Dancing, drawing, maths, storytelling, calligraphy, singing and others. None lasted very long though! I walked to school every morning and home at night. After school, we all played together and really had no worries at all. It was not like now. As a mother, myself I'm always worried about the safety of my sons. There are so many stories of children being kidnapped and I worry so much about their safety and about society now. Times have changed – for the better in many ways – but not in some."

Yuli experienced the childhood of so many Chinese of the 1970s generation. Away from the major cities, life moved much as it had for generations. But change came with the Cultural Revolution and the years thereafter saw an explosion of industry across China, even to the further reaches of the more remote provinces.

"When I was at middle school it was only a short walk from our house. It was a beautiful walk to school and back each day as there were so many trees along the roads. They were tall, straight and very old poplar trees. They were so green in the summer time. Walking along in the shade of the trees was a delight, especially because there was a small book store on the side of the road where I often used to stop off to browse through the books. It was a happy time and when my mother told me that the trees had all been cut down not so long ago for a municipal development plan, I couldn't help crying as it was under those beautiful trees that I met my first love. It was a treasured place and now, like so much, it has gone. Even now I don't like to go back to my home town to face those destroyed memories."

Yuli's senior middle school years brought tragedy to the family with the sudden and inexplicable death of her father after a short illness in 1994. It was the second year of her senior middle school and at the age of 16 her life changed forever.

"It was so sudden. It was then that I swore I wanted to leave that place forever and move to Beijing. Two years later I came here to study at the Beijing Second Foreign Language Institute. I majored in marketing and tourism and also studied English. Those four years of study really gave me such a rich experience, not just in study terms but also living in this enormous metropolis."

Yuli stayed in Beijing. Her first job was at a secondary tourism school as an English tour guide and class teacher. The salary was low, at around ¥800 (£80) a month so she, like so many in Beijing, could only afford to return home at the major festivals and then at the basic level of travel. The slow trains, with no reserved sleeping cabin. Spending up to 13 hours overnight in a packed seat-only carriage, she would swelter in the summer and freeze in the winter journeys.

"Then it was a sleepless and very tiring journey. Now it's a one hour flight home. So much easier!"

After just over a year and a half teaching, Yuli left her job and went to Wall Street English in 2002, one of China's top English teaching organizations. She was there as a study advisor until 2005, earning considerably more money than she had done before at ¥3,000 (£300) a month. However, there was a penalty for leaving the private school. The school had given her the chance to gain a Beijing *hukou* and a fee was payable to the owner when she left to allow her to retain the all-important *hukou*. The 'fee' was over ¥20,000 (£2,000) and almost unaffordable, so she had to borrow money to pay the fee but felt it was worth the trouble.

"Then, in 2003, SARS hit China and Wall Street English changed their business model to a much more sales-orientated one, which I found much more difficult and I decided to leave in 2005. I had a short time with an investment company who were involved in Inner Mongolia to develop a coal site into a diethyl ether plant. However, because of the pollutants and likely environmental problems, the National Development and Reform Commission refused the licence. The whole project collapsed and the job with it! I was then introduced to my next job by a friend. It was with the Czech Tourist Authority in Beijing. I didn't even know where Czechoslovakia was when I started or what the capital city was! I had a 30-minute interview, mainly doing translation, and I got the job because my English was much better than another young girl's. I worked there from 2006 to 2013 and really enjoyed it."

Yuli was caught up in the changes affecting China as it opened up to foreign tourism and the Chinese started to travel more. Travel agencies were initially the only way foreign countries could work to advertise in China and then Czechoslovakia entered the Schengen Agreement on 21 December 2007, allowing the freedom of movement across the European Union borders. Suddenly Chinese people entering Czechoslovakia could visit neighbouring countries easily.

"Working as a destination promotion representative was really fun as the tourism industry was suddenly taking off in China. I was working not only with tourism offices but also the media, running seminars, doing road shows, training and news conferences. I was able to travel and see the world. Cooperating with the Austrian, German and Hungarian tourist authorities allowed me to visit those countries too."

Yuli, now firmly established with her English name of Sunday, started to travel to the US. Introduced to the role by a friend, she had never thought she would have so many opportunities from her small beginnings as a young girl from Inner Mongolia.

"I travelled extensively in the US, to Michigan, Florida, Oregon, California and then also to Alaska. When I first set foot in Alaska, I felt that life was so wonderful."

Sunday is a product of the new China and the China Dream extolled by President Xi Jinpin as he came to power in China in 2012. Now, at the age of 38, she has resigned from her job and set up her own business undertaking public relations and events for some US companies, as well as building her own contact base as a travel expert and high end translator.

"It's all new and quite hard. A couple of friends and I decided now was the right time to start out on our own. China is encouraging people to do this sort of thing so we feel we have a chance as the country goes global. I work from home which is very convenient for me. I really hope I can do well."

Sunday also believes that she has something else which will help her in her new venture. She is a Buddhist.

"I started to understand something about Buddhism in 2005 and I started to read books and scriptures. I also listened to radio programmes about Buddhism. I found it really interesting and then in 2010 I became a Buddhist. After studying hard I was awarded a certificate to confirm my knowledge as a student of Buddhism. What I learned in my studies is that Buddhism is not only a religion, not only a philosophy, it's not a superstition, but an education. Mr Sun Yat-sen, the first president of the Republic of China, said that people without a belief are people without hope. I think it is good that there are now television programmes about Buddhism and the government now promotes Buddhism in China. I believe that now the morality of China and the Chinese people should be improved and this will start from religious education. Family education, school education and societal education are the three aspects of moral education which go together. I study every day and do my Buddhism homework every day too."

We are oblivious to the hustle and bustle of the coffee shop around us. The epitome of modern capitalistic, some would say, morally tarnished China sit and surf around us. But we are transported to a different possibility in our thoughts.

"Now the standard of success is money. The lack of morality is not a big city thing. It is a China thing. Only moral education will solve this problem. It is good that the government is calling upon people to have a deeper morality. The new classes in schools are on Confucianism, Buddhism and Daoism. They are all now taught in primary schools. The government knows you have to start when children are young and instil the right moral foundations in them for life. This new initiative will change China in the long term. As more people learn to love the traditional Chinese culture and to have a strong belief in religion, then things will change for the better."

Sunday is one of many Chinese I know who are devout Buddhists. Many are passing believers, practising as part of the turn of the seasons to visit the temples and light incense and pray in their homes at the appointed time. The religion is growing, as too is Christianity in China. The government, far from suppressing needs and beliefs, is an active supporter of the moral code underpinning the ancient and intrinsically Chinese beliefs of Confucianism, Buddhism and Daoism.

"Education is the answer. If we cultivate a society of good, kind and considerate people, then history will judge us well. I have joined a charity which is the largest non-governmental organization in China. It is called 'Great Love Budda'. The group provides finance to support children of poor and disadvantaged families to be able to take the university examinations, the *Gaukao*. I am so happy to be a member of this organization and to play my small part in the development of society."

Sunday reflects on her own beliefs and her family.

"I really want to have everything go well for me and my family. It is not important to have a lot of money. It is much more important to have good fortune when I am in the next life. I want to be good to people. Too many people take advantage of your kindness and I do not want to be one of these types of people. I try to avoid people who are a drain on me and to be with positive people. My only real regret is that I did not spend as much time as I would have liked with my eldest son. As a result, he is a bit shy. I want him to have a good temper and I have encouraged him to be a member of a basketball team. He is a bit stubborn though, like his father, but I believe he will turn out ok. My second son was born in Hong Kong. I went there, even though it cost a lot of money for the hospital there. I needed to have him in Hong Kong so we could avoid the problems and fines of the one-child policy. It cost over ¥160,000 (£16,000) for the doctor and hospital in Hong Kong, as well as the agency costs to get it all arranged, but it was worth it. I am very happy as he has a Hong Kong passport so can go anywhere in the world when he is older. We have to go back to Hong Kong every five years to renew his papers but it was, and is, the right thing to do."

Despite the pride Sunday has for China, she is not above spending the efforts and money to get what she wants for herself and her family. Even she has seen great change in China during her 38 years.

"In 1996, when I first came to Beijing, I went to Tiananmen Square for the first time, to McDonald's for the first time and on the subway for the first time. It was amazing. Back then the subways had just started working and they were almost empty, not like the crowds today. You could actually sit down and even read a newspaper properly. Not like the crush today. In 2008 I remember there was only one shopping centre in the whole of Beijing and Guomao was the only luxury office block area in the city. It's all changed so much in a few brief years. In my home city there was only one street that actually had a name back then! The city used to have a nickname. It was called the Oriental Little Paris, with wide streets and parks. No longer! It's all gone, all changed. The old flat houses have been replaced with high rise blocks of apartments. Now Tongliao has a Burger King and a KFC. Now China's tier-one cities are very Westernized, almost unrecognizable from their historic past."

As Sunday bemoans the changes that have become so synonymous with the developing China, she also acknowledges that the China of ten years ago wasn't all good. The poverty of the old *hutongs* and flat houses, the poor sanitation and privations which faced so many citizens of Beijing and beyond. She accepts that progress has come at a price. Although her preference is for a wider harmony and higher morality, she seems to be reluctantly resigned to the time it will take to renew and rekindle the values she holds so dear in the majority of the population.

"I hope more charity groups will appear and grow stronger in China. Everyone has his or her family to look after, but also we should attend to society as a whole. We all have a social responsibility to fulfil. The famous British historian Dr Arnold Joseph Toynbee (the prolific historian and philosopher of history 1889–1975) said, 'Only Confucianism and Mahayana Buddhism can save the world.' I believe that."

We sit in quiet contemplation for a few minutes as I absorb what Yuli has said. She is, without doubt, a true product of China. A realist and an eternal optimist of the possibilities this amazing country could aspire to. If only it can hold on to its traditional culture, learn from its prodigious past and embrace the future which now opens up before it with its consummate sensitivity and humility.

POSTSCRIPT: A PERSONAL LETTER TO THE READER.

Dear Reader,

If you are browsing to the back, or have finished and turned the last page, I am grateful for your time.

I am not in Beijing.

I am not in my favourite Beijing coffee shop.

I am in another coffee shop more than 8,350 km from Beijing.

The internet is working, the noise of cups and coffee is much the same, but I am in my home town of Harrogate in Yorkshire in the north of England. While in China, New Year looms and there is the mad flurry of activity before Chinese New Year which falls this year (2017) on 28 January.

A year has passed since I last sat here and started to write. I am sitting and thinking; reflecting on the many people I have met and stories I have heard, noted and recorded in Beijing, many of them now included here, though some still languish in the dog-eared pages of my note books, a few respecting their post-interview request of anonymity.

The stories keep coming and I am still receiving invitations to interview, and probably will. The story of modern China and modern Beijing continues to unfold every day in the honest and uncensored words of the ordinary Chinese people to whom I talk. I sat and listened, they sat and talked. The Western foreigner and the indigenous Chinese. Very different, yet so similar in so many ways. We are human beings, we share the same emotions and the same needs, though we do not share the same history, language or culture. The seeming gulf between us, I feel, is more in our perception than in reality. A willingness to talk and share, to seek out common ground, was a solid bridge which overcame almost all of the misunderstanding and stereotypical prejudices we both initially brought to our shared space.

I have been incredibly fortunate to have been able to meet the people I have met and even more privileged that they have shared their stories and thoughts.

I have tried very hard to act as a mirror, true and fair, to the shared confidences, dreams and perspectives of my interviewees. I have, no doubt, made some errors. I trust they will forgive me for those. The notes which I have drawn together are my own, including the personal reflections on life in China and Chinese life. They are not an official or corporate review or assessment, certainly not a full audit of China, but they are my genuine perspectives and views on what I have heard and experienced.

I hope you find them of value and of interest.

Let me know.

Kind regards,
Jonathan

ACKNOWLEDGEMENTS

Almost every book you ever read has this page so you will find it no surprise that this is here. However, just as this book is, I hope, a little different from those others you have read, so too is this page a little different. To be honest, the book was easy to write. I'd like to be able to say that it was hard to get people to agree to see me but that was relatively easy too, once they had spoken to those supporting me. Then, when we started to talk, the stories have written themselves. They are, after all, just the words, expressions, hopes, fears and truths of the Chinese who were gracious enough to talk to me.

However, we all shared one vision; that the story of the real China, as it is now, needs to be told. So much is written and depicted of this seemingly impenetrable country in Western media. People like to believe in the demons and bogeymen of the past and the notion of a different narrative, as that told here, perturbs and unnerves us. My heartfelt thanks and gratitude go to all those who were open hearted and trusting enough to go 'on the record' in these pages. I can honestly put my hand on my heart and say that all the words here are true to those who uttered them. No one shirked from any questions or avoided answering my often naive, and sometimes direct, probing. China has had its turbulent past, as has any country you care to bother to examine in any detail, but the difference is in the rawness of history that lives today in the words, experiences and hearts of all Chinese.

Without the candour and openness of so many people, and those who shared but could not be included, this would have remained as a pile of coffee-stained napkins and dog-eared notes. Special gratitude goes to Joyce Chao and Sunday Wang, who opened up both books of contacts and their hearts for me to explore and draw upon.

I suppose I also have to thank Paul Gordon, long-time friend, as well as business and personal coach. He has been the keeper of my conscience, as well as voluntarily taking the position of irritating, annoying, pushy surrogate pre-editor. He knows me well enough to push the right buttons to get the best out of me, for which I am forever grateful.

Thank you to you too, 'dear reader'. Thank you for buying this book. I hope that in return for your hard earned cash I have repaid you with a genuinely unique suite of stories from the real lives of ordinary, by and large, middle-class Chinese people today.

I was never asked to write this by anyone in China. It has not been through any form of censorship or political filter. It is the raw, unadulterated truths of China lives.

AN INTRODUCTION TO
JONATHAN
GELDART

Jonathan Geldart was born in Pembrokeshire in Wales in 1958 and brought up in Yorkshire in the north of England. The son of a Professor in chemical engineering, he gained his MA at St Andrews University in geography and archaeology, specializing in underwater archaeology. After a short time training to be a brewer, he went on to pursue a career in marketing. Outside work, he competed in motor rally sport for almost 20 years, eventually at an international level, but his real passion is the outdoors and exploration. In 2006, he was part of a team that trekked unsupported for 26 days in sub-zero temperatures to the Geomagnetic North Pole from Canada. He has climbed in the Himalayas and undertaken expeditions in Norway and the Canadian Arctic. In his 'spare' time he still runs leadership training and team development courses for business people that requires them to climb mountains and sleep outside, often in sub-zero temperatures. He is a Fellow of The Royal Geographical Society and a council member of The British Exploring Society.

Jonathan started working in packaged goods for major blue chip consumer brands and subsequently focused on professional services where he spent significant time within two of the largest firms in the world in various strategic, marketing and business development roles. At PwC, he ended a 16-year distinguished career, as UK marketing director for their mid-market practice, joining Grant Thornton International Ltd in 2006 to become international marketing director.

Having spent a number of years with extended visits to China, in 2013, Grant Thornton International Ltd appointed him as executive director, markets development, with a specific remit in emerging markets, and China in particular. He has now worked in China, on and off, for almost seven years and full time since 2013.

Jonathan is captivated by China as an economy, by its long history and fascinating culture but, in particular, by the people. Everyone has a compelling story and this book tells some of them.

Together, they serve to paint a picture of China through the eyes of real Chinese people who represent all ages, social groups and backgrounds.

Through a series of interviews, conducted mostly in a variety of Beijing coffee shops, Jonathan simply asked a few questions and let the people speak. What he learned was insightful and compelling and is recorded here for the reader to draw their own conclusions and some additional insights from the words of those interviewed, coupled with a personal commentary from Jonathan.

He decided to write this book as a follow up to *The Thoughts of Chairmen Now*, a book he co-authored with David Roth from WPP plc, the world's largest communications group with multiple businesses across China.

The Thoughts of Chairmen Now was a different sort of business book. It used the stories and words of CEOs and chairmen in China to add colour and human interest to the miracle that is China's emergence as the world's second, soon to be largest, global economy.

This is not a business book. Nor is it a Beijing guide book, although it provides an insight into life in this extraordinary city. It is a book for anyone interested in China who wants to see beyond the obvious, and often extraordinary, facts and figures. It is written in 'bite-sized' segments so the reader can dip in and out as they wish. It is also almost short enough to finish in a single sitting, or during a long plane journey.